J. G. Hoyt

MISCELLANEOUS WRITINGS:

ADDRESSES, LECTURES, AND REVIEWS.

BY

JOSEPH G. HOYT, LL.D.

BOSTON:
CROSBY AND NICHOLS,
117 WASHINGTON STREET.
1863.

University Press:
Welch, Bigelow, and Company,
Cambridge.

PREFACE

By REV. A. P. PEABODY, D. D.

BEFORE it was possible to commit the contents of this volume to the press, the author had passed away. The book certainly needs for those who knew him no other Preface than his own, with its sweet solemnity and sad beauty, written as the death-shadow was fast closing over a life than which few can have been more vigorous, sanguine, and happy. But there may be readers who will be glad to know how dearly he was loved and prized, how sincerely respected and honored, and why. We first became acquainted with him, when he commenced his duties as one of the instructors of the Phillips Exeter Academy. It is impossible to overestimate his worth as a teacher. It was not that he was more assiduous or successful than many others, as a mere taskmaster in the mechanical drill or in the finer analysis of the school-room. We doubt whether the term examinations of his classes would have fully justified to a stranger the warmly eulogistic way in which his character as an instructor was uniformly spoken of by the friends, patrons, and alumni of the Academy. But one who sat by him during an ordinary recitation-hour could discern the secret of his success in the complete vivifying of the lesson in his own and to his pupils' consciousness. He brought the minds under his discipline into intensely vigorous action, and on a wide range of subjects collateral with or suggested by the main subject of the hour. Large reading, an exhaustless memory, and a fertile fancy, were all brought into liberal use, now to supply analogies from an entirely different realm of knowledge for some mathematical proposition, now to pour a flood of transfiguring light on some passage in a classic which had before seemed clear enough, but as trite as clear, and now to trace a Greek word back to phonetic elements closely akin in sound to its meaning, and on to its remotest derivatives in our vernacular tongue. Thus trained, his pupils carried with them much more than a mere technical preparation for college. They acquired habits of investigation and reflection, which were often more distinctly recognized in the later years and in the philosophical portions of the college course, than in the routine study of the mathematics and the ancient languages.

But he was much more than a good teacher. His pupils were indebted to him for the highest moral impulse and example. He made himself their friend, and they were uniformly his friends. He had a strong sympathy with boyhood, and with every festive, sportive aspect of life; and while there could not have been a hardier style of manliness than his, he retained his love of mirth, fun, and frolic unimpaired. Thus brought by community of taste and enjoyment in this one particular into the most intimate intercourse with the young persons about him, he used this leverage to raise them toward his own elevated plane of upright purpose, loyal endeavor, and conscientious fidelity, Godward and manward. His broad, generous, hospitable nature invited confidence, and suffered no official distance of age and station to intervene between himself and his pupils; so that he stood to them in the relation of an elder brother, whom they profoundly respected indeed, but from whom they would keep back nothing of which they were not ashamed, while they were heartily ashamed of whatever they could not communicate freely to him. This influence, so justly and worthily obtained, he regarded as too precious to be wasted or imperilled, and he husbanded it so wisely, and adopted such timely methods of exerting it, as to bestow its whole weight and might in behalf of a high and ever higher standard of moral excellence.

At the same time he never forgot in his official cares and labors his obligations as a man and a citizen. No one can have been a kinder neighbor, a more loving and assiduous friend, than he, and none can have felt more sacredly the obligations imposed by the larger public, and by every cause of human emancipation, progress, and well-being. Whatever the community really needed, he was among the foremost in devising and furthering. Not content with the educational duties which belonged to his office, he devoted much time, labor, and talent for a long series of years to the improvement of the public schools in the town of his residence, and of the school system for the State at large; and, aside from his general services, there are numerous specific benefits in this department for which his fellow-citizens are indebted to his sole agency.

It need hardly be added, that Mr. Hoyt was pre-eminently a religious man, and that his friends could trace the beauty, wealth, and strength of his character to Christian faith, trust, and hope. Though with an intelligent, definite, and decided belief as to subjects of religious controversy, he had too large a sympathy and too comprehensive a fellowship to be a sectarian, and he was always glad to recognize the Divine Master's image in the disciple of whatever name or form. His piety only deepened the fountain of his charity, and rendered dogmatism and intolerance as utterly impossible for him as indolence or selfishness seemed to be.

One word as to the papers in this volume. Some of them failed of the last feeble touch by which the writer, in his wearisome and painful decline, sought to revise a part of them. They were none of them written with reference to publication in a permanent form, and most of them were prepared in haste, and under a heavy pressure of duty, to meet special occasions. They represent the affluence of the author's learning, the copiousness of his thought, and the wide range of his fancy; while they must needs appear at the disadvantage which always attends the posthumous publications of an able and gifted writer. They are all of them rich in thoughts peculiarly his own, and some will, we know, be regarded as masterpieces of their kind. The Inaugural Address, especially, will vindicate Mr. Hoyt's distinguished reputation as an educator, and must awaken in every intelligent reader profound regret that one who understood his work so thoroughly, and had the energy requisite to embody his plans and actualize his conceptions, has been so early withdrawn from a service in which he had few equals, hardly a superior. Our consolation is, that he has only been removed to a higher sphere of service, where the powers which wrought so vigorously under the burden of growing infirmity have no longer clog or hinderance. He leaves in the hearts of all who knew him, and most with those who knew him best, profound regrets, and dear, honored, hallowed memories.

PREFACE.

OF the miscellaneous articles which constitute this little volume, some are reprints and others appear in type for the first time. I have been induced to gather them up and throw them into their present form, partly because those to whose judgment I have been accustomed to defer advised it; * and partly because I hoped, perhaps vainly, that a book containing some of my best thoughts and most earnest convictions upon subjects of permanent interest, lying on the table of my friends, might, when this sensible warm motion has become a kneaded clod, help me to survive for a time in the memory and kindly regard of those I love. I shrink from the cold obstruction, — the oblivion of the grave. Like a timid child, I dread to go out alone into the darkness. The fire-light on the hearthstone of home is more attractive to me than the brightest star in the far-off heavens. *Ἡ φυγὴ μόνου πρὸς μόνον,* — "the flight of a lone soul to a lone God,"— is a fearful thing to poor

* "ST. LOUIS, November 1, 1862.

"DEAR SIR: —

"Believing that the publication of your Essays and Addresses would not only afford deep gratification to your friends, but would promote the interests of education and sound learning in the land, we respectfully invite you to publish a volume of your writings.

"S. WATERHOUSE,
W. G. ELIOT,
W. CHAUVENET,
GEORGE PARTRIDGE,
JOHN HOW, and others.

"CHANCELLOR J. G. HOYT."

human nature. In its immediate prospect, though impatient of delay, —

> "I falter where I firmly trod,
> And falling with my weight of cares
> Upon the great world's altar-stairs
> That slope through darkness up to God,
>
> "I stretch lame hands of faith, and grope,
> And gather dust and chaff, and call
> To what I feel is Lord of all,
> And faintly trust the larger hope."

If, as the western "shadows fall longer" upon our earthly pathway, they were not met and dispersed by the auroral light of an immortal life, — a life made radiant and beautiful by the prospect of reunited human friendships, — then should we be "of all men most miserable."

But a brief Preface is not, perhaps, the place for the expression of one's personal feelings. It only remains for me to say, that, if otherwise able, I am too far away from the printing-office to read the proof. Of course there will be mistakes, and therefore the more urgent necessity for the "charitable speeches" of my pupils and friends, to whom the volume is affectionately dedicated.

J. G. HOYT.

St. Louis, November 5, 1862.

MISCELLANEOUS WRITINGS.

AN INAUGURAL ADDRESS.*

THE RELATION OF CULTURE AND KNOWLEDGE IN A UNIVERSITY EDUCATION.

IT is the tendency of human nature to adapt itself to the circumstances of its position. Society is the complex resultant, not only of antagonistic forces within itself, but also of a variety of influences constantly exerted from without. Let a civilized community be begirt with savage tribes, and its standard is gradually lowered, the line of demarcation grows fainter and fainter, until at length nearly all traces of high social and religious culture have disappeared.

The Dutch Boers, intelligent Protestant Calvinists, who began a settlement in Cape Town, South Africa, about the middle of the seventeenth century, have become, within the period of our own history, nomadic, lawless, sanguinary barbarians, hardly less wild and gross than their Hottentot neighbors. If during the last few years they

* The Inauguration of Joseph G. Hoyt, LL. D. as Chancellor of Washington University, in the city of St. Louis, took place in the Hall of the Mercantile Library, on Tuesday evening, October 4, 1859. A prayer, offered by the Rev. Truman M. Post, D. D., commenced the services, after which the Rev. William G. Eliot, D. D., President of the Board of Directors, made a statement explanatory of the progress and present condition of the University, and, in behalf of his associates, committed to the Chancellor elect the insignia of his office. The following Inaugural Address was then delivered, and ordered to be printed by the Directors.

have exhibited indications of improvement, it is because newly established commercial relations with the enlightened countries of Europe are producing the legitimate effect of a national regeneration. But so late as 1820 there was not within their borders a school-house, or a bookstore, or a newspaper. The women, descendants of the fair-haired daughters of German princes, were menial slaves, beasts of burden, whose characters were as low as the degrading services which they performed ; and the whole colony, though still nominally Christian, under the Synod of Dort, had descended to the level of brutal savages, a living illustration of the fact, that it takes only two centuries to change the high civilization of our boasted Anglo-Saxon race into unmitigated heathenism.*

Our New England colonies suffered a similar, though less striking, retrogression. The first settlers at Plymouth were, to a large extent, men of fine scholarship and polished manners, graduates of the English Universities, skilled as civilians and courtiers, compatriots with Milton, Hampden, and Cromwell. But they came into the wilderness, and, in accordance with the inexorable laws of our nature, were tempted of the Devil. The restraints of civilized life, the thousand nameless influences of cultivated society, did not follow them. Their dress, manners, homes, soon began to partake of the coarseness of their rude exemplars. Refinement, sentiment, education, all languished in the shadows of the overhanging forests. In two or three generations, though the spirit of political and religious freedom was not extinguished, yet the whole aspect of the colony was changed. Instead of the scholarly culture which had come, only a few years before, from Cambridge and Oxford, we find in the civil and ecclesiastical records a crudeness of style and an absurd capriciousness of orthography characteristic of a degenerating race. The enlight-

* Horace Bushnell, D. D., "Barbarism the First Danger."

ened religion of Owen and Robertson had caught from the woods the taint of a worse than savage superstition, and the whole community, ministers and people, rulers and subjects, were alike trembling in terror at the wrath and diabolical enchantments of infernal spirits.* But the constant influx of an intelligent immigration from the mother country, together with the early establishment of public schools, and especially of Harvard College, saved New England from the barbarism toward which in her early conflicts with savage life she had steadily approximated.

But the end is not yet. In every young State springing up on our shifting western frontier, the great problem of American society must be solved anew. We are solving it to-day in Missouri; not, however, for Missouri alone, but for this whole Mississippi Valley. St. Louis can hardly fail to be the metropolitan city of the largest and richest and most populous territory which the sun ever shone on. If the Moors, in their exultant pride of country, could believe that the Paradise of the Prophet was situated exactly in that part of heaven which overhung the kingdom of Granada, we may be excused for recognizing the commanding nature of our position in the world, especially if this knowledge awaken in us a vivid sense of our responsibilities. The great valley watered by the Mississippi and its tributaries, containing, as it does, an area of one million and a fourth of square miles,† is equal in extent to the whole European continent, with the exception of Russia, and could be carved up into a dozen kingdoms as large as Great Britain and Ireland combined. Within this valley are ocean-like prairies of exhaustless fertility, immeasurable strata of lead and zinc and copper

* See Cotton Mather's "Observations, as well Historical as Theological, upon the Nature, Number, and the Operations of the Devils." Published by the special command of his Excellency, William Stoughton, the Governor of the Province of Massachusetts Bay, in New England, 1693.

† United States Census, 1850, p. 29.

and coal, hills of solid iron, mighty forests of timber, and, on its western boundary, mountain streams, whose sands are richer in gold than the fabled Lydian Pactolus. These multiform products of a teeming soil come by steamboat or rail-car to this central point of navigation and travel, where they are transformed by our manufacturing and mechanical skill, or are exchanged for the various commodities of civilized life. Besides this, when the railroad, whose achievement is but a question of time, shall have connected New York and San Francisco, the Atlantic and the Pacific, deep answering unto deep, the riches of India and of China, the commerce of the world, will pass by our doors, and St. Louis will become the half-way caravansary on this continent for the nations of the earth. Now it will not be denied that this city, thus situated, thus related to the world's affairs, rests upon the broad foundation which, as Adam Smith affirms, underlies every great city, — agriculture, commerce, and manufactures; nor can it be doubted that she must exert a mighty influence on the intellectual and moral character, as well as on the material interests of the thronging millions who will gather around her in this immense valley, and who, by their suffrages, will erelong determine the destiny of a republic before whose colossal proportions and political power the empire of the Cæsars dwindles into insignificance. How shall she be prepared to accomplish the high mission which Providence has assigned her? Manifestly there can be but one answer to this question: she must *first educate herself*, in the most comprehensive sense of the term, and then let her light shine until the humblest dwellers in the shadows of mountain and forest shall rejoice in its warm radiance.

In a monarchy or arbitrary government, it is, comparatively speaking, a matter of small consequence whether the people are educated or not; their first and highest duty is unquestioning obedience. But with us, so far at least as our civil relations are concerned, every individual is a ruler, and must exert an influence upon every other individual in the republic. It is a proposition in natural philosophy, susceptible of demonstration, that every foot-fall of every child jars the earth, and not the earth only, but the whole universe of God. It is a proposition which needs no demonstration, that every member of a free government affects for good or ill every other member. The boy now flying his kite on Washington Common, or blowing soap-bubbles under the eye of his mother, may attain to the highest office of the nation; for, as a distinguished statesman has intimated, every man in these days is *liable* to become President of the United States. But if he should reach no official dignity, yet he is a voter, and as such holds up the hand that sways the sceptre of power, or strikes it down at his pleasure. It has been well said, that "to know how to cast a ballot in a free country is of far more importance than to know how to cast a spear." A nation may recover from a defeat in battle, or even from the disastrous consequences of an unsuccessful, or, what perhaps is worse, a successful war; but from the effects of popular ignorance, or rather of misdirected education, there is no recovery. It is an abiding consumption at the vitals of the body politic. Ignorance among the people in a democratic commonwealth reaches, in its leprous influence, to every fibre and function of the state. It stagnates the currents of health, palsies the right arm of labor, debases a cheerful and intelligent worship to a fear-stricken superstition, pollutes the fountains of justice, renders contemptible the decisions of the jury, degrades and brutifies our social intercourse, exchanges the discussions of freemen met in council for the yells of a mob or for voices of command from military despots. The sovereignty of intellectual power is supplanted by unreasoning force. The pen gives place to the sword, the book to the bayonet, the majesty and authority of law to the reign of "chaos and old night."

A perfect system of popular instruction involves the necessity of institutions for common, intermediate, and higher education. The first already exist in our primary and grammar schools; the second, in our high schools and academies; the third, not yet adequately provided, must be found, if found at all, in well-endowed, well-appointed colleges and universities. The public schools of St. Louis, with their present able and efficient corps of teachers, and under their present admirable supervision, are securing to all our children the rudiments of a good English education, and, to those who desire it, a thorough discipline also in those classical and mathematical studies which are preparatory to a still more liberal culture in higher seats of learning. It is of this latter class of institutions — our *Universities* — that I wish to say somewhat on this occasion.

The University, in its original scope and meaning, was *Universitas doctorum et scholarium*, — a community of learned men, pursuing their studies under a municipal organization of their own, amidst the parchment rolls and black-letter volumes of the earlier and middle ages. The subjects and objects of study had no reference to the outward world. Scholarship was sought for its own sake, and was its own exceeding great reward. But this is changed. The University now is rather *Universitas Literarum et Scientiarum*, — a repository of the highest learning in every department of human knowledge,* represented to the public eye, not merely in its scholarly Professors, but also in its Libraries, Laboratories, Observatories, Philosophical Apparatus, Cabinets of Minerals, Museums of Natural History, Botanical Gardens, and Galleries of Painting and Sculpture. It is a place where the student

* "Omnis doctrinæ ac scientiæ thesaurus altissimus."

is furnished with every possible facility for pursuing his studies to the highest range of thought, in any direction, throughout the whole domain of science and letters. Of course, the University is altogether more comprehensive in its character than the College. Its instruction is ordinarily divided into four faculties, having charge respectively of Law, Medicine, Theology, and the Arts or Philosophy. The first three of these belong to professional schools, the last to the college proper. In addition to these, the recent rapid development of the physical sciences has rendered eminently appropriate the establishment of special departments of Natural History, of Mathematics applied to engineering and mechanics, and of Chemistry in its relations to manufactures and agriculture.

The English University at Cambridge is a union of seventeen colleges or corporate bodies,* each of which, like the several States of our own confederacy, is represented in a congress, consisting of a senate and council. It is exclusively in this *federal* capacity that degrees are granted, and then only after the most searching and severe examinations. In this way, a diploma is, what it always should be, the seal of profound scholarship.

We have, strictly speaking, no University in this country. Harvard and Yale, perhaps, approximate the nearest to it; but there is a wide distance between them and Berlin, with its 175 professors and its library of 7,000 manuscripts and 500,000 volumes. With us, the College, which was originally a mere eleemosynary hall for the accommodation of poor students, has usurped the functions and prerogatives of the University, essaying to teach, in four years, the whole circle of liberal arts and sciences, and lavishing its honors upon men of whom it knows as little as the favored recipients of its cabalistic letters-patent know of sound learning.

* Cambridge University Calendar.

As a people we are yet in our childhood, exuberant with untamed life. The sutures of our national cranium are closing slowly and with difficulty over the wildly throbbing brain. It is just here in this fact of our youth, that we, especially at the West, encounter the greatest difficulty in building up an educational institution which shall be commensurate with our intellectual necessities and conservative of our vast material interests. We may as well look this difficulty full in the face. We are young, and it is because we are young that our life, like an oration of Demosthenes, is full of thrice-repeated "*action.*" We are content to leave all meditation to our ministers and maiden aunts. An ague-fit is preferred to a fit of reflection. The crash of falling trees, the clang of machinery, the buzzing of spindles, the shriek of fire-winged locomotives, are pleasanter far to our ears than the quiet hum of academic halls, or the swelling organ peal of ivy-crowned cathedrals. He only is supposed to live who finds something in the outward world to do, and does it, — something, too, which is palpable, visible, striking. We pay more honor to the strong arm than to the thinking brain. We call the men we employ our hired hands, not our hired heads. We are never easy, always possessed of a spirit of unrest. If we sit, unlike the rest of the world, we must rock. Indeed, a rocking-chair under full swing would be no inappropriate heraldic national emblem. If we pretend to sleep, we talk, like Lady Macbeth, to our "deaf pillows." If we stop to think, we whittle a stick, or masticate with increased vigor "the weed." It is true, as a German paper says of us, that we chew more tobacco and burst more steam-engines than any other nation on the earth. We are eminently a *fast* people. We charge upon our daily business with as much *élan* as the French cavalry exhibit in charging upon the serried ranks of a hostile army. The veteran missionary, Dr. Goodell, recently visiting his native country, after an absence in Syria of some thirty years, was struck, on landing in Boston, as he tells us, with the extraordinary hurry in which everybody — men, women, and children — seemed to be, and he could hardly be persuaded that there was not, somewhere in the city, a *fire*, which the jostling multitude was hastening to extinguish. Even our letters of friendship are scrawled with the most business-like despatch, and the boarding-school maiden subscribes her first perfumed epistle to her adorable lover, — "Thine, dearest, *in haste!*" The student, catching the spirit of the street and the exchange, grows impatient over his books in his classic retreat, and pants for an intenser life on the levee, or a freer one among the placers of Pike's Peak. He does not believe in the necessity of spending seven or eight years, the best part of his valuable existence, in poring ingloriously over "dead languages" and abstruse mathematics. He is sure the world is waiting and anxious for him, and so he will not tarry in our academic Jerichos until his beard be grown, but goes forth with his bow and arrow to the "world's broad field of battle," to see if he, like the smooth-faced Paris, may not hit some great Achilles in the heel. Or if, made of finer mould, he should covet the reputation and badge of scholarship, still he must be allowed to attain his object with the least outlay of labor and in the briefest possible time. If ostriches hatch their young, as the Arabs believe, by merely looking at their eggs, why may not scholars be hatched in quite as summary a way? Educators, so called, have not been wanting, who have taken this oviparous view of the subject, and who, with a zeal for the cause of learning as disinterested as that of the goldsmith, who fell in love with the diamond eyes of the idol of Jaghernaut, have furnished the kind of institutions demanded. They are scattered all over the country, though, like "the course of empire," their tendency is decidedly "westward." A young man in six months may fit himself, in one of these temples of Minerva, to enter college a year in advance, with a wide margin of Hebrew and Geology besides. If not favored with a premature degree, he sallies forth, in due time, against the Philistines, a Bachelor of Arts, and achieves wonders with the same famous weapon which Samson once wielded at Ramath-lehi!

> "Non tali auxilio, nec defensoribus istis
> Tempus eget."

It takes the cypress-tree a thousand years to accomplish its full size. The education which the exigencies of our country and the times demand cannot be the work of a day. It must be a process, not a spasm; a healthy growth, not a sudden "swell"; a development of trunk and limb, not a whitewashing of the bark. "The gods," says an old Greek, "sell all good things at the price of labor," * not for money. The rich man who bought the study-lamp of Epictetus for three thousand drachmas, in the hope that it would light him into the very adyta of Philosophy, awoke the morrow morn a sadder, but not a wiser man.

No nation since the world began has required a tithe of the disciplined talent which is now absolutely indispensable to us. Look at the democratic character of our institutions; at the great experiment of a free government, cut loose from the precedents and prescriptions of antiquity; at the heterogeneousness of a population speaking in all the "cloven tongues" of the ancient Pentecost, and bound together by no common bond of historic associations; at the undeveloped resources of a territory outstripping in the rapidity of its expansion the speed of the pioneer, and putting to shame the unreliable charts of the chorographer;

* . . . . . τῶν πόνων
Πωλοῦσιν ἡμῖν πάντα τἀγάθ' οἱ θεοί.
Epicharmus.

at the restless activity of the masses, heaving and tossing with the irrepressible energy of a storm-driven sea; — look at these things, startling in their present reality and more startling in their prophecies of the future, and tell me if there is not need, here and now, of a keener intelligence, of more thoroughly furnished faculties, of a loftier virtue, of a profounder and more comprehensive culture, than any of the civilizations of the Old World ever knew? The very difficulties which, as we have seen, lie in the way of a great University, are the strongest arguments for its necessity. The terrible activity of our physical life must be guided and elevated, or it will waste itself in aimless exertion, if not in suicidal violence. The nation, not less than the individual, should be educated in youth. It is then, if ever, that we may "wield at will the fierce democratie" of untamed passions, and open through green meadows channels for undisciplined affections. It is then, when gross materialism is the preordained law of our being, that we should stir our grovelling nature with thoughts of a higher life, and quicken its sight with visions of spiritual beauty.

The highest institutions of learning are not of necessity, as some suppose, the slow growth of centuries. The University of Berlin is foremost among the Universities of Europe, and yet it is not so old as our own Harvard by a hundred and seventy-two years. It was but sixteen years of age when it contained one thousand six hundred and forty-two matriculated students. It is true, Prussia is a densely-peopled country, while in our Western States the camp-fires of the Indians have hardly yet gone out. But the population of this Mississippi Valley, according to the census returns for the last two decennial periods, is doubling in a little more than thirteen years, so that, at the same rate, in 1900, a point doubtless within the lifetime of many of my hearers, we shall have become a hundred and sixteen millions! St. Louis, the geographical centre, not only of this valley, but of the whole country, will be to a fearful extent responsible for the intellectual and moral character which shall be impressed upon the American people. It was in view of considerations like these, that a few far-sighted and large-hearted men, of whom the famous verse of Terence —

Homo sum; humani nihil a me alienum puto * —

was written, laid the foundation of WASHINGTON UNIVERSITY. It has grown to its present dimensions through the fostering care, not of the State, but of unostentatious private individuals, whose pathway in society we discover by the fruits of their generous munificence, just as the Eastern traveller can trace from afar the course of a river in the desert by the trees and verdure that spring up along its banks, — a waving line of green in a waste of sand. Harvard, Yale, and Dartmouth in this country, and the Universities of Oxford, Cambridge, and Paris in Europe, were, in their inception, the result of private liberality; but when, in process of time, they had given proof of their public utility, they were, in their further development, materially assisted by the state. It has been for a long time well understood by the profoundest statesmen, that learning, art, faith, have an economic value, — are worth money; that education not only elevates the intellect, but economizes also the public purse; that it costs less to support a boy at the school, than it does to support a man in the penitentiary; that high moral culture is the cheapest police; that society, if thoroughly interpenetrated with the spirit of the New Testament, would have no need of jails and gibbets, and the sheriff's occupation would be gone; in a word, that a high-toned, well-appointed institution of learning pays good dividends to the community, and the

* Heauton Timorumenos, Act I. Scene 1.

stock taken in it by the state is well invested. In saying this, however, we have no fell intentions upon the Treasury in Jefferson City.

WASHINGTON UNIVERSITY is not yet "finished," — only begun. It is the order of nature to grow. The shell-fish, when he feels himself "cabined, cribbed, confined," crawls forth from his stony incasement, and slowly builds for himself another and a larger house. We expect to conform to this universal law of growth. We have now in the University five departments, — a Preparatory or Academic, a Collegiate, a Scientific, a Polytechnic, and, under the same charter and general supervision, though in separate buildings and grounds, a Seminary for female instruction. In the Academic department, the course of study has been so arranged that pupils of eleven years of age and of good natural ability may, in four years, fit themselves to enter upon either of the two higher courses, — the Collegiate or Scientific. The College, corresponding, like those of New England, very nearly to the German Gymnasium, furnishes facilities for a good English and Classical education. The studies in the Scientific department are *special* and *practical* in their character, — looking, on the one hand, to the higher and subtler investigations of science in Mechanics, Astronomy, and Chemistry, and, on the other hand, to the every-day employments, in the shop or field, of the industrial classes, for whom the liberal provisions of the Polytechnic Institute are particularly intended. Such, in brief, is the outline and framework of our University. But it is Carlyle, I think, who says, "The house that is a-building looketh not like the house that is built." If it be objected, that, without the present reality and fulness of a University, we have no business with so august a title, we answer, that parents do not wait until their children have become full-grown men before they name them. The great American statesman, the expositor and defender of the Constitution, — who, whether in the cabinet or senate-chamber, always stood

> "With Atlantean shoulders, fit to bear
> The weight of mightiest monarchies, whose look
> Drew audience and attention, still as night
> Or summer's noontide air," —

was once a mere child, chasing butterflies in the clover-fields, or catching minnows with a pin-hook from the silver streamlets of New Hampshire, and the name which the world will pronounce with reverence and pride "to the last syllable of recorded time" was that which his mother gave him when he lay an infant on her knee.

It may not be inappropriate, in this connection, to indicate briefly my idea of a University, — not what it might be in some far-off imaginary Republic, like Plato's, but what it should be in this section of this country at this time. The Academic, or preparatory studies, prescribed for admission to the best Colleges in New England, do not, in my judgment, demand any serious modification at our hands. The common evil of careless and inadequate preparation we can remedy by a more rigid and pitiless examination. The ground already occupied is broad enough, — it only needs a deeper and more thorough tillage. Of the constituent elements of a true University, the first and most important is the College. Its faculty of instruction and government should consist of a corps of Professors, having charge respectively of the English, the Latin, and the Greek Language and Literature, of pure and mixed Mathematics, of Chemistry, of Rhetoric and Oratory, of Ancient and Modern History, of Metaphysics and Political Economy, of Modern Languages and Literature, and of the Natural Sciences. This last topic could be taught only in outline, as preparatory to an ampler discussion in the post-graduate course. A College thus constituted and furnished would be the grand foundation. The superstructure built upon it would be naturally divided into various apartments of different dimensions, each of which would be devoted to a special pursuit, and presided over by a special Faculty. In one, we should have a Faculty of Science in its application to Mechanical, Agricultural, and Commercial industry; in another, a Faculty of Natural History, embracing the whole range of Physical Sciences; in another, a Faculty of the Arts, both useful and ornamental, including Painting, Sculpture, Design, and whatever in civilized life may be connected with beauty, form, color, or sound; in another, a Faculty of Philology; in another, a Faculty of Law; in another, a Faculty of Medicine. As Scientific Theology is necessarily sectarian in its character, it belongs exclusively to denominational schools. In our own case, it is wisely prohibited by our charter. Upon the honorable completion of the college course of four years, the graduate should receive the degree of Bachelor of Arts. Two years more spent upon the studies of either one of the special or professional departments of the University, according to his option, would entitle him, on examination, to the degree of Master of Arts.* In the ideal University which I have been portraying, and which is nothing more nor less than Washington University, rounded out into symmetry and fulness of proportion, there might be arranged for those students who, like the members of the intermediate classes of Oxford and Cambridge, cannot afford the time and means necessary for a thorough education, a three years' scientific course, running parallel with the first three years of the college course, and securing to those who complete it the degree of Bachelor of Science.† It is obvious that

* Columbia College, New York City, under its recent re-organization, proposes to confer the degree of Bachelor of Arts at the end of three years' study; and that of Master of Arts, after two years additional.

† In the re-arrangement of the system of instruction at Brown University, in 1850, provision was made for a three years' Scientific course, terminating with the degree of Bachelor of Philosophy.

in the constitution of a University there must be, in addition to the several faculties which have been specified, books in every field of research; apparatus, chemical, mechanical, and astronomical; cabinet specimens from the whole realm of Nature, animal, mineral, and vegetable; models of implements invented for the use of man; and galleries of art, appealing to his sense of beauty.

The different branches of study indicated in the foregoing enumeration of professorial faculties are distributed between the College proper and the various departments of the University, not at random, but in accordance with the universally recognized nature of man, as a subjective and objective being, requiring on the one hand, for his perfect development, the discipline of his own original powers, and on the other, an intimate acquaintance with the phenomena, properties, and laws of the outward world.

In the highest institutions of learning, then, we aim at two results, — CULTURE *first*, and KNOWLEDGE *afterwards*. These are the two grand essentials to intellectual power, to an imperial manhood. Neither is sufficient of itself, *nor can their order be inverted.* Strength of muscle is a prerequisite to success in the harvest-field. The bending wheat is not for the puny arm; the wonderful facts in science are useless to the undisciplined mind. Those modern reformers in our educational systems, with whom the "be-all and end-all" of life is the *practical* and *real*, are striving to gather fruit from a tree which has neither stem nor roots. Far be it from me to undervalue *utility*, in this "working-day world," as a *leading object* in the University. I believe, with Bacon, that it is the mission of sound learning "to work effectively for the purpose of lightening the inconveniences of human life." * I only object to the unphilosophical, and therefore inefficient,

* "Efficaciter operari ad sublevanda vitæ humanæ incommoda." — *De Dignitate et Augmentis Scientiarium*, Lib. VII. c. 1.

method of accomplishing so beneficent an end. The first question, then, which presents itself to us is,— How shall we, within the prescribed college olympiad, secure to our students, not the maximum "knowledge," but the highest possible "culture"? To this question the scholars of all ages and in all places have given this one uniform and emphatic answer: The best human culture is attainable only through the earnest and indefatigable study of the mathematics, and of the Greek and Latin languages. Homer and Xenophon, Virgil and Cicero, Euclid and Archimedes, have been for ages past, and must be for ages to come, the great educators of our race.

But it is not to be denied, that the "dead languages," so called, and the higher mathematics, are denounced at the present day by some intelligent men as serious obstacles in the pathway of all rational progress. It is fitting, therefore, that something should be said in their vindication. Their relation to each other and to the human mind is such, that they must either stand or fall side by side. They may both be abandoned with impunity, or else to neglect either one is to abdicate the functions of a well-balanced education altogether. In defending their common cause, I shall maintain their importance in the University curriculum, both as a means of "culture" and as a source of "practical knowledge." Though many of the arguments which might be urged in behalf of the classics are equally pertinent in a defence of the mathematics, yet, as a matter of convenience, I shall separate them in this discussion.

In the first place, then, let us consider whether the languages of Greece and Rome, which have hitherto occupied so conspicuous a place in the highest institutions of learning throughout the world, should, in the clearer light of these modern days and under the severer pressure of the progressive sciences, be condemned and banished from the recitation-room.

It is certainly something in their favor, that they have, by common consent, constituted a principal part of sound learning in every civilized nation of the earth ever since the mediæval darkness, which they did more than all things else to dissipate; something, that the profoundest scholars of past centuries have gratefully acknowledged their indebtedness to them, while the profoundest scholars of the present day plead, in all the various tongues of Christendom, against

"The deep damnation of their taking off."

The enlightened public sentiment of the world, or even of a single community, upon other questions, whether educational, social, civil, or religious, is considered of some value; but we will not insist upon it in this case.

It is argued, that, when the classics are tried in the crucible of *utility*, they cannot stand the fire, but vanish into thin air, — *in tenues auras.* The popular mind is not a little befogged in its conception of the meaning of this eternally recurring word, "utility." It is forgotten that it is not an absolute term; — a thing is useful or useless just according to its fitness or unfitness to produce some required result. Uselessness will not be predicated of a plough because it cannot reap wheat, nor of the sickle because it cannot till the ground. It does not follow, as a logical *sequitur*, that, because a knowledge of international law cannot be turned to any practical account by the chemist, Vattel therefore will not be a useful text-book to diplomates and statesmen; nor can we fairly infer, that, because the retort and blow-pipe are not the best armor for the forum and deliberative assembly, they are not, for that reason, indispensable to the laboratory. It is quite possible that the Greek Slave of Powers, though it can neither pick cotton nor tend a sugar-mill, may not be altogether destitute of utility. Ask Miss Hosmer whether that drooping figure, with its face of wondrous beauty, in whose expression the lofty spirit of a Pythian priestess and the wounded delicacy of shrinking womanhood are so mingled and blended as to vitalize the chiselled marble, has no value in her "heart's just estimation"? She might not know its relation to the often-repeated questions, "What shall I eat, what shall I drink, and wherewithal shall I be clothed?" but she would answer you, in the language of the poet,

"A thing of beauty is a joy forever!"

The Psalms of the great Hebrew Prophet are of very little material worth, — a few dollars could buy enough of them to supply the whole heathen world; but yet, who that has drunk at these sweet springs in the desert of life, when travel-stained and way-worn, and been refreshed by them to pursue his journey onward and upward to the end, would think of counting up their value on his "anxious fingers,"* like a speculator in the waters of a Blue Lick fountain or sulphureous Artesian well?

There are two lights in which a man may be regarded: in one, he is a means to an end; in the other, he is an end himself. The training adapted to render him a dexterous instrument amidst the actualities of life is not the same as that which is suited to develop in harmonious proportion all his original faculties, whether of thought or feeling, to their highest power and perfection. The two, however, differ more in degree than in kind. The former is absolutely necessary; the latter is always desirable. We must eat to live; we need not live to eat.† Of the utility of those branches of knowledge which are fitted to prepare us for industrial conquests in the shop or on the prairie, enabling us by the fruits of our toil to satisfy the crav-

* ". . . . sibi quid sit
Utile, solicitis supputat articulis." — Ovid.

† "Edere oportet ut vivas, non vivere ut edas." — *Ad Herennium.*

ings of our animal nature, and which have been called by the Germans *Brodwissenschaften*, the Bread-and-Butter sciences, nobody entertains an unbelieving doubt. The controversy is restricted to those studies, on the other hand, which look primarily to the elevation and expansion of our intellectual and moral powers for their own sake, and because of their exalted nature and destiny, and which are known among scholars under the generic appellation of the "Liberal Arts and Sciences." The utility of these, including as they do the classic languages of antiquity, are questioned not only by those who believe that it is the sole mission of humanity "to draw existence, propagate, and rot," but also by sharp-minded, practical men, who, not to be imposed upon by visionary enthusiasts, weigh every article of alleged value in the scales of the money-changer, and proclaim to the world its exact worth in the Arabic characters of our federal currency. Woe to the unfortunate commodity, whatever it may be, which cannot be coined into drachmas;—it is good for nothing but to be cast out and trodden under foot of men. The Greek language, with its artistic beauty, its sinewy strength, its exhaustless capabilities, its adaptation to every variety of scene and subject and manifestation of genius, speaking to us in the sounding line of Homer, in the commanding eloquence of Demosthenes, in the subtile and shadowy philosophy of Plato, in the grace and touching pathos of Sophocles, in the gossiping freedom of story-telling Herodotus, in the conciseness and fiery energy of Thucydides, in the elegiac sweetness of Moschus, in the pastoral simplicity of Theocritus and Bion, in the delicate characterization and two-edged satire of Aristophanes,—the Greek language, I say, the instrument of thought to a people who have drawn deeper lines on the rind of this old world than any other nation of the earth, must not be studied, forsooth, because in this busy country it will not "pay"! "Malebranche," says Mirabeau, "saw all things in God; M. Necker saw all things in Necker." There are those who see all things in money, and look only for money in all things. The most beautiful landscape in the world to them is a corner city lot; the most graceful tree, that which will make the biggest pile of cord-wood; the most accomplished lady, she who is heir-apparent to the largest fortune. The sun shines to save the expense of gas or coal-oil; the "books that are books" are the ledger and the bank-book, and the eloquence which stirs their blood like the sound of a trumpet is that which offers two per cent a month with good security. Their Lydian Stone —the sole criterion of the quality of things, material and immaterial—is the market value. It is of one of these that Wordsworth wrote,

> "The primrose by the river's brim
> A yellow primrose is to him,
> And it is nothing more."

The divine effluence which is shed from Corinthian column and blossoming tree, from emerald lawn and blushing fruit, the matin song of birds among the leaves, the fragrant breath of summer flowers, the ethereal essence of nature, her beauty and her glory, are, in the dialect of trade, "of no account," because they cannot be sold by "samples" in the exchange on short credit, or, what would be a better "operation," "realized" at once. Now all this material philosophy is based upon the assumption that we are mere creatures of sense, and that the late Lord Orford, as a fair type of our race, was not far out of the way in expecting that his stomach would survive the rest of his person. But it is not all of life to live. There is a bitter irony in the words of the poet:

> "We eat, and drink, and sleep; what then?
> We eat, and drink, and sleep again."

There are other and nobler functions of the human organism than the digestion of quails and oysters. The gastric juice is not the universal solvent, vainly sought, amidst smoke and toil, in the laboratories of the old alchemists. We have hearts as well as a digestive apparatus; heads as well as hands. It is in this realm of our higher nature the liberal arts and sciences find their place and mission. It is here the ancient languages vindicate their claims to utility.

1. In examining them, therefore, in the clear atmosphere of this high table-land, we observe, in the first place, that they are admirably adapted to the purpose of severe *mental discipline.* However philosophers may differ in their distribution of our cognitive faculties, they all agree in asserting the fundamental importance of a habit of intellectual *attention.* Now in the Greek and Latin languages syntactical relations are not expressed, as in English, by any law of juxtaposition, but by the terminational endings of the principal parts of speech. The eloquent periods of Cicero are each an organic whole, whose force and significance cannot be apprehended little by little; but the definitions of the separate words, one after another, must be held in the memory by a special intellectual effort, until the last one, the final verb, having been reached and conquered, the glowing thought or sentiment flashes like an electric spark from the conclusion to the commencement. There is no room here for drowsiness or indifference. Let the mind relax its grasp for a moment, and the meaning of some captured word will escape and return to its hiding-place in the lexicon. It is easy to see, therefore, that, in the version of a Latin or Greek sentence, the mental faculties must be awake and at home, intensely occupied with the work before them, and that, as we acquire habits by acts and strengthen them by exercise, it is only necessary for the student to pursue this translating process to the proper extent in order to secure for himself the power of a *patient and prolonged attention,* — an achievement of more value to him than all the knowl-

edge contained in all the books of the Mercantile Library. No man, without the ability to concentrate all his energies upon any given subject for any reasonable length of time, has ever accomplished or ever will accomplish anything extraordinary in human affairs. No man with this power of abstracting himself from the invasion of surrounding objects, and of devoting himself for the time being to some one overmastering purpose, lacks the golden key which may open to him the temple of science or fame. "Genius," says Helvetius, "is nothing but a continued attention," — *une attention suivie.* Not unlike this is the saying of Buffon: "Genius is only a protracted patience," — *une longue patience.* The difference between a Newton and a common man is found chiefly in the fact, that the former is able to apply himself to any subject of inquiry for an indefinite period, with all his powers under his entire control, connecting conclusions with premises in one continuous chain of reasoning, until a determinate end be reached and the far-off truth brought within the circle of positive knowledge; while the latter, the undisciplined man, cannot command his intellectual forces at all, much less lead them in battle array, by long and painful marches, to conflict and victory. In a striking passage in his *Traité de Morale*, Malebranche, as quoted by Sir William Hamilton, has beautifully said: "The attention of the intellect is a natural prayer by which we obtain the enlightenment of the reason." It was the opinion of Condorcet, indorsed by Dugald Stewart and Professor Playfair, that any ordinary student may, under competent teachers, acquire all that Newton or La Place *knew* in *two years.* But it need not be said, that to acquire their *regal power of intellect*, asserting its empire over more worlds than would have satisfied the wildest ambition of Alexander, were quite a different thing. *This* comes only as the fruit of long years of persistent, self-imposed discipline. A habit of attention, such as the school-boy may form over his

Cæsar and Virgil, was strengthened in them by repeated exercise, until, as its culminating result, we have those star-crowned monuments of sleepless labor, the *Principia* and *Mécanique Celeste.*

In the act of translating from the classics, the necessity of constantly discriminating between the several meanings of every word, and determining their rival claims to a place in the English version, not only cultivates in the student the utmost precision and exactness of language, but it serves also to give him that dispassionate and judicial habit of mind which distinguishes a man of sound judgment from a person of mere impulse and caprice. It does not require much observation to see that speaking accurately always implies thinking clearly. Whatever facilitates the former cannot fail to promote the latter. It was not a matter of accident, that reason and speech are both denoted in Greek by one word, λόγος. Words have a soul as well as a body, and the study of them in connected discourse is the study of the high themes of which they treat. It is not strange, therefore, that a prolonged and critical examination of the classical productions of antiquity, the most faultless models of thought and speech, should, by a beneficent law of our being, produce in the youthful devotee a purity and correctness of taste, an elevation of sentiment, a warmth and truth of feeling, a beauty and splendor of imagery, a wealth of allusion and illustration, — in a word, all those various qualities and accomplishments of mind and heart which are fitted to give a man, and always do give him, a sovereignty over his fellow-men. The ennobling influence of such writings as the dialogues of Plato and Tully upon the *moral* nature of the student, is not to be overlooked. It is impossible for him to listen, in the stillness of his night-watches, to the pure and persuasive teachings of Socrates in the *Phædo* and *Memorabilia*, and of Cicero in his *De Senectute* and *Tusculan Questions*, without feeling the divinity stirring within him and kindling aspirations after immortality. We cannot wander through Sabean groves of bloom without catching the perfume in our dress; we cannot "sit down to a symposium with the gods, and rise from the banquet wholly mortal."

2. A familiar acquaintance with Greek and Latin is indispensably necessary to any exact knowledge of the modern languages, our own included. It is a rule of masonry, I believe, that in building a structure we should always begin at the bottom. The Latin is the foundation of the French, Spanish, Portuguese, and Italian. The latter are mere dialects of the former; and the only philosophical and practicable way of learning thoroughly the Romanic languages of Europe is first to learn thoroughly the old Roman language which underlies them. It is possible, I know, by force of iteration and reiteration, after the nursery or Ollendorff method, to acquire the power of speaking intelligibly in any modern tongue. But such an acquisition, based on no knowledge of the fundamental laws of universal grammar is merely empty sound, — *vox et prœterea nihil.* To a person ignorant of the Latin, the Southern European languages must appear a set of unmeaning jargons, with no resemblance between any two and no consistency in any one, but all alike rioting in wanton, incoherent lawlessness. Whatever may be said of the origin of the Teutonic languages of Germany and the North of Europe, it is certain that, in their capability of continued development from their own substance, in their pliability of construction, in their flexibility and scientific precision, and in the picturesque beauty of their words, they bear a striking resemblance to the more perfect Greek; and it is safe to say at least, that a knowledge of the language of Plato and Aristotle cannot be otherwise than an admirable preparation to the student who aspires to comprehend the teachings of Kant and Hegel.

It may seem to some of my audience a hard saying, but I have no hesitation in affirming that it is impossible to be an accomplished scholar in our own native tongue without an intimate acquaintance with the classic tongues of antiquity. The English is a composite language, and its principal factors are the Latin, Greek, and Anglo-Saxon. To understand the former without a knowledge of the latter would be as impracticable as to apprehend the aggregate value of a numerical expression without knowing the individual value of the figures which constitute it. The Anglo-Saxon furnishes us, to a large extent, with the little monosyllabic, bullet-like words, which we shoot back and forth in the common "will and won't" dialect and dialectics of every-day life. But all those words which win the ear in the eloquent harangues of the orator, or lend music to the rhythmic cadences of the poet, or give precision to the definitions of science as well as to the discussions of the metaphysician, came to us from Greece and Rome. Before they were ours they had been pronounced in that "assembly of kings" on the Capitoline Hill, or had passed the searching ordeal of the polished and hypercritical Attic Demos, whose delicate and scrupulous ear tolerated no barbaric utterance from the stage or *βῆμα*. The English language, thus constituted, is an instrument of thought and speech worthy of the two great nations of modern times; and it is no wild anticipation, that he who learns to wield this instrument with skill and power may yet, in the progress of events, command the listening attention of the world. But this skill and power does not come by inspiration; is not inherited like money and beauty; cannot be bought like blood stock and patriotic politicians. He who, by a wide-reaching comparative philology, and, above all, by a patient and laborious analysis of the two scientific languages whose harmonies and concise energy so greatly enrich our own forms of speech, — he who has thus studied universal grammar, and he alone, "knows the structure, the laws, the liberties, the powers of his mother tongue. He is the master, not the slave, of language. He can mould its forms at pleasure. He can sweep every cord of the many-stringed harp, and draw from it the unfailing echo of his own thought and sentiment." *

Our whole literature is interfused, in every part and parcel of it, with the writings and spirit of antiquity. I do not refer merely to the numerous quotations from Greek and Latin authors, which are found in almost every standard English work, whether of prose or poetry; but rather to the multitudinous allusions to the facts and fictions of ancient history and mythology, an acquaintance with which is as much presupposed in our literature as a knowledge of the alphabet; and, more than all, to that indefinable something, that *nescio quid preclarum ac singulare* of Cicero, which we may call the classic style. To the mere English scholar, Milton's Paradise Lost, and even Sir William Hamilton's Lectures on Metaphysics, are almost as unintelligible as the Iliad of Homer and the Ethics of the Stagirite. If we come down from the airy realm of poetry and speculation to the solid ground of fact, we encounter the same difficulties, enhanced and multiplied. Every page of our text-books on the exact and progressive sciences is dark or light, according to our scholarship, with words of classic origin. It is an unnatural effort, which some are making,† to array the Physics against the Humanities; — it is an attempt to strike down the eagle with an arrow feathered from his own plumage. The nomenclature, the terminology, of all the physical sciences is wholly borrowed from the Greek and Latin, and a knowledge of these languages is not more absolutely necessary to any exactness of classification on the

* A. P. Peabody, D. D., Address before the United Literary Societies of Dartmouth College, 1843.

† "Damnant quod non intelligunt." — Cicero.

part of the writer, than it is to the comfort and edification of the reader. If any one, whose studies have been confined to his mother tongue, is sceptical on this point, let him undertake to read intelligently or intelligibly some scientific treatise on botany or zoölogy, for example, and he will discover, before he reaches the end, if I mistake not, that there are a great many *deader* things in this world than the "dead languages."

In speaking of the importance of the classics to a right understanding of our own tongue, it would be improper to omit all allusion to the fact, that a knowledge of revealed religion is communicated to us in the *Greek* Testament. We would not undervalue the English version. It is worthy of the patient scholars who made it, and of the lofty themes with which it has to do. But still it is a fact, not without significance, that God chose to make his revelations of mercy to a fallen world in the Greek language. In this language Christ preached his Sermon on the Mount,* and Paul harangued the Athenians from Mars' Hill, and wrote his letter to the Corinthians developing the great doctrine of the Resurrection. If, therefore, we would understand the Christian Scriptures, in all their exactness and intensity of meaning, we must avoid the diluted mixtures of the commentators, and go back to their original sources. We cannot judge of the flavor of the Rocky Mountain springs by drinking the soil-stained waters of the Mississippi.

* The proposition that *Christ spoke Greek* is not, we are aware, universally admitted. Those who deny it rely upon the statements of the Greek Fathers; those who maintain it, not only impugn the authority of the Fathers, but appeal to the internal evidence of the Gospels themselves. Three things on this point are, we think, especially worthy of notice: — 1st. Papias, whose testimony in the negative is the fullest and most positive, was, as Eusebius affirms, *σφόδρα σμικρὸς τὸν νοῦν*, a man of imbecile intellect; while Jerome, as he himself acknowledges, and Epiphanius, as his writings show, mistook the spurious *Gospel to the Hebrews* for the genuine "Gospel according to Matthew." 2d. Christ, in his frequent citations from the Old Testament Scriptures, almost uniformly quotes, *not from the Hebrew text, but from the Septua-*

3. The careful study of the Greek and Latin is the only thing which can save our own language from impurity and disintegration. The elaborate beauty and lofty diction of Athenian eloquence are a perpetual rebuke to the Congressional and forensic orators, who are polluting good old Chaucer's "well of English undefyled" with the foul expectorations of Parisian *poissardes* and bar-room politicians. The barbarous idioms, the base-born provincialisms, the grotesque anomalies, which are constantly creeping up into the language from the lower strata of society, or pressing into it from beyond the outer rim of civilization, can be prevented only by a more thorough training of our youth after such models of exquisite taste and chastened elegance as are furnished in the simple narratives and moral discussions of Xenophon. In the same culture, too, must be found the cure for those extravagances of speech, which are not unfrequently heard in our withdrawing-rooms, and which are eminently characteristic of *sensational* young ladies. It would be difficult to find anything in the Attic tongue corresponding to such high-sounding phrases as "gorgeous sponge-cake" and "splendid mince-pie"! The Greeks, in their severe simplicity, did not think it necessary to break on a wheel the butterfly which might be crushed under a sandal, nor to carry their kittens to the Hyper-

gint Greek version, — an absurdity if his disciples did not understand Greek, and an impossibility if he did not himself understand it. 3d. That the Greek language prevailed among the people with whom our Lord mingled in daily intercourse may be inferred, without violence, from two facts: first, Syria, including Palestine, had been under *Greek rule* from its subjection by Alexander the Great, A. M. 3681, until it was conquered by Pompey, a few years before the advent of Christ; and, second, the Evangelists were always careful to *translate into Greek every Hebrew word* which they employed in their own narrations, — a precaution they certainly would not have taken if they had been writing for Hebrew or Aramaic readers. (Matt. i. 23; xxvii. 33, 46; Mark xv. 34; John xix. 13, &c., &c.) See Prolegomena, pp. 25 – 29, to 3d ed. of Greek Testament, by Henry Alford, B. D., Minister of Quebec Chapel, London.

borean Ocean when they could be drowned at home in a puddle just as well. The Latin, with its terse and nervous vigor, spurning all circumlocution and unmeaning expletives, impatient alike of the rose-colored verbiage and diluted twaddling of the modern novellette and of the outrageous solecisms and loose-jointed compounds in which Thomas Carlyle plays off his radical conservatism, a

"Disguised Apollo changed to Harlequin,"

is the strong manilla cable on which we rely to hold our language to its moorings. Sunder this, and we float out to sea, — a sea, too, like that amidst the Arctic wastes, without harbor or headland, and whose only beacon-lights are the wild flashings of the Aurora Borealis or the dim phosporescence of its own tumultuous billows.

It is not unfrequently asked why the salutary influence exerted, as we have maintained, by the classics, may not be secured through the translations which now abound. This question, of course, leaves out of view their disciplinary effect upon the student, as well as their fundamental and living relation to the modern languages. But, aside from this, there is another important consideration, which meets us at the threshold of the subject: *works of art and taste cannot be translated.* The best versions which we have seen, whether they have appeared under the guise of Professor Anthon's voluminous annotations or in the literal interlineations of Hart and Clarke, are as inferior to the original as the daubing of a journeyman sign-painter is inferior to the touches of Raphael or Michel Angelo. They are the Apollo Belvidere and Venus de Medici imitated in plaster of Paris; they are oaks of Dodona, "high-haired" and wide-branching, vocal with the utterances of the gods, hewn down and lying trimmed and inglorious in the ship-yards of Naupactum. There are no articulate words in English, nothing but the most delicate intonations of voice, which correspond at all to those correlative particles, μέν and δέ, which play so important a part in all Greek writings, and whose force is so finely illustrated in that perfect model of elaborate eloquence, the Funeral Oration of Lysias. No translation can give to us the faintest idea of the contemptuous emphasis with which Demosthenes hissed that *Μάκεδων ἄνηρ* through his teeth in his Philippics, or of that mingled horror and indignation with which Cicero, in his fierce denunciation of the blood-thirsty Prætor of Sicily, portrayed the crucifixion of a Roman citizen. We may undoubtedly learn some facts in ancient history and science from our common English versions; but even here we miss that primeval grace and beauty, which made dry details a living reality. We feel that, though the body remains, the soul is gone. Instead of the full-robed kings and priests, who walked the streets of hundred-gated Thebes in all the pride of power, we have the shrivelled, eviscerated, brainless mummies of the Upper Nile.

4. The study of Greek and Latin literature brings us into immediate and sensible contact with the life of antiquity, from which our own is an outgrowth. Lord Bacon has said, "Antiquitas seculi, juventus mundi"; which has been rendered by Jeremy Bentham, "*We* are the ancients." We have no objection to this epigrammatic statement of fact, though we do object to the inference which its author has drawn from it. The classic nations of the past are not to be blamed for their youth. They might have been wiser, perhaps, if they could have read the *Novum Organum;* but there was no *a priori* method of doing it. There is a profound truth in the simple line of Wordsworth, —

> "The child is father of the man."

It is as applicable to nations, in their lineal descent, as to individuals. The roots of our intellectual life are deep in the soil of Attica and Latium. We are what we are, because Greece and Rome were what they were. We can no more assert our independence of them, than the child, who has within himself the tendency to certain forms of physical development or the germs of certain peculiarities of character, transmitted to him from generation to generation, can assert his independence of his ancestry. The present age is connected with all the ages. We are heirs to the riches of them all. Their great thoughts and great deeds, their treasures of art and of learning, are ours by inheritance, and may be ours by individual possession, if we choose to make them so. Hitherto, we, in common with the countries of lettered Europe, have been wise enough to avail ourselves of this accumulated wealth of centuries. The key to this repository of the past is a knowledge, not of Bohn's translations, as we have intimated, but of the Greek and Latin languages. These, as taught in the schools throughout the civilized world, have been the fountains of modern civilization. Whether Plato lighted his lamp at the altar of Moses or not, it is certain that he found favor with Justin Martyr, Clemens Alexandrinus, and other Christian Fathers; while it is not less certain, that his speculations and sentiments still affect, in no inconsiderable degree, the discussions and theoretic faith of our modern schools of theology. Macaulay is not extravagant in asserting of early Christianity, that "the rites of the Pantheon had passed into her worship, and the subtilties of the Academy into her creed."

In that department of the science of morals which regards man, not in his subjective nature, but as an active being, having duties to fulfil and evils to shun, the classics are full, teaching us in every form, by dialogue, by allegory, by positive precept, "to hate the cowardice of doing wrong," and to love the beauty and goodness (τὸ καλὸν καὶ τἀγαθόν) of a true and manly life. The allegory of Prodicus and the picture of Cebes are familiar illustrations of this kind of writing; and not a few of the best books in our Sunday-school libraries are indebted to them, to a greater or less extent, for their efficiency in winning the young to virtue. The argument of Paley and of most modern *a posteriori* writers in moral philosophy, proving from the evidences of design in nature the existence and benevolent providence of a Supreme Being, is only a dilution of the famous conversation between Socrates and his devoted, though sceptical disciple, Aristodemus.*

It is not much to say in respect to the *laws* of modern times, that Roman jurisprudence still bears sway in all the courts of Christendom. When the shadows of the Middle Ages began to rise from the nations of Continental Europe, the Pandects of Justinian, a compilation of the legal lore of thirteen hundred years, all revised and purged of what was arbitrary and technical by Cujacius and the civilians, so as to be equally well adapted to all ages and peoples, were hailed with joy and gratitude as a collection of written reason, a revelation of the holiest mysteries of justice. Chancellor Kent, who was himself a brilliant illustration of the use which may be made of the enlightened equity of the Roman jurisconsults, traces the great improvements in our jurisprudence to "the study and influence of the civil law." Such a result could hardly fail to follow from such a cause. For, unlike some of the pettifogging *pragmatici* of the present day, who, in Dr. Arnold's opinion, are not fit for heaven, the Roman lawyers looked upon law as a branch of ethics, whose foundations lay in right reason and the unalterable feelings of human nature.† They believed that it was, as Cicero has portrayed it, not a thing thought out by the ingenuity of man, not a decree of the people, but an

* Memorabilia, Lib. II. c. 4.

† "Neque opinione, sed natura constitutum est jus." — Cicero.

eternal entity,* coeval in its origin and harmonizing in its operations with the Divine Mind; that it was the recorded morality of a nation, a rule of social duty not less than of civil conduct; that it was the sacred embodiment of the public will and understanding, the unanimous assent of a great people to the principles of a refined equity and enlarged benevolence, reduced to practice in the daily concerns of life with the precision, the consistency and uniformity of an exact science. It is not strange, therefore, that the jurisprudence of the old Romans, drawn thus from the very depths of philosophy, —*penitus ex intima philosophia*, — should outlast the changing polities of nations and look down through the ages with serene contempt upon the unjust, and therefore perishable, legislation of unprincipled men.

But without pursuing this topic further, it is obvious that the Present is only an outgrowth of the Past, and that he who would see our life and civilization in its germinant state and early developing, must go back to the prolific soil of Greece and Latium; — to a period when the world was new, and wondering eyes were taking their first earnest look at the beautiful objects of outward nature, or, filmed and dreamy, were watching with philosophic ecstasy the workings of the human soul; to races of men who left no field of thought unexplored, but who, whether "up-looking" or "earth-gazing," † whether creating works of art or elaborating an ethical science, always saw clearly, felt intensely, reasoned profoundly, and wrought each in his own sphere with the hand of a master. It may well be to us a matter of self-gratulation, that in literature at least we are their legitimate heirs, —

* "Hanc, igitur, video sapientissimorum fuisse sententiam, legem neque hominum ingeniis excogitatum, nec scitum aliquod esse populorum, sed Eternum Quiddam." — Cic. Leg. II. 8.

† The generic word for *man* in Latin is *homo* (akin to *humus*), the *earth-born*; in Greek, *ἄνθρωπος* (*ἀνά* and prob. *ὁράω*), the *up-looker*.

Κάδμου τοῦ πάλαι νέα τροφή;

that the study of their poetry, art, eloquence, and philosophy brings us near to their great, beating hearts, and not only unites us to them in more vital bonds of sympathy, but also introduces us into the goodly fellowship of scholarly minds all over the world.

The moral efficacy of the classics in uniting cultivated men of every age and nation in one communion and commonwealth of letters, leads me to suggest that philological facts are of more consequence in discussing the question of the physical unity or plurality of our race, than all the speculations of geology or anthropology, however subtile and ingenious they may be. If forms of speech the most diverse have numerous *common roots*, as they undoubtedly have, it follows as an inevitable inference that they are only dialects of one primeval tongue. The unity of the race is a mere corollary to a demonstration of the original unity of language.

5. The Greek and Latin languages are worthy of study not merely for their own artistic excellence, but also because of their connection with the highest works of art.* There is no man so entirely material, so utterly destitute of imagination, as to be altogether content with the mere utilities of life. There is inherent in our very being a longing after something higher and better than that which ministers only to our physical wants and appetites. The eye turns away from the dusty thoroughfares of business, from the uncouth objects which lie along our daily path, to find repose and pleasure in symmetry and proportion, in comeliness of shape and beauty of blended colors. If, in the most hapless conditions of humanity, as in the hovel of the Russian serf, or the snow-built hut of the Esquimaux, or the sightless cabin

* "Nec levis, ingenuas pectus coluisse per artes,
Cura sit; et linguas edidicisse duas." — Ovid.

of the Southern slave, life shrunk within itself asks only for food and shelter, it is because the heaven-enkindled aspirations for what may grace this earthly existence have been extinguished in the souls of men. There is a use of Beauty as well as a beauty of Use. The two are mutual helpers, and should never be separated. They have their prototype in the famous Persian bird, the Juftak, which has but one wing, on the opposite side to which the male has a hook and the female a ring, so that they can fly only when fastened together. Just so, it is only when Art and Utility are united that a national civilization reaches its highest development and perfection. The old Roman built the Pantheon and Coliseum when he was the busiest in constructing legal systems and in carrying his conquering eagles to the remotest boundaries of universal empire. The modern Italian, despising stern labor in his devotion to cameos, mosaics, hand-organs, and poor copies of the old masters, has lost the glow and inspiration of genius as well as the fruits of industrial conquest. Of his country, from which the last "bright dream of commonwealths" has just faded, the poet has written truly:

> "There tiny pleasures occupy the place
> Of glories and of duties; as the feet
> Of fabled fairies, when the sun goes down,
> Trip o'er the grass where wrestlers strove by day." *

In our own country, hitherto, we have furnished an illustration of indomitable energy consecrated chiefly to utility. We have been too much engrossed in the present to paint or build or write for the future. The bayonet of necessity has been at our back. The sunlight must be let into the gloom of untraversed forests. Savage beasts and savage men must be driven before the advancing line of a new civilization. Gold, gleaming through the crevices of distant mountains, has caught the eye and quickened the

* Walter Savage Landor, Hellenics.

pulse. Everybody has been in too great a hurry to stand still long enough to admire the beautiful in nature or to create the beautiful in art. It is said * that the dogs in Egypt never stop to lap the waters of the Nile, but always run while they drink, afraid lest the crocodiles should seize them. So with us, the eagerness to achieve some present good, or the fear of some impending evil, has kept us in a perpetual "dog-trot." From the tanning of a calf's skin to the development of a child's brain, all has been haste. But we are now approaching another era. Accumulated wealth has brought with it ampler leisure, and Art is beginning to lend her embellishments to the monuments of our industry. It is at this point, and in this relation, the classics assert their claims with special emphasis to our attention. I do not mean to say, that a good linguist must of necessity be a good painter or sculptor, but simply that a careful study of those languages, whose very words are pictures, whose sentences in their construction are models of artistic skill, and whose subjects are borrowed from all that is attractive and thrilling in human observation and experience, — from outward nature with its visible shapes and images of things, from the soul dark with passion or warm with affection, from the boundless world of fable, — cannot fail to quicken our sensibilities to the power of beauty, and to prepare us for a higher appreciation of every form of art.

Simonides has defined a picture to be a silent poem, and a poem a speaking picture.† We are impressed with the propriety of this definition in reading the Iliad, — an epic which is not so much a portrait-gallery of heroes as it is a pictorial representation of heroic life. The characters of

* By Phædrus. "Ut canis e Nilo," is an old proverb, applied to anything done in haste.

† "Si poema loquens pictura est, pictura tacitum poema debet esse." — *Ad Herennium.*

Homer never sit in attitude till he has sketched them off, but all are up and in motion, full of lusty, sinewy vigor. Councils gathered on Olympus, gods and goddesses in high debate, tents dotting the plain in the moonlight, the son of Thetis sitting gloomy apart, war-cars dashing over the battle-field, heroes stalking in their strength over the slain, wounded divinities flying from the carnage back to heaven, Trojan maidens moving in sad procession to the temple of "the fair-haired terrible goddess," the smoke of burning victims curling round the tomb of Patroclus, the "white-armed Andromache" plying her loom in silence or bewailing on the city walls the "god-like Hector," — all pass hurriedly, but clearly, before the eye, like the shifting scenes of a panorama. It was not without reason, that Lucian declared Homer to be the greatest of painters, and Pliny bestowed no slight compliment upon Apelles, when he expressed the opinion, that his chief work, the painting of the sacrifice of Diana, surpassed even the description of the great poet. Historic Painting and Epic Poetry, in their imitations of nature, both alike study its most perfect forms, and abstract from them an idea of absolute beauty and virtue; both, too, exhibit with similar skill the passions and interior life of man.* Strength and energy distinguish the characters of Homer and Michael Angelo; grace and propriety, those of Virgil and Raphael. Landscape Painting and Pastoral Poetry present an analogy hardly less striking. Titian and Claude Lorraine are in the one what Theocritus and the author of the Bucolics are in the other.

But it is not fitting for one who cannot speak of the great works of the artist *ex cathedra*, to pursue this topic further in this direction. We are happy to know, that the Directors of Washington University are not unmindful of this branch of an accomplished education, but that provision

* "Pictoribus atque poetis
Quidlibet audendi semper fuit æqua potestas." — Horace.

is making for a department of the Fine Arts,* so organized that, while it may subserve the important interests of Architecture and of Design in its infinite applications in manufactures and mechanics, it may also afford alike to youth and age, to refined leisure and to toiling industry, the means of gratifying that love of the Beautiful, which not only dwells in each human heart, but is manifested also in all the graceful and gorgeous drapery of external nature as one of the attributes of the all-creating, all-pervading Spirit. It has been said, that a man should enter his house every day between rows of magnificent statues to make him magnanimous. That our characters are modified by whatever surrounds us, whether animate or inanimate, does not admit of a question. We are all chameleons in this respect, and our thoughts take their coloring from the objects on which they rest. The legislators of ancient times, in the light of this law, studied to render the arts subservient to public virtue and morality. The statutes of Harmodius and Aristogeiton were placed in the Forum, where they stood as the perpetual champions of Athens, and for ages kept alive the holy flame of liberty. In the courts of justice, the marble forms of Solon and Lycurgus overlooked the judges on their bench, and watched with stern regard and scrutinizing eye the administration of law. Every portico and public walk presented some memorial of departed merit, fitted to kindle the enthusiasm of the young and urge them on to glorious deeds and a similar immortality. The history of Greece might be studied in the streets of her capital by its sculptured heroes, statesmen, and poets, almost as well as in the closet with Herodotus and Thucydides.

The great work on this American continent, which now lies first and nearest to us, is the blending of the grace and

* The School of Fine Arts in Paris has twenty Professors; and the School of the Industrial Arts, fourteen Professors.

refinement of Greek cultivation with our own Roman energy and religious faith. Let this be done, and then shall there arise upon the eye of the world the lineaments of a republic far transcending the loftiest conceptions of Plato,—a republic of which poets have dreamed and prophets spoken, the flowerage of centuries, the bloom and perfume of a Christian civilization.

I have thus presented a few of the many considerations which justify an institution of learning in insisting upon the ancient classics as one of the two great means of that *intellectual culture* which, constituting the principal work of the college, must precede and underlie the various branches of *knowledge* taught in the special departments of the University. It remains for me to speak briefly of the Mathematics as the other means of this intellectual culture.

It must be remembered, that, notwithstanding the innumerable applications of mathematical science to the practical use of man, yet the primary object, in the order of time, is not so much to store the mind with facts and principles, as it is to give it skill and power; not so much to surfeit the student with the stale thoughts of others, as it is to teach him to think himself; not so much to deck the garden of the mind with flowers, or even to fill it with fruits, as it is to enrich the soil and render it capable of indefinite growth and luxuriance. It is not enough that the classics furnish us with a refined and elevated taste, a nice and accurate discrimination, a ready flow and copiousness of language, and a bold and fertile imagination, teeming with the beautiful creations of the poet and orator. Graceful acquisitions in literature as well as the facts and data of science, though in themselves good, do not reach their highest efficiency without the ability to arrange and classify and employ them by well-directed means to some determinate result. The power which can reduce these elements to order, and give to them an harmonious and effective energy, must be sought in a strong and highly cultivated *reason*. That the mathematics are eminently adapted to the accomplishment of this end, will become apparent from a brief examination of their nature and effects.

1. We observe, in the first place, that there is a regular gradation from the plainest and easiest process of reasoning to the most complicated and abstruse. From the intuitive axiom or the child's simplest proposition up to the startling conclusions of a Kepler or Newton or Le Verrier, there is a natural and easy succession of steps, — a sort of ladder reaching from earth to heaven as in patriarchal vision. At each step, the student, so far from being fatigued, is invigorated to take the next and the next with greater facility, and the more sublime the height attained, the firmer his foot and the clearer his vision. If it be objected, as it sometimes is, that some persons are so constituted as to be incapable of success in mathematical studies, we answer, that, if a mind can deduce consequences from general principles on any other subject, there is no conceivable reason why it may not do the same thing in mathematics, where, from the definiteness of the relations and the clearness of the language, reasoning must be far easier than amidst the obscurities and equivocations attendant upon most other subjects of investigation. It is safe to say, that a man who is not suited by nature for mathematical reasoning is not suited to reason at all.

2. There is, again, another advantage belonging especially to the study of mathematics: not a particle of the real acquisitions which the student may make can be lost; for it is incorporated into the very constitution of the mind itself, and becomes a part of its substance. He may, indeed, so soon as he is free from college regulations and out of hearing of the college bell, shut up the hated volume of Curves and Functions, and follow in funeral procession old Euclid to his burial; but yet their influence will be

manifest through life, in every manly act he performs, in every page he writes, in every speech he makes. He may forget all their rules and formulæ and captions, but still the intellectual power which the rigid demonstration of their correctness has given him is not a thing of memory. The giant may not be able to recollect the household receipts for preparing the food which matured his strength and turned his gristle into bone; but, in spite of forgotten receipts and lost cook-books, he is a giant still. History and the natural sciences are, to a large extent, useful only as we remember the facts which they reveal; but in case of mathematics the highest virtue is not in the information, but in the discipline; not in the answers obtained, but in the obtaining of the answers; not in the truth demonstrated, but in the demonstration of the truth. Whether the student shall succeed at last in solving a knotty problem, which has been haunting him for days, is a matter of small consequence, if it was only fitted to fasten his attention and produce in him the power of abstraction and the habit of persevering, courageous thought.

3. It is to be observed, in the third place, that the mathematics present a field for mental exertion, where there is nothing to affect the free and unbiassed exercise of the reasoning powers and the judgment. We learn to swim in still waters, — not in the rapids. On a vast majority of the subjects presented to the mind for investigation, prejudice, passion, and interest become powerful disturbing forces, and thus give a wrong direction to our researches, and lead us by a way we know not to barren results or to conclusions widely at variance with the truth. Many a fierce contest on the field of ethical polemics, which a mathematical exactness in the statement of the question at issue might have prevented, has accomplished nothing more definite and satisfactory, than to demonstrate to the world that controversialists, especially in metaphysics and speculative theology,

fight most readily about those doctrines of which they know the least, and fight with most acrimony when neither party understands his opponent or himself. Who expects, in our political assemblies, that the discussion of great questions of interest and duty will be conducted to their legitimate results with a logical regard to truth and an honest desire to promote the right? Who does not know that party ties are too often stronger than principle, and that party zeal cannot listen to argument? No one can reason fairly, or reason at all, when under the influence of any overpowering passion. To persons in such a state, as Burke once said of the French Jacobins, "a whole generation of men is of no more consequence than a frog in an air-pump." But in subjects of a mathematical nature, the mind may pursue its inquiries unimpeded and undisturbed. The clamors of party strife, the caprices of fancy, and the conflictings of interest have no power here.

It is alleged, I know, that the mathematician is, by his very training, unfitted to reason on moral or probable questions, because in these the perfect precision of thought and expression to which he has been accustomed are impossible. The fallacy of this assumption is obvious from the fact, that the mind pursues the same process and calls into play the same intellectual powers, whatever may be the subject of logical investigation. We see no plausibility in the pretence, that a man who has been weighing evidence or anything else all his life by a perfect standard should be thereby incapacitated from making any estimate upon what could not, for want of a just balance, be exactly weighed. If we had no instruments with which to measure a field, we should rather trust the eye of a practised surveyor to determine for us its probable area, than the eye of a man who had never seen a gunter's chain and did not know whether six square miles or six miles square would make the larger township. It is absurd to suppose that he who has been conversant with perfect proof should be less likely to estimate the approximate value of that which is imperfect, than he who has no just conception of what perfect proof is. Dr. Samuel Clarke, next to Newton, his great master, was perhaps, in his day, the foremost mathematician in England; but in his argumentative writings on moral subjects, the fatalists and philosophic infidels of that age found him, to their discomfiture, "a reasoning machine," as Voltaire expressed it. Pascal was a mathematician of the highest order, and yet the productions of his pen on religious themes show a subtilty and power of which the acutest metaphysician might be proud. How highly Plato esteemed mathematical studies, and how necessary a preparation he thought them for philosophical speculations, may be inferred from the inscription which he placed over the door of his school: *οὐδεὶς ἀγεωμέτρητος εἰσίτο*, — Let no one unacquainted with geometry enter here. *Μαθήματα*, from which our word *mathematics* is derived, implies that, in Greek estimation, they contain the sum of all essential *learning*.

4. But the crowning excellency of the study of mathematics is its eminent fitness to induce the habit of concentrated, continuous, and patient thought. The highest object in all systems of education is, or should be, nothing more nor less than this, — *to teach the pupil to think*. The art of thinking is a mystery, into which, as into the Eleusinian mysteries, the many have never been initiated. What passes for thinking among men resembles it about as much as a column of words in a spelling-book resembles a demonstration in geometry. The continuity in it is a matter of collocation, regulated by accident or whim, and not a rigid, truth-developing process, controlled by immutable laws. The thoughts of most men lead on in no one pathway to any definite conclusion; they ascend from day to day to no higher heaven of invention; but merely go forth in the

morning, without method or aim, just as domestic fowls leave their roosts with the sunrise and scatter over the fields, with no guide but appetite, to return again to the same old roost at sunset. Very few of those who are reckoned wise in the world's esteem could say, with the questionable logic of Des Cartes: *Cogito, ergo sum*, — I think, therefore I am. If the correctness of the philosopher's conclusion depended on the truth of his hypothesis, how little conscious existence there would be in our crowded streets and thronging thoroughfares! It is, however, undoubtedly true, that there is less vicarious thinking — *fides carbonaria* — now than in any former period of history, and yet there are not a few who are willing to surrender the prerogative of free, earnest thought to any self-constituted leader; not a few who are content to stand in the shadow of a great name, and to "crook the pregnant hinges of the knee" at the bidding of any great man; not a few who are always prompt to cough, as the phrase is, whenever some favorite hero happens to take cold.* The old Romans had a way of stitching up the eyes of their poultry and then stuffing them with dough in the dark. Some men are happy to be treated in the same way. But, thanks to the discipline of the schools, the number of these men is growing "fine by degrees and beautifully less." In a process of mathematical reasoning, there is a continual series of propositions, each immediately connected with the one that preceded it and each requiring a distinct intellectual effort. To trace out, therefore, this chain of simple propositions, the mind must be constantly active, or, in other words, must *keep thinking*. In this way is formed that habit of long-continued and intense thought, which underlies every splendid achievement in art or science, and which constitutes the genius of investigation and invention.

It is true, that some of our text-books in mathematics

* "Si dixeris, Æstuo, sudat." — Juvenal.

have been ruined by the *keys*, which compassionate authors and publishers have "printed for the use of teachers only." It is true too, perhaps, that some teachers, so called, may need them, and equally true, that all their pupils get them. This evil will be easily remedied, when our instructors, in the exercise of a proper self-respect, shall look with unmitigated contempt upon the efforts of benevolent book-makers to chew their food for them, or to substitute for the invigorating meat of mathematics a sort of sweetened milk for babies. As it is, the mischief is restricted to certain elementary branches. The comforting assertion, "There is no royal road to Geometry," is as true to-day as it was in the time of King Ptolemy. The calculus and higher mathematics must, from the nature of the subject, escape the desecration of the spoilers. The sordid avarice for money cannot destroy them as efficient agents of intellectual culture. No Midas will bend over them with pendent ears, or turn them by his touch into miserable gold.

But mathematics have an objective relation to society, as well as a subjective relation to the human mind. Up to this point in our discussion, we have considered them only as a means of mental discipline, — as constituting with the ancient classics the two great sources of college culture. But nobody, whose eyes are in his forehead, can have failed to observe, that the grand characteristic of the present age — that which especially marks the progress of the race — is the application of mathematical science, either by itself or in connection with the laboratory, to the every-day, material use of man. Its principles, whether simple or recondite, are not locked up in mystical formulæ, to be deciphered two thousand years hence by some enterprising Champollion; but they are organized and stand forth in tangible shape, and we see them reaping our harvest fields; or whirling, with terrific speed, strange carriages from far city to far city; or sailing up our rivers and across the ocean in spite of wind and current; or writing down the words of a friend the moment he utters them a thousand miles away;* or searching for lost treasures in the depths of the sea with a success which would have astonished the pearl-divers of Delos; or revealing to our enlarged vision, in the midnight sky, new worlds of light, and thus giving us clearer conceptions of the greatness and glory of Him whose "Spirit hath garnished the heavens."

Mathematics, then, are mixed as well as pure, and it is their thousand-fold application to the useful arts and sciences in practical life, which renders necessary the special departments of the University and gives peculiar importance to the Polytechnic Institute. It will not be forgotten, that, in an accomplished education, there must be *knowledge* as well as *culture*. The former should be to the latter what the fruit is to the tree, or rather what the whitening harvest is to the teeming soil. It is not possible to teach even the well-prepared student everything within the four years of the college course. This experiment has already been tried in our country again and again, but always with the most unsatisfactory result. When Cambridge and Oxford were first established, a liberal education might be obtained in this brief period. But since that time the field of knowledge and research has been rapidly growing broader: the exact sciences have made wonderful advances, and numerous natural sciences, then unknown, have been either entirely developed, or, like

> "The tawny lion pawing to get free
> His hinder parts,"

are struggling, half formed, into shape and being. If, therefore, we are not willing to impair the culture to be obtained

* For connection between the telegraph and higher mathematics, see "Address to the Alumni of the University of the City of New York," by Prof. J. W. Draper, M. D. 1853.

from the disciplinary studies of the college, nor yet to forego the advantages which would accrue to the community from enlarged scientific knowledge, we must, as the only remaining alternative, organize a post-graduate course; — in other words, we must make provision, as I have already said, for at least two years' *special* or *professional* study in whatever direction individual taste or genius may lead. It is not by any means necessary, that every college in the country should thus become a University, but it is greatly important that a few should furnish the amplest facilities, to the graduates of other institutions as well as to their own, for the highest attainments in any department of letters and science. Such a University carefully organized and adequately endowed, the grand repository and dispenser of knowledge, cannot be otherwise than of incalculable advantage to any people. Such it is intended WASHINGTON UNIVERSITY shall become, — aiming especially, in addition to the general culture secured to its Baccalaureate graduates, to promote, through its special departments, scientific and scholarly investigations in every field of industry and art. The principles to which these investigations may lead will not be permitted to remain idle in the class-room of the Professor, mere embellishments to the dreamy abstractions of the student, but will be brought, by means of the Polytechnic Institute, into immediate and vital connection with the material interests of society. In this way, the scholar with his theory and the artisan with his practical experience will come together face to face, and both will be benefited by the friendly contact. The former will learn to adapt his researches to human use; the latter will find a reason for rules which before were arbitrary, and be able to walk with assured step in the light of science, instead of groping his way falteringly in the penumbra of conflicting traditions, or stumbling hopelessly in the darkness of ignorance. One of our own citizens, whose leisure, wrung from a laborious profession, is sedulously devoted to the best interests of productive industry in St. Louis, has forcibly asked: "If all workmen, from the proprietor and foreman to the youngest apprentice, combined with his manual skill and dexterity a thorough knowledge of the mechanical laws and of the properties, both mechanical and chemical, of the various substances on which he works, — knew how to avail himself, to the greatest advantage, of every principle, property, and agency in nature, — in short, if science and art should unite and work together, and through the same person, who could place a limit to the progress of either, to their expansion and growth, under such never ceasing action and reaction on each other? And what as yet unimagined and wonderful discoveries in science and productions of inventive genius might not flow therefrom?" These questions, it is hoped and believed, will find their solution in the Polytechnic Institute.

There is no subject about which the community has not more rational notions than those which it entertains in respect to the economic value of a scientific truth. How many persons ever dreamed that there was even the slightest connection between Malus's discovery of the polarization of light and the remunerative manufacture of beet-sugar? Who ever associates in his mind Priestley's decomposition of the oxide of mercury with the metallurgic success of the miner? or Scheele's hydrochloric-acid experiments with the immense productions of the paper-mill? or Eli Whitney's invention with the cheapness of the cotton fabrics which clothe the world? or the simple pile of Volta in his laboratory at Pavia with the electric wires which now stretch in every direction across the continent, and thrill with thought and feeling like the living nerves? We do not render unto Cæsar the things which are Cæsar's. The world not unfrequently lets its best institutions of learning and its profoundest scholars beg or starve, while it waxes fat and kicks, like Jeshurun of old, over the fruits of their labor. Yale College is made to depend largely upon the tuition of its students, and, as a necessary consequence, the salaries of its eminent Professors are not so well suited to these flesh-and-blood times as to that ideal age, predicted by the great Persian philosopher, when men should neither need food *nor cast a shadow!* How intensely significant to President Woolsey and his compeers must be the etymological relationship between our word *salary* and the Latin word *sal!** Every thorough scholar is a public benefactor. Every profound thought lifts a shadow from the earth and casts out a demon of fear or superstition. Every repository of science, whether it be a laboratory, library, or observatory, is a dispenser of wealth as well as light to the community. The able and eloquent President of the Mississippi University is far from extravagant, when, in speaking of the vast commercial importance of determining a ship's place at sea, he says of the Observatory at Greenwich: "That single institution has done more for the increase of the world's wealth, than would have sufficed to support at their ease all the astronomers and physicists that ever lived since the days of Hipparchus; to build and furnish all the observatories the world ever saw; to establish and endow all the universities, colleges, and schools, of every grade from highest to lowest, throughout the globe; to erect and provide for all the hospitals, almshouses, and eleemosynary institutions of every kind, in all civilized lands; and to build all the churches and parsonages, as well as defray all the other expenses attendant on the support of religion, in every Christian country, from the advent of our blessed Saviour down to the present hour." †

I have thus spoken, "not as I wished, but as I was

* The Professors receive less than $ 1,150 per annum. President Woolsey's Historical Discourse, 1850, p. 123.

† Letter of F. A. Barnard, LL. D., to the Board of Trustees, 1858, p. 63.

able," upon the University, in its origin, constitution, and various relations to wealth, civilization, and refinement, — of the *culture* which it secures to the intellectual and moral powers, and of the *knowledge* which it sows with liberal hand in every field of human toil. There are peculiar circumstances, I apprehend, which render this general discussion applicable, at every point, to WASHINGTON UNIVERSITY. If nothing has been said in respect to physical education, the omission is not the result of an inadequate appreciation of the importance of the subject, but because, in its intimate relations to health and life, and the harmonious and efficient action of the mental faculties, it is deemed altogether too important to be made subsidiary to the other topics which necessarily engross the present hour. It demands an occasion of its own.

It must not be forgotten, that, *without ample endowment*, an institution of learning cannot command the highest educational talent, and stand firm amidst the fluctuations of popular favor; that, without a rigid *classification*, consulting the best interests of the pupils and permitting no ill-advised interference, it cannot change the heterogeneous materials which come to it, shapeless and confused, from *chaos* to a *cosmos;* that, without a *patient persistence in study*, in spite of the attractions of a money-making city, its students, at the end of their course, cannot go forth from it every one a chieftain, as Cicero says the disciples of Isocrates went forth from his school, — *tanquam ex equo Trojano, meri principes exierunt.*

It is a most fortunate circumstance, indicating the wisdom as well as catholic spirit of its founders, that our University is elevated, by the explicit and imperative language of its charter, above the narrowness of *sectarianism* in every shape and guise, now and forever; still we may devoutly hope that the light which glows in the Divine philosophy of the New Testament may permeate every science and give new lustre to every classic page; and that teachers and pupils alike may not only unseal the springs of Helicon and Parnassus, but drink also at

"Siloa's brook that flows
Fast by the oracle of God."

It would hardly be excusable in me, on this Inaugural occasion, so far to forget the amenities of social life, the consideration due to the "better half" of my audience, as to make no further allusion to the MARY INSTITUTE, which, though it has an individual organization and life of its own, is nevertheless a Department of the University, subject to the exclusive supervision of its Directors, and entitled to the immunities of its charter and to the instruction of its learned Professors. "Should women be taught the alphabet?" was the subject of a recent article in one of our most popular monthlies. The question proposed received from the author an answer quite different from what would have been given to it several centuries ago. "The happiest mother of daughters is she who has only sons," was an old proverb not without significance. In the most cultivated as well as the barbarous nations of antiquity, woman was trampled on by the lords of creation as an inferior being. The followers of Mohammed to this day look upon her as a mere temporary convenience, suited well enough to the present world, but poorly fitted to grace the Elysium of their future life. In one of the earlier Christian councils, it was proposed as a serious question, "whether woman was a human creature or not." It should be added, that, after long and grave debate, it was decided in the affirmative. Still she was everywhere made to feel that there was an impassable distance between her position and the lofty elevation from which man affected to look down upon her. We do not forget the Sapphos and Aspasias and Zenobias and Hypatias, who shed a light upon the darkness of the past;

but we remember, too, that they were "bright *particular* stars," high above the horizon of their sex, and all the brighter because there were no other luminaries around them. Considered of small consequence in the machinery of society, or regarded at best as a sort of necessary evil, woman was tolerated rather than courted in the most prominent nations of antiquity. The Jews married without affection and divorced their wives without compunction. Josephus observes on one occasion, with the utmost coolness, "About this time I put away my wife, not being pleased with her manners." Aulus Gellius assures us that Metellus Numidicus, the Censor, declared to the Roman people, in a public oration, that, "had kind Nature allowed us to exist without the help of woman, we should have been delivered from a very troublesome companion; and he could recommend matrimony only as the sacrifice of private pleasure to public duty." It is not to be denied, however, that the history of the Roman nation furnishes numerous instances of female virtue and nobleness, and that wives and mothers were nowhere treated with greater regard than among the Romans; but this regard, it must be remembered, was paid to them, not as women, but as the wives and mothers of brave and patriotic men. So far as intellectual culture was concerned, woman was, by common consent all over the world, either shut out entirely from the commonwealth of letters, or merely allowed, in rare instances, as an especial favor, to stand in the harvest fields of knowledge, like Ruth among the alien corn, a gleaner where others had reaped and bound up the sheaves. Dr. Milne quotes from a Chinese writer, who, in exhorting husbands to instruct their wives, encourages them in the arduous task by reminding them, that "monkeys may be taught to play antics, cats to run round a cylinder, dogs to tread in a mill, and parrots to recite verses"; and therefore he infers that woman may be taught something!

A school for the higher education of girls was never heard of even in the most polished of the ancient nations. The popular sentiment of the world was well expressed in the old aphorism: "To cultivate virtue is the science of men; to renounce science is the virtue of women."

But a change has come over the spirit of this dream. The world has awaked to a consciousness that woman does play an important part in its affairs; that she is an element, not to be overlooked, in human civilization; that she really has a soul, and should be educated in the light of this interesting psychological fact. This impression, which is becoming popular, is deepened and quickened by Christianity. In the Catholic worship, the Virgin and the Child, Mary and Jesus, are inseparably connected. The deified image of female purity and virtue, which graces the walls of gorgeous churches and dwells as an object of reverence in the minds and hearts of men, invests the sex with a peculiar sacredness. Everywhere in Christendom, whatever may be the form of religious faith, a willing homage is accorded to virtuous and intelligent womanhood. Out of these chivalrous sentiments of respect have grown the various means and appliances for the education of girls which distinguish the present age. Sources of improvement which were once sealed are now open to them, both in the public and the private school. The same studies which give strength and acumen and light to the minds of our sons are now pursued by our daughters. While the former are allowed to drink with a pitcher at the fountain, it is not thought necessary to compel the latter to absorb weak dilutions through a straw. It is not forgotten that Apollo and Diana were twins of one heavenly birth. It has been found, that even the higher mathematics, from which girls used to be excluded as carefully as farmers exclude their young cattle from black-cherry leaves, have nothing in them poisonous or hurtful to the most delicate female constitution. Mary Somerville in England and Miss Mitchell in Massachusetts are living illustrations of the healthfulness as well as safety of a mathematical regimen. The facts in physiology and the laws of health, of which a large majority of the community, a few years ago, were as ignorant as they were of the anatomy of Job's Leviathan, are now taught to both sexes alike. The saying of Coleridge, that "the largest part of mankind are nowhere greater strangers than at home," is gradually ceasing to be a truth, at least so far as our material being is concerned. The bony architecture of these houses we live in, and the furniture of the rooms which the spirit occupies, are painted for our school-children by Cutter and Hooker with as much precision as an architect would draw the plan of a ship. The physical sciences and the languages are now deemed eminently appropriate in the course of studies prescribed in every well-appointed Female Seminary; and young ladies are no longer reckoned "*blues*," even though they may have extended their researches into natural history somewhat beyond what is implied in the constant care and admiration of a pet cat and poodle dog. Their education is not now regarded as "*finished*," when they can work a fire-screen, and dance a polka, and drum a sentimental tune upon an unhappy piano, and paint a pastoral scene in some imagined Arcadia, and write a love-ditty on gilt-edged, perfumed note-paper to some gilt-edged, perfumed dandy. To sit up for show, like mantel ornaments or rare birds or exotic flowers, is not thought to be "the chief end" of their being, nor is their mission considered fulfilled when they have, like the heroines of our popular novels, got married. John Wilkes has said, that "hanging is the worst use a man can be put to." We think, with all deference, that marriage is the worst use an *ignorant* woman can be put to. A law, making it a penal offence for any one, man or woman, to perpetrate matrimony, until he or she can pass a strict examination in certain specified branches of study, before the superintending committee of the town in which the parties reside, might be of some service to the state. Napoleon never uttered a graver truth than when he said, "The fate of the child is always the work of its mother." It is true in every sense, physical, intellectual, and moral,— true in respect to the laws of natural descent and true in respect to the influence of early education. *Similia similibus gignuntur* — like produces like — is a law as fixed and inexorable in the rational as in the vegetable world. A perverse habit of mind, as well as a vice or weakness of body, may be transmitted to posterity and wreak its vengeance upon children's children "to the third and fourth generation." Ignorance is not a mere negative state of being, inefficient alike for good or evil. An ignorant person, as a late Chief Justice of New Hampshire used to express it, "is full of all manner of emptiness." Suspicion, jealousy, low cunning, bigotry, intolerance, superstition, and deceit are the seven spirits which always hold possession of the empty, swept, and garnished apartments. The influence of an individual thus "possessed" is bad enough anywhere; but when exerted by a woman, whether as a mother or a teacher, upon the unsuspecting and susceptible nature of the child, it is evil and only evil, and that continually.

> "A pebble in the streamlet scant
> Has turned the course of many a river;
> A dew-drop on the infant plant
> Has warped the giant oak forever."

If the influence of an ignorant woman is thus potent for evil, it is manifest that the influence of an intelligent, thoroughly educated woman, working with augmented power and a well-directed energy upon the same plastic materials, is wellnigh omnipotent for good. But to reach this high position of usefulness, either in society or in the family, there must be not only facilities for the utmost development and expansion of every faculty of mind and heart, but there must be unremitting, self-reliant, individual exertion. Our daughters should be taught at home, as well as in the school-room, that a genuine woman cannot be made wholly of cotton and crinoline; that the small head which surmounts her vast circumference * should be radiant with thought, — the dome of a pure and broad-visioned soul; that her heart, striving, perhaps vainly, to beat beneath her encircling zone, was intended for something more than to flutter with hope under the smiling glance of a glistening exquisite, or to tremble with fear at sight of a spider or a cow.

In the MARY INSTITUTE we shall endeavor to secure to the young ladies the mental discipline, and to impart to them the knowledge, which shall render them, in the highest and best sense, intelligent and womanly women. We do not desire to enkindle the intellect to such a consuming flame as to dry up the fountains of affection. We shall not aim to make Deborahs, whose wild chants shall wake the echoes of our temple-worship; nor Jaels, whose massive logical hammers shall nail to the floor, like sleeping Siseras, the stupid dogmas of an oppressive conservatism; but we shall strive rather to train up those committed to us to be MARYS, who, in this street-sweeping age, shall "*sit still in the house*," bright exemplars of the domestic virtues, the light and joy of every home which their presence shall purify and bless.

And now having discoursed, at such length as the occasion seemed to demand, upon the various topics connected with the great educational enterprise in which we are engaged, I close, — thanking you for the courtesy of

* "Pars minima est ipsa puella sui." — Ovid.

your patient attention, and commending WASHINGTON UNIVERSITY, with all its interests, immediate and prospective, first to the liberal regard of the citizens of St. Louis, and, next and highest, to the beneficent guardianship of the Infinite Father.

> "For He doth sway the tides of thought,
> And hold the issues in his hand
> Of all that human toil hath wrought,
> And all that human skill hath planned."

POPULAR FALLACIES.*

[North American Review, January, 1863.]

PORSON, a close observer of men as well as a sound Greek critic, once jestingly remarked, that he would some time write the history of human folly in five hundred volumes. Our author has given us but two volumes on this prolific subject, commencing with the "Mississippi Scheme" of John Law, which turned the head of all France, and ending with a chapter on the insane admirers of relics, — "men who have made fools of themselves for the jaw-bone of a saint, the toe-nail of an apostle, the handkerchief a king blew his nose in, or the rope that hanged a criminal." We shall not follow Mr. Mackay in his interesting discussion of the extraordinary delusions of the race in earlier times; but we propose rather to speak of the popular fallacies which, notwithstanding our vaunted progress, still bewilder the mind and conscience of the people. Out of the many which readily occur, we shall touch upon five; selecting them not because they are the most striking which could be introduced to notice, but because they are severally connected with the five grand departments of our general education, and correspond to the intellectual, industrial, civil, social, and religious elemental forces in our national life.

* Memoirs of Extraordinary Popular Delusions and the Madness of Crowds. By Charles Mackay, LL. D. London: G. Routledge & Co. 1856.

The first popular fallacy to which we shall advert relates to the intellectual element in our national education. It is *the confounding of profound learning with practical uselessness.*

Physical activity, in this country, is considered by the many the chief end of man. The study-lamp of the student, in the general apprehension, shines upon an idle dreamer, a drone in the great hive.

As a question preliminary to a fair discussion of this topic, it is important to ask, Who are laborers in this world? Certainly not those only who till the soil, or make music with saws and hammers, or toil in subterranean mines, or do business upon the great deep; but all who contribute, in any way, to the physical, intellectual, moral, or political well-being of their race. If we do not greatly mistake, it will be found, even on a slight examination, that there is no interest of society, however material, which is not intimately and inseparably connected with the researches of the scholar. Behind and beneath the activities of the outward world, the motive power lies out of sight, and is therefore unappreciated. The furnace-fires, which work the piston, and keep the wheels revolving, and vitalize the whole vessel, are down in the darkness of the hold. What is it but the thought of dreamy scholars which now guides the rich freights of the merchant over pathless seas, drives the mysterious shuttles of the manufacturer, reveals to the farmer the hidden resources of his wasted acres, points the miner to the metallic treasures of the sunless earth, and flashes instant intelligence, whether pertaining to business or pleasure, across a continent? Look at the steam-engine, with its Titanic sinews, its Briarean arms, "breathing softly as a sleeping child," and yet endued with a force as mighty as the swelling of the sea. It is but the outward garb of thought. Villages, Thebes-like, spring up at the sound of its Amphion music, and around it gather troops of laughing girls, each of whom is "a living story of love, and hope, and courage," more beautiful than any which Scott or Dickens has ever told.

"It would not be difficult," says one of the profoundest philosophers that England ever produced, — "it would not be difficult, by an unbroken chain of historic facts, to demonstrate that the most important changes in the commercial relations of the world commenced in the closets or lonely walks of uninterested theorists; that the most important of those discoveries and improvements in the mechanic arts, which have numerically increased our population beyond what the wisest men of a preceding age deemed possible, had their origin, not in the cabinets of statesmen or in the practical insight of men of business, but in the visions of recluse genius." A less close observer than Coleridge could hardly fail to see that the mere inventions of Watt, Whitney, and Morse have not only changed the world in its outward seeming, but have modified the intellectual and social condition of entire races. In truth, there is not an implement of husbandry, not a tool of the artisan, not a piece of machinery, not a human habitation, which has not felt the transforming touch of genius.

It is the glory of this nineteenth century, and especially of this country, that every department of human industry is luminous with thought, — thought which becomes at once the property of the Present and the heritage of the Future. It is not engraved in mystical hieroglyphics upon stone, but it is multiplied by the press, and scattered like winged seed on every wind. It is caught up by school-boy and proletaire, and discussed in reference to its *use* with an earnestness which would have shocked and disgusted the refined idlers of the Porch and the Academy. Time was when greatness among men was determined by the pound, just as we settle the weight and value of beef and pork. The strongest man was the king among his fellows. Red brawn was the badge of royalty. The suitors of Penelope despised and insulted her long-lost husband when he first, as a disguised mendicant, ventured in among them in their revels; they trembled and grew weak in their knees when they found he could bend the bow of Ulysses. But the reverence and terror which brute force once inspired have become a matter of history. Samson would make poor headway with his jaw-bone against the smallest Zouave with a Minie rifle on his shoulder. The great Pyramid of Cheops, which required in its erection a hundred thousand workmen, relieved every three months, for twenty years, could now be built in half the time by a dozen Manchester engines, managed by a hundred skilful engineers. It is getting to be understood that he succeeds best in his undertaking, whatever it be, who brings to it, not the greatest physical power, but the keenest intellect. The strength which could toss the mountain crag far out into the sea was of little use to Polyphemus after the wily Greek had bored out his eye. There never was a great act which had not, nearer or more remote, a great thought for its ancestor. The old rhymester believed this when he wrote: —

> "He that good thinketh good may do,
> And God will help him thereunto;
> For was never good work wrought
> Without beginning of good thought."

The sneering assertion is too often made without rebuke, that high themes of state are by no means fitted to the closet of the student; that the mighty interests of confederate and yet conflicting sovereignties cannot be subjected to the canons of scholastic rhetoricians or to the crucibles of experimenting chemists; that the wheels of government are too wide-sweeping in their revolutions and too complicated in their adjustments to be controlled or regulated by the feeble strength of white-handed theorizers; in a word, that practical affairs, moral and political as well as mechanical and agricultural, are not suited to men

> "Sicklied o'er with the pale cast of thought."

The world is too apt to associate power with the noise and pomp which attend its exercise. Because the cackling of geese once saved the Capitol of Rome, it is thought to follow as a logical *sequitur*, that the senseless gabbling of featherless bipeds is always of more efficiency and value to a people than the counsels of a Cicero or the philosophy of a Seneca. Wisdom is sought in the camp and in the agora; seldom in the halls of learning. Warriors show the wounds which the happy accident of a Mexican copper bullet may have inflicted, and they are forthwith inducted without the laying on of hands into the sanctuary of our national government.

Far be it from us in this "working-day world" to disparage the achievements of the doers in any field of honorable enterprise. But after all, where but in the brain of the thinker are forged all constitutions and polities and laws? Who but he adjusts the mechanism of society, and knows where to touch the invisible springs of human action? The garret in which the scholar sits among his books, is higher than the saloons of wealth or fashion. The mists which rest upon the lowlands do not rise so as to shut out or refract the clear white light of the noon-tide. His narrow room is radiant with a brightness not of the sun, and he looks forth as from a mount of vision. His eye scans the wide and teeming Present. The Past, with all its treasures of wisdom and experience, are his. The goodly fellowship of sages, poets, orators, and philosophers inspire him in his prophecies for the Future. The proud exclamation of the great leader of modern science, "We are the ancients," is eminently true of the scholar. For him Virgil told the adventures of Æneas, the fall of Ilium and the rise of Rome; for him Demosthenes declaimed on the sea-shore, and from the sounding Bema

> "fulmined over Greece
> To Macedon and Artaxerxes' throne";

for him Socrates discoursed of life and death and immortality; for him Plato and More created ideal republics; for him Cicero hurled his anathemas at Catiline, and talked as no one had ever talked before, of patriotism, justice, and law; for him Bacon laid deep and broad the foundations of experimental philosophy; for him Hampden and Sidney, Washington and Lafayette, fought the battles of freedom; for him Burke and Chatham, Marshall and Story, expounded the principles of constitutional liberty; for him artists, famous or unknown, touched with magic power the stones of Rome, of Greece, of Egypt, and of half-fabulous Assyria, so that they speak to him an intelligible language from far-off centuries. There has not been a poet, who has not burned and sung for him; not a philosopher, who has hidden from him his profoundest and most subtile thoughts; not an orator, whose eloquence has not stirred, like the angel of Bethesda, the fountain of his being; not an earnest student, whose midnight lamp has not shone for him; not a champion of human rights, whose valor he has not witnessed on the red field of battle; not a martyr to truth, whose blood does not cry to him from the ground. The brilliant intellects and brave hearts of remote ages have sent their great thoughts and great deeds down to him, as the fountains of the Apennines sent their pure waters, through far-reaching aqueducts, into the city of Rome. All that is valuable in liberty, in science, in philosophy, in religion, in law, the past has poured at his feet. How preposterous, then, to maintain, that the profound scholar, thus situated in the light of other days, rich in the wealth of buried centuries, should be regarded as incapable of good or ill in the exigencies of society, while the great interests which belong to the well-being and existence even of nations are committed to the hands of trading politicians, impudent pretenders to patriotism, eel-fishers in the Copais Palus,* brazen demagogues whose reverberating sciolism is as empty as their heads!

The unobtrusive thinker, then, is not a cipher at the left hand of society. He has a power for good far transcending the conception of those who look upon the student's life as one long holiday. To the service of his country he brings a sterner culture than can be found in a listless wandering amid Sabean odors, — a higher consecration than a baptism in rose-water can give, — a larger experience than those who live only within the horizon of the passing hour can know, — a clearer prescience than the leaves of the Sibyl or the utterances of the rapt Pythoness can impart. He stands a daysman between the Past and the Future, and can lay his hand upon them both. Without him history would have no lessons for the Present, but would be a "dreamy, aimless procession of lost spirits descending into the pit." Without him the ship of state would drift in darkness on a perilous sea, with no charts of hidden rocks and lee-shores, and with no beacons on the headlands. Without him to feed and guard the lamp of thought, the light would grow dim, and the flapping of a conqueror's banner would extinguish it forever. Without him to discover and invent, the hum of industry would be hushed in our work-shops, and the music of machinery would cease to mingle with that of our mountain streams. In estimating the value of men, and determining their rela-

* *ὅπερ γὰρ οἱ τὰς ἐγχέλεις θηρώμενοι πέπονθας·*
ὅταν μὲν ἡ λίμνη καταστῇ λαμβάνουσιν οὐδέν·
ἐάν δ' ἄνω τε καὶ κάτω τὸν βόρβορον κυκῶσιν
αἱροῦσιν.

Knights, v. 864–867.

tive importance in society, we must look beneath the surface of things, and remember that one great principle, either in science, morals, or political economy, distinctly enunciated and clothed with organic life, outweighs the armies and navies of the world, is more decisive of the destiny of the human race than all the great battles which have ever been fought, from Márathon to Magenta.

The next popular fallacy to which we shall refer relates to the industrial element in our national life. It is *the confounding of wealth with material riches.*

The distinction here is not a subtile one, as might at first glance seem; but it is broad and radical. The word *wealth* belongs to a numerous family. Its nearest relatives are the English words *weal*, *well*, *heal*, *hale*, and the Latin *valeo.* The primary idea in it, therefore, is *soundness*, — soundness of mind and body, a symmetrical wholeness; and *wholeness*, we know, is etymologically, if not theologically, synonymous with *holiness*. *Riches*, on the other hand, is allied to *rex*, *rego*, *regnum*, and to our English substantives *reach*, *region*, and implies, therefore, extent of possessions and power. Wealth we see, then, is a subjective term, relating primarily to the quality of the man; while riches is an objective term, and refers exclusively to the external world, to farms and flocks, ships and merchandise. The man who does not own a rood of land, nor even a single share of fancy stock, may have a wealth of affection, of intellectual culture, of moral sentiment, which all the "barbaric pearl and gold" of the East could not buy. Most men look upon the earth only as a great farm, suitably divided into mowing, tillage, and pasture-land, with numerous water-privileges and orchards. They see no footprints in the old red sandstone, but they are sharper than Lynceus to detect infinitesimal gold or platinum specks in quartz rock. "Put money in thy purse," was the precept of Iago, and it is obeyed with more relish than the Decalogue in every profession and rank of life.

"Lord Stafford mines for coal and salt,
The Duke of Norfolk deals in malt,
The Douglass in red herrings;
And noble name and cultured land,
Palace and park and vassal band,
Are powerless to the notes of hand
Of Rothschild or the Barings."

But while too many make the acquisition of money the overmastering passion of life, we would not be understood as decrying its value. That it is a good thing for the individual and for the state, does not admit of a question. The constituent elements of our civilization — our manufactures, commerce, and agriculture, our educational and religious institutions — require, one and all, a capital, immense beyond the conception of those who flippantly talk of the utilitarianism of the age. If the material riches necessary to a high state of civilization could be more equally diffused, it would undoubtedly be a blessing to rich and poor alike. It is an unhappy fact, that nine tenths of the property of this country is owned by one tenth of the people. But this is the result of our individuality, and our individuality is the result of our civil and social liberty. It is, like sin, the consequence of the freedom of the will. But it is a consolation to those of us who are fellow-citizens in poverty, — who look forward to affluence as the Hebrew, faint with watching in a strange land, looks forward to the coming Messiah, with a hope fringed and shadowed with despair, — to know that riches are not the true wealth, that money is not all of property. Your neighbors across the street live perchance in magnificent houses, and occupy large estates. They point to certain dingy scrolls in the Register's office, and call these buildings and grounds their own. But it is your fault if they are not essentially yours as well as theirs. They may, it is true, range at will through drawing-room and boudoir, as you may not, and consume the fruits which spring up along the garden paths; but the divine effluence which comes from marble colonnades and "speaking oaks," the incense shed from the thousand swinging censers of blossoming trees, the morning music of singing birds and lowing kine, — these cannot be held by title-deeds, or shut in by high walls and triple-thorned acacia. It is only the grosser products of the dull earth which can be appropriated to individuals; — the ethereal essence of nature, its beauty and its glory, are free as the chainless air. They were meant for all who have the seeing eye, the hearing ear, and the understanding heart. It is quite possible that the rich man may reap a smaller harvest from his broad acres than the gardener who trains his vines and trims his trees. The greatest loser by the destructive fire in New York city, in the summer of 1842, was not the millionnaire whose massive structures sunk to ashes in an hour; but it was the poor negro woman who only lost the two trees and the little bed of flowers which glorified her tiny garden, and upon which she had expended the strength saved from incessant toil, and the watchful care which the full heart must lavish upon the sole objects of its yearning affections.

It is a significant question which Mrs. Child asks in one of her letters, "Which would a mother value most, the price of the most elegant pair of Parisian slippers, or a little worn-out shoe, once filled with a precious infant foot now walking with the angels?" There are a thousand things which make up the sum of our real wealth, over which money has no power, — with which it has nothing to do. Who would cut down for the market the tree which sheltered his childhood, or sell the portrait of a friend in heaven? These things, and such as these, have an intrinsic and permanent worth, irrespective of the rise and fall of stocks, independent of the fluctuations of society and the progress of the race. But material riches have no absolute value; they are only relative, and therefore always changing. What is a luxury in one age becomes a want, or even a necessity, in a succeeding age. Our aristocratic ancestors in the fifteenth century sat on wooden benches, drank their beer in wooden bowls, and ate their salt-fish or joint of beef on pewter plates. Now the Catawba of their descendants sparkles in cut-glass or gold, and the richest meats exhale their fragrance from Sevres China. Chimneys and window-glass were wonderful domestic rarities, and bleached shirts and cotton umbrellas were personal extravagances, at periods not very remote from this. An Irish shanty by a railroad-cut is a palace compared with the human lair which a troglodyte of the Upper Nile calls his home.

It was a characteristic remark of Lord Falkland, "I pity unlearned gentlemen on a rainy day." The educated man is never alone. He may not be admitted to the first circles, or to "our set"; but Plato never sends his servant to the door to say "Not at home" to him, and Shakespeare never "cuts" him in the streets. In nature, too, there is no "Fifth Avenue," no favoritism, no exclusiveness, no costly pews along the cathedral aisles of her grand old woods. When Michael took Adam up into the highest hill of Paradise,

> "To show him all earth's kingdoms and their glory,"

he not only "purged with euphrasy and rue the visual nerve," but he also

> "from the well of Life three drops instilled,
> E'en to the inmost seat of mental sight."

It is here where we find the grand distinction between men, — a distinction deeper and broader than that which lies between poverty and riches. Money, at best, is but the complement of the senses. It can, like the angel, introduce us into new fields of vision, spread out before us the colossal grandeur and profuse luxuriance of a tropical clime, or fling open the doors to galleries of painting and sculpture in Rome or Corinth; but, unlike the angel, it cannot give us the intellectual power of appreciating either nature or art, or the delicate taste which can relish and enjoy them.

> "We may not hope from outward forms to win
> The passion and the life whose fountains are within.
> O Lady! we receive but what we give,
> And in our life alone does nature live."

Our own poet-philosopher, whose scholarly pen has rendered classic the fields and river which the first blood of the Revolution made sacred, has brought to this subject, as to many others, the discrimination of a clear-seeing intellect. "The moral sensibility, which makes Edens and Tempes so easily, may not be always found, but the material landscape is never far off. We can find these enchantments without visiting the Como Lake or the Madeira Islands. The stars at night stoop down over the brownest, homeliest common, with all the spiritual magnificence which they shed on the Campagna or on the marble deserts of Egypt. The uprolled clouds and the colors of morning and evening will transfigure maples and alders. The difference between landscape and landscape is small, but there is a great difference in the beholders."

The distinction between wealth and material riches is as clearly marked in the state as in the individual. The immense territory of our own country, washed by oceans three thousand miles apart and stretching wellnigh through a zone; our inland seas and majestic rivers, bearing on their bosom the products of a teeming soil; our interminable coasts, scalloped with bays and "broad-armed ports"; the white wings of our commerce, beating, like the albatross, the air of every clime; our panting engines, running on their iron tracks across the continent, or raging in the streets of our cities, like the fiery chariots of Nahum; our mountain streams, weaving and grinding for a naked and hungry world, — these are not to be overlooked or forgotten. But it should be remembered that a state has other and better property than that which serves its material uses. The great thoughts which have illuminated it, the great words which have been spoken in it, the great deeds which have been done in it, the great works of art which have been wrought in it, the heroic self-sacrifice which has sanctified it, — these are a nation's chief and choicest possessions.

Another wide-spread popular fallacy relates to the state, — to the τὰ πολιτικά of Aristotle. It is *the confounding of Law with legislative enactments.*

We do not mean to say that these are never accordant, but we do mean to say that they may be, and often are, in direct and open antagonism. In discussing this point we shall of course leave out of view all those regulations of public conduct which have no moral quality, but are merely prudential. There is no inherent right in catching alewives in Taunton River on Fridays; no inherent wrong in catching them on Saturdays. Whether a young man shall pay a poll-tax at the age of sixteen or twenty-one, is not a question of morals, but of political economy. There is in the world, especially in despotic governments, not a little solemn quackery about the inviolability of human legislation, the awful and unapproachable majesty of mean and wicked enactments promulgated by mean and wicked men.

Law in its highest and proper sense is either the mode in which God acts, or the property which, in the constitution of things, he has impressed alike upon mind and matter. Unlike human statutes, it is uniform, universal, immutable. This distinction, too little recognized in modern times, did not escape the acutest mind of antiquity. "Law," says

Cicero, "in accordance with the opinion of the wisest men, is not a thing thought out by the ingenuity of man, nor is it a decree of the people, but it is an eternal entity, coeval in its origin and harmonizing in its action with the Divine Mind." Few truths of more vital importance in their relations to man have ever been uttered by uninspired lips.

The great mass of the people have yet to learn, that far above the conflicting opinions of men, far above the clashing statutes of deliberative bodies, Law has "its seat in the bosom of God," unchanged and unchangeable, the same yesterday, to-day, and forever. We desecrate the name of law, whenever we apply it, as men are wont to do, to the capricious decrees of despots, or to the fiats of a fickle populace. The greatest enormities that have ever darkened and disfigured the history of the world have been perpetrated in strict accordance with the forms and spirit of legislative enactments, or in the common but false and deceptive phrase, "according to law."

Hancock and Adams rebelled against British rule, and trampled under foot stamp-acts and writs of assistance, and, because they succeeded in the struggle which followed, they are held in grateful remembrance by worshipping millions. But had they been defeated, they would have been hanged with their compatriots on the highest tree — "according to law."

Algernon Sidney was suspected of opposition to tyranny and a love for constitutional freedom, and because he failed in his efforts to overturn the one and secure the other, he was convicted of treason before the infamous Jeffries, and beheaded on Tower Hill — "according to law."

A slave of Pedanius Secundus, Prefect of Rome, had, as Tacitus tells us, bought his liberty, and because the boon for which he had toiled and paid was unjustly withheld, he in his desperation murdered his master. For this act, the guilt of which, whatever it might be, attached to him alone, all his fellow-slaves, four hundred in number, of every age, from helpless infancy to the decrepitude of years, of every shade of complexion, from the fair-haired daughters of German princes to the captive soldiers of Indian kings, were tried for their lives. It mattered not that they were innocent; it mattered not that the people were inclined to mercy; the Senate was inexorable, and they were all executed in cold blood, without pity and without exception, but the butchery was done — "according to law."

Socrates, the brightest genius in the dark past, whose "low-roofed house" had been made radiant by the light of philosophy, if not of love, was arraigned before the popular tribunal of the Heliæa, by a majority of three voices was condemned to death, and, therefore, drank the hemlock — "according to law."

It is fitting that we, as constituent elements of a free government, as men who cannot delegate our duties and responsibilities to priest or judge, should discriminate between the true and the false, — between that legislation which is but the re-enactment of the Divine law, and therefore a "terror to evil-doers," and that legislation which is but the expression of human prejudice and passion, and sets his heel upon the sanctities of Eternal Justice. The one demands our reverent obedience; the other deserves our indignant maledictions. We need not raise the bloody flag of revolution. That is the prerogative of the down-trodden victims of despotism; in this country it would be an atrocious crime. In a republic we may appeal to the people, with a confidence proportioned to their intelligence, and await the remedy of the ballot-box. Meanwhile it should be remembered, that when citizens, through loyalty to the government, attempt to obey a statute which is in contravention of all right, they set their nature at strife with itself. They are compelled to annihilate in themselves conscience, instinct, principles, all those qualities and attributes of character on which alone law can rest. It is as if the great goddess Diana, as Coleridge somewhere expresses it, had commanded her priests to dig up the charcoal foundations of the mighty temple of Ephesus in order to furnish fuel for the burnt-offerings on its altar! "That which is not just," said Algernon Sidney, in his epigrammatic way, "is not law, and that which is not law ought not to be obeyed." We cannot, like the Samaritans of old, "fear the Lord" and at the same time "serve graven images."

No wise prince, much less an enlightened deliberative assembly, will ever promulgate an ordinance which a patriotic people can obey only by sacrificing their self-respect, and trampling under foot the immutable principles of right. The "Antigone," foremost among Greek dramas, forcibly exhibits, in the impassioned dialogue between Creon and the heroine of the play, the conflict between the divine law and human decrees. We know of nothing grander than the reply of the condemned though fearless maiden to the tyrant's question, "Hast thou dared to transgress these edicts of mine?"

> "I had it not from Jove, nor the just gods
> Who rule below; nor could I ever think
> A mortal's law of power or strength sufficient
> To abrogate the unwritten law divine,
> Immutable, eternal, not like these
> Of yesterday, but made ere time began."

It is not enough that judges lend to the obnoxious statute the sanction of their approval. However honest and hearty may be our reverence for the judicial dicta of the Woolsack, it is not to be forgotten that William Scroggs and George Jeffries once wore the ermine, and that the intuitions of our own moral sense are sometimes clearer than the vision of Lord Mansfield and Sir Matthew Hale. There have been, and still are, not a few judges whose faces are always turned towards the pyramids, — men in whose estimation dead "authorities" are of more consequence than living justice. An extensive knowledge of books is valuable in the highest degree to him who has the faculty of making the great thoughts of other men enkindle his own intellect to a whiter heat; but not unfrequently the fuel is green and puts out the fire. A case adjudicated by some trembling minion of tyranny, anxious to retain his judicial robes and fearing to displease his master, in the reign, it may be, of Henry VIII., or of some despot still nearer the flood, is not necessarily of more weight and value in determining questions of right, than the unbiassed opinion of an intelligent man who happened to be born in the nineteenth century. Robbers in the East, as we are told, formerly used a certain kind of lantern, the candle for which was made of the fat of a dead malefactor.* The mouldier the fat and the greater the scoundrel from whom it was taken, the surer the light which it furnished and the richer the spoils to which it led. Black-letter judges, slaves to musty "precedents," are the dupes of a similar superstition. Men are slow to learn that the highest "authority" is that of enlightened reason, and that the only irreversible "decisions" are the decisions of common sense. When these are violated, either by the enactment or by the interpretation of a statute, it is not less the duty than the right of every law-abiding citizen to utter his earnest protest. Nothing can be infallible or final which is not just. The people are a higher tribunal than Star-Chambers or Inquisitions. The bench and the throne cannot feel the ground-swell of

* It is in allusion to this custom, that Moore, in his Lalla Rookh, stigmatizes the judges of his day: —

> "Ye wise, ye learn'd, who grope your dull way on
> By the dim twinkling gleams of ages gone,
> Like superstitious thieves, who think the light
> From dead men's marrow guides them best at night."

the heaving millions, without toppling to their fall. We have not forgotten that Chief Justice Hutchinson decided that writs of assistance might be lawfully issued; but the people thought differently, and the world knows the result. We remember that the twelve English judges in the case of Hampden decided unanimously that ship-money might be levied, in accordance with law, by the crown, without the intervention of Parliament. But the hard-headed Anglo-Saxons, so far from submitting in cheerful acquiescence, "agitated" until these same ermined functionaries reversed their decision in every particular.

The next popular fallacy which claims our notice relates to the social element in our national life, — to our manners. It is *the confounding of reverence with servility.*

The confusion of terms here indicated is perhaps peculiar to this country. It naturally grows out of the freedom of our institutions, — out of the levelling tendencies of our democratic ideas. We do not, in the intensity of our independence, discriminate between reverence and its counterfeit presentment. The dread of appearing servile has led us to be irreverent alike to age, to station, and to things sacred.

We read in relation to the entertainment given by Joseph to his brethren, that "they sat before him, the first-born according to his birthright, and the youngest according to his youth." Herodotus tells us that the young men of his country and time yielded the road to age, and rose from their seats before the hoary head. It is a noticeable fact, that Demosthenes, the foremost man in the Athenian Senate of Five Hundred, was compelled to apologize, in his first Philippic, for rising to speak before all the older members had delivered their sentiments. The liberty and national existence of Greece were at stake, every heart was glowing, every ear was erect to hear the burning words of the greatest orator in the world, and yet Attic patriotism was subsidiary to Attic politeness. Xenophon, in his Memorabilia, says: "The older citizens were in the habit of inquiring of the youths whom they met in the streets of Sparta the place of their destination and the purport of their errand, and reprove those who refused to answer their interrogatories and those who attempted to give an indirect reply." It may be proper in this connection to say, that there was one single exception to this rule. That class of the community which they called *οἱ ἄγαμοι*, and which we call "old bachelors," were not considered by the Greeks as entitled to the ordinary courtesies and amenities of social life, and to them, therefore, boys and girls alike might be as saucy as they pleased, without fear of punishment.

Cicero, in his "De Senectute," declares, that "the respect which is paid to age forms an infallible criterion by which to determine the moral advancement of a people." We are not disposed to question the truth of this assertion. It is a significant fact, that the connection between the demeanor and the character was deemed so intimate and inseparable by the two most deep-seeing and philosophic nations of antiquity, that in the Greek and Latin languages good manners and good morals are the same thing. There is but one word in each for both. The most careless observer of the present day cannot have failed to notice, that the boundary line between them, like some of the lines in geography, is only an imaginary one. We cannot gather grapes of thorns, or figs of thistles. The soul imparts its own hue and quality to the external life. Or, as Spenser has said in his own quaint way,—

> "'Tis of the soul the body form doth take,
> For soul is form and doth the body make."

Dr. Johnson was a bear in social intercourse, because he was a bear in spirit and feeling. Good manners are the blossom and fragrance of good morals.

The fear which many parents feel, lest their children may not be sufficiently independent in character, coupled with the anxiety of babes and sucklings to grow up and be brought out, has created a feud between nature and fashion, and introduced into society between childhood and mature life a new order of beings, a sort of third estate. We have now in many communities no boys and girls, but a nondescript class of bipeds, waiting to be classified and named. It is certain that our great naturalist, should he undertake the task, will not find in all of them the modest reserve, the respectful demeanor, and the reverent spirit, which were once the characteristics and the glory of the young.

The spirit which animates men is naturally reproduced in boys, and re-enacted in the nursery and at the public schools. In the increasing activity of our people, in the intensity of our haste to be rich, we cannot wait to be respectful. Parents once brought up their children; children now bring down their parents. Formerly, the traveller in passing the school play-ground was saluted by deferential bows and courtesies from its party-colored columns of light infantry; now, the hat adheres to the head as firmly as the scalp, the "pregnant hinges of the knee" have forgotten how to crook except where "thrift may follow fawning," and the traveller is happy if he can dodge between the snow-balls which fly around him like bomb-shells from a Malakoff. There is no station high enough, no place of power dazzling enough, to inspire Young America with awe, or to call forth any show of reverence.

We have read of an honest Hibernian who plunged into the water when George IV. was landing at Kingston, to shake hands with his Majesty, and who was ever afterward so proud of the circumstance, that no earthly inducement could prevail upon him to wash the hand his Majesty had pressed. It is difficult for us to understand and appreciate the spirit of loyalty which animates the subjects of European monarchies. We do not associate the government with any substantive reality. It is an idea, not a person; a majority of votes, not a crowned head; the result of a popular election, not one of God's anointed. The humblest man among us is a Warwick, and can make and unmake kings as easily as the Duke of Northumberland. We are living in the enjoyment of the largest liberty. We look up with reverence to no titled nobility. We despise the obsequious fawning of little men. We practise no genuflections before lazy dignitaries. We train our backs to bend and our eyes to droop in presence of no earthly potentate. It is not true of us, as Juvenal expresses it,* that "death alone divulges how little are the bodies of men." We measure with unquailing, curious look the tallest and the proudest, long before we dig their graves. The terms of deferential address, which are always demanded from the lower classes in a country whose government recognizes a distinction of rank among its subjects, are all barbaric jargon to us, and he who should use them here would be regarded as a grotesque caricature of manhood. In the thoroughness of our contempt for the servile homage paid to blood and birth and place, we have gone so far in the other direction as to emancipate ourselves from the restraints of good breeding, and to maintain our independence of the beautiful amenities of life.

But perhaps the most unsatisfactory aspect in which our want of reverence can be viewed, is in its relations to things sacred. There is in our temples no veil through which the high-priest alone may enter. The foot-fall of the curious inquirer may be heard in the innermost *penetralia.* We do not often take off our shoes because the ground whereon we stand is holy. The Urim and Thummim are only bright buttons on a flashy vest, and the halo

* "Mors sola fatetur
Quantula sint hominum corpuscula."

around the priestly head is moonshine to us, and nothing more. We do not see anything wrong in laying hands on the ark, and we wonder that the anger of the Lord was kindled against Uzzah at Nachon's threshing-floor. The Mahometans will not tread on the smallest piece of paper in their way; "for," say they, "the name of God may be written upon it." We are troubled with no such scruples. The sacred pages which contain the glowing words of Isaiah and David would be deemed quite as appropriate to light our cigars as to kindle our devotions. The old Hebrew had such a veneration for the name of Jehovah, that he would not pronounce it, even in holiest forms of speech, but used instead of it Adonai or Elohim. There are among us not a few who feel that a simple assertion or plain statement of obvious facts will pass for nothing, unless they swear to its truth by all the names of the Deity, and blister their lips with every variety of hot and sulphurous oath. If we observe such persons closely, we shall generally find that the fierceness of their profanity is in inverse ratio to the affluence of their ideas. We know not but that this may be regarded as a general formula. Byron seems to recognize it when he says of Jack Buntin,

> "He knew not what to say, and so he swore."

At any rate, we venture to affirm that the profanest men within the circle of your knowledge are afflicted with a chronic weakness of intellect, and that their half-dozen thoughts rattle in vacant heads like the brazen pebbles we read of. The utterance of an oath, though it may prevent a vacuum in sound, is no indication of sense. It requires no genius to swear, — to "swear terribly like our army in Flanders." The reckless taking of sacred names in vain is as little characteristic of true independence of thought, as it is of high moral culture. In this beautiful and breathing world, filled as it is with the presence of the Deity and fragrant with incense from its thousand altars of praise, it would be no servility should we catch the spirit of reverent worshippers, and illustrate in ourselves the sentiment that the Christian is the highest style of man.

The last popular fallacy to which we shall allude relates to the moral element in our national culture. It is *the confounding of a religious life with a theological creed.*

The Protestant traveller, who for the first time visits Milan and joins the thousands who, at the vesper hour, throng the avenues and courts of its magnificent cathedral, may amid the gathering gloom of twilight bow with the Catholic devotee at the shrine of the Holy Mother, and yet not assent to the Biblical interpretations of Papal Œcumenic Councils, nor forsake for a moment the faith of his fathers. As he gazes upward upon the immense dome, and around upon colossal statues and long-drawn aisles, the one sentiment of stupendous grandeur, of vastness that dilates rather than humbles the beholder, overpowers alike his prejudice and his pride, and his full soul must flow forth in devotion. The massive columns, the gorgeous paintings, the music chanted by unseen choirs, the tapers faintly burning, dark-eyed maidens kneeling at ancient altars, — all appeal to him with an eloquence which cannot be resisted. They do not ask him to believe in the infallibility of the Pope, nor in the intercessory power of the Virgin Mary, but they ask him to lift his heart in adoration.

A man may be a good man with a very poor creed, or even with no well-defined creed at all. "In unnumbered cases," as Professor Park well says, "the real faith of Christians has been purer than their written statements of it. Men, women, and children have often decided when doctors disagreed, and doctors themselves have often felt aright when they reasoned amiss." It would be difficult, not to say impossible, to frame any written document, however short and simple, which should receive from its readers the same mental interpretation. Words take their meaning, not from their component letters, but from our own natures and associations.

As no two persons ever saw the same rainbow, so no two persons, Christians though they may have been, ever worshipped the same conception of the Deity. We are differently constituted. Our physical temperaments, our intellectual habits, our moral susceptibilities, our hereditary proclivities, separate us. Each has an ideal of the Supreme Good, peculiar to himself. The strong, severe man, who regards human weakness with contempt and sin with indignation, naturally endows the object of his worship with the qualities of his own mind, only in their highest degree. The Infinite One is to him, therefore, an impersonation of inflexible Justice, and his reverence for him is enhanced by the assurance, that he "will by no means clear the guilty." On the other hand, the man of gentle character, who would not "needlessly set foot upon a worm," does not appreciate the sterner attributes of the Godhead, but looks up only to a loving Father whose "tender mercies are over all his works." John Foster in his boyhood "abhorred spiders for killing flies, and abominated butchers." We are not surprised, that, in his manhood, this same John Foster, in all the ripeness of a beautiful Christian character, with his great heart still more tremulously tender than a woman's or a child's, could not accept the doctrine of eternal punishment. On the contrary, Calvin, equally honest, equally earnest, equally profound, could contemplate with composure the burning lake as the necessary and chosen abode of the incorrigibly depraved. He, like Dante, believed that in the future world, as in the present, there must be mingled with an infinite pity an infinite rigor of law. He saw, that here sunny skies are darkened with lowering clouds, from whose depths "leaps the live thunder"; that the spiced and favoring wind, wafting the white sail over the tranquil sea, is changed into the fearful tornado, whose wild wail mingles with the "bubbling cry of some strong swimmer in his agony"; that flowery lawns and June blossoms are charred and wasted by the burning lava of volcanic wrath; that faces, mantled with the smiles of birthday and of bridal, are stained with tears and overshadowed with hopeless pain; that Olivet had not only rung with the songs of vintage and the glad voices of children, but had also in the gray of the morning echoed to the tread of a brutal soldiery and witnessed the crucifixion. His quick eye had marked the misery which had been permitted in this world, and he had no doubt that a similar economy would prevail in the next. John Calvin and John Foster were both Christians, nominally of the same school; but, so far as the Divine character and government are concerned, they could hardly have subscribed to the same creed.

We do not mean to intimate that it is of no consequence what we believe, but simply that a difference of opinion on subjects beyond the range of knowledge may not only be honest, but even a constitutional necessity. Charles V. was right when he inferred that, if he could not make two clocks keep time together, it were folly in him to attempt to constrain his subjects — thirty millions of thinking men — to a cordial adoption of the same prescribed formula of faith.

So intimate is the relation between soul and body, that our theology almost always tastes of the cask from which it is drawn. Disease, especially if it disturb the normal action of the brain, is likely to modify essentially our creed. To say that Coleridge varied from the most liberal latitudinarianism to the strictest adherence to the "Thirty-nine Articles," somewhat according to the quality and quantity of the opium which he consumed, would not be an extravagant assertion.

But not only is the conception of the Supreme Being different in different persons; the future blessedness to which we aspire varies in character according to our views of the highest good. The poor washerwoman in Hyperion, weary and toil-worn, longed to die and go to heaven, that she might sit in a clean white apron and sing psalms all day long. Plato, when asked what would be the employment of heaven, immediately answered, "The study of geometry." To the one, heaven was a place of quiet rest; to the other, a field for thought and for unending progress.

Not only can no two persons, though of equally high religious character, adopt precisely the same creed; it is obvious, also, that no one person can be expected to entertain through a life of ordinary length the same views on any moral subject, especially on one so eminently speculative as that which concerns his spiritual being, its essence and its relations. It is the order of nature to grow. "I could never," says Sir Thomas Browne, "divide myself from any man upon the difference of an opinion, or be angry with his judgment for not agreeing in that from which within a few days I might dissent myself." The thinking man outgrows his beliefs as he does his clothes. The swaddling-bands of infancy cannot encompass the stalwart loins of manhood.

"Build thee more stately mansions, O my soul,
As the swift seasons roll!
Leave thy low-vaulted past!
Let each new temple, nobler than the last,
Shut thee from heaven with a dome more vast,
Till thou at length art free,
Leaving thine outgrown shell by life's unresting sea."

We know that there are numerous exceptions to this law of growth. There is a large class in society whom Sydney Smith calls the "sheep-walkers," — men who never deviate from the beaten track, who think as their fathers have thought since the flood, who recoil from a new idea as they would from guilt. These persons never disturb society and are never disturbed by it. Only those who have the intellectual vigor necessary to independent thought and fearless expression "turn the world upside down," and, like Paul and Silas, "trouble the people and the rulers of the city." It is among these alone, whose loyalty to truth and duty is stronger than their devotion to sect, that the dungeon, the rack, and the stake have, in all ages, found their victims. The humanizing influence of popular education and a more liberal intellectual culture have softened the asperities of religious persecution; yet even now any departure from the established belief may subject the venturesome wanderer to social discomfort and disabilities. Not a few good men have so identified religion with their own creed, that they look upon every dubious question, every uncanonical conviction, as an alarming approach to unpardonable heresy. The first buddings of thought they regard as incipient excrescences on the body of Christian faith, and woe betide the luckless wight whose spiritual growth should be found to exceed the knot on their measuring-line!

"Here," said a student to Casaubon, as they entered the old hall of the Sorbonne, "is a building in which men have disputed for more than four hundred years." "And," asked Casaubon, "*what has been settled?*" There is a mournful significance in the question of the old Genevan Professor. Four things, however, amid the chaos of conflicting opinions, we think are in a fair way to be settled. First, men fight most readily and with the most bitterness about those doctrines whose influence upon the life is the least. Secondly, persecution for opinion's sake is not only a crime, but a folly. When the Aurora Borealis can be put out by a fire-engine, then, and not till then, can a religious principle be extinguished by blood. Thirdly, the right claimed by Protestants of interpreting the Sacred Scriptures each one for himself, involving, as it does, not only the possibility, but the necessity of an honest difference of opinion, demands of us, as reasonable men, that we be intolerant of nothing so much as of intolerance. Fourthly, the religion of the heart is higher and better than the scientific creeds of the head, and he is not the best Christian who is the best reciter of formulas, but he whose life is most like that of our Great Exemplar. In aspiring to reach the lofty height of his virtue we shall resemble pilgrims climbing up different sides of the same mountain, who draw nearer at every step, not only to the sunlit summit, but also to one another. Fallen men are to be saved now as eighteen hundred years ago, and here as in Palestine, not so much by the sharp subtilty of their logic as by the earnest beneficence of their lives.

THE THINKER IN SOME OF HIS RELATIONS TO THE COMMUNITY.*

"WE cannot conceive," says an eminent physiologist, "even in the remotest manner, in what way the brain — a compound of water, albumen, fat, and phosphate salts — operates in the generating of thought." Of the house we live in, its various apartments and wonderful architecture, and more especially of its mysterious occupant, we know comparatively nothing. We are nowhere strangers so much as at home. We have only learned, by watching our neighbors, that the connection between the physical organization and the intellectual operations is most intimate, and that in their reciprocal action they seriously and constantly modify each other. The great difference in human countenances is a difference, not in features, but in *expression*, — an expression which is the outward exponent of the spiritual life. No face can attain the highest degree of manly or womanly beauty of which it is capable, until it is informed and interpenetrated with thought and feeling. It was not of a passive, waxen doll, but of an intellectual, thinking woman, that the poet said:

> "Her pure and eloquent blood
> Spoke in her cheeks, and so distinctly wrought,
> That one might almost say her body thought."

The influence of the mind upon the body is seen, not only

* A Lecture delivered before the Lyceums of Springfield and Woburn, Mass., Concord and Portsmouth, N. H., and in other places. 1854 - 55.

in the prompt obedience of the muscles to its will, not only in the flashing eye of indignation, the quivering lip of some strong agony, the mantling blush of ingenuous shame, but also in the power which the rapt spirit has of triumphing over physical torture. The exultant song of the martyr has often risen above the flames which were consuming him.

We are by no means to infer from this, that the material organs are of slight importance in the development and exercise of the mental powers. The mind cannot act perfectly through a diseased and dilapidated body. The literature and theology of the world always indicate, with more or less of distinctness, the character and condition of the brain which produced them. Byron tastes of gin; Bulwer smells of tobacco; every gland in Dr. Johnson is distended with scrofula; the mighty thoughts of Coleridge and the capricious imagination of De Quincey are alike obscured and distorted by the fumes of opium; many of the sombre speculations and repulsive dogmas of the great Christian Reformer are easily traceable to the abnormal action of a diseased physical system.

But it is not of the mutual relations of mind and body that we propose to speak. We wish rather to say somewhat upon *the Thinker in some of his Relations to the Community.*

The most obvious fact in respect to the thinker of the present age, and especially of this country, is the efficient influence which he exerts in quickening and elevating the intellectual character of the common people.

In those nations of antiquity which occupy the proudest position in the history of the world, the persons who thought sat apart, or at most allowed access to a chosen few. Plato and Zeno and Aristotle gathered around themselves a few favored disciples, and sought to elevate *their* minds to a communion with their own, but for the improvement of the great body of the people they felt no concern. They had no sympathy with the unwashed, vulgar herd. The feelings of the refined philosopher towards the unlettered tradesman or laborer are well expressed in the motto of the Rosemary in old Herbals: *Sus, apage, haud tibi spiro!* — "Be off, brute! my fragrance is not for thee." Hence it happened, that, while the mind in some instances received its last finish of elegance, the masses grovelled in ignorance and superstition. Airs from heaven floated around the top of leafy Olympus, but death-bringing miasmata exhaled from the marshes at its base. Light illumined the domes of gorgeous temples, but the people knelt at the altar below in darkness. If in the observations of the astrologist any fact in astronomy was discovered, it was not thought worth recording, unless it might have some influence on the destiny-revealing horoscope. If in the experiments of the alchemists any great truth in chemistry * revealed itself, it was looked upon as a matter of no interest, and so was either lost or locked up in mystical formularies. Men searching for the philosopher's stone, and the universal solvent, and the elixir of life, cared little for scientific principles, which could only be made subservient to the common people in the physical interests of material life. The student lived in rapt reverie, or dreamed of imagined perfection in some Utopian state or far-off Islands of the Blest.

A man of intellectual vigor and acumen valued himself according to his skill in discussing those questions which were most remote from the wants and necessities of "this working-day world." His constant employment was an interminable logomachy, — a battle not of swords, but of words, — a fierce dispute, not on strictly metaphysical subjects, not in respect to the soul and its faculties, but about "airy nothings and impalpable inanities." The dialectics in which the time of whole schools of philosophy was con-

* Becker and Boyle were the first to give anything like plausibility of system to chemical science.

sumed were mere eristic syllogisms, which went by different names according to their individual peculiarities. One of them, called, from the example which illustrated it, "The Lying," was perhaps as famous as any. "If, when you speak the truth, you say you lie, you lie; but you say you lie when you speak the truth; therefore, in speaking the truth, you lie." In discussing the momentous interests involved in this ridiculous quibble, Chrysippus wrote six ponderous volumes! Diodorus of Caria, a great adept in this kind of verbal combat, invented the extraordinary argument against *motion*, which was afterwards employed by Sextus Empiricus in his controversy with the mathematicians. "If any body be moved, it is either moved in the place where it is, or in a place where it is not; but it is not moved in the place where it is, for where it is, it is; nor is it moved in a place where it is not, for nothing can either act or be acted upon where it is not; therefore, there is no such thing as motion." How entirely absorbed men became in this strife of words may be inferred from the fact that this same Diodorus, in the height of his fame, actually died of vexation, because he could not answer one of these dialectic questions proposed by a rival philosopher. The respect which we entertain for such a man is second only to that which we feel for the royal French cook, who, because a chowder, a favorite dish with the king, was spoiled in preparing, took the accident so much to heart that he went to bed and died a martyr to fish.

The whole Megaric sect — a sect which sprung directly from the school of Socrates — deemed it the highest aim of philosophy, the chief end of man, to be able to construct a syllogism or disentangle a logical puzzle. Its disciples, therefore, could "cavil upon the ninth part of a hair," but in relation to those principles which underlie human society, and contribute to the happiness and well-being of the struggling multitude, they knew as little as they cared. There was not a word nor a sentiment in all their teachings which was meant for the masses, or which spoke, however faintly, of a human brotherhood. While Plato, therefore, was speculating sublimely in the groves of the Academy, and building the airy fabric of his ideal Republic, infant children, whose feebleness or deformity of limbs gave no promise of brawny strength in future martial conflicts, were cast out by their parents to the wolves of the mountains or left to starve in baskets by the wayside. While Pericles was adorning Athens with magnificent works of art, whose ruins even are the wonder of the world, thousands of slaves were fleeing from tyrannical masters to the Temple of Theseus, or cowering in terror amid the shadows of the Parthenon. While Hippocrates was discoursing on the principle of life and the nature of disease, there was not throughout all Attica, nor in fact in the known world, a single hospital for the sick, not one retreat for the deaf and dumb, not an asylum for the insane. While Gorgias and his fellow-sophists were paid enormous amounts to train the sons of the rich in all the sharp subtilties of logic and the graceful refinements of a splendid rhetoric, not a drachma was ever raised by individuals or by the state for the purpose of educating the children of the poor. While poets and orators and historians were constructing a literature richer in its natural simplicity, and more varied and brilliant in its beautiful creations, than any the world had ever seen, the people, who thronged the busy streets, or toiled in the vineyards and olive-grounds, or fought at Marathon and Mantinea, knew as little of letters as they did of the mysteries of Eleusis or of the secret rites of the Cabiri. The common school, whose instruction and supervision command the warmest interest and highest talent of this country, is an element of strength and perpetuity in the state never dreamed of by the philosophers and statesmen of the ancient republic. Had district school-houses dotted the hillsides of Attica and the Peloponnesus, the poet never would have been compelled to sing:

> "The isles of Greece! the isles of Greece!
> Where burning Sappho loved and sung,
> Where grew the arts of war and peace,
> Where Delos rose and Phœbus sprung, —
> Eternal summer gilds them yet,
> But all except their sun is set!"

When Athens was the eye of Greece, and Greece the intellectual head of the world, the physical sciences, with all their manifold applications to practical life and human happiness, had hardly the rudiments of an embryo existence. Her scholastic philosophy frowned upon all attempts to investigate the works and laws of nature; her learned men could not descend from their lofty speculations to this foot-worn world of sense. One of them used to say, that "those who studied particular sciences and neglected philosophy were like Penelope's wooers, who made love to her servant-women." The few allusions which we find in their writings to these great departments of knowledge serve only to render visible the darkness which rested upon them. The earth,* in their geographical systems, was a great, flat, circular body, floating upon unfathomable waters, and surrounded by an ever-flowing, all-embracing river, in whose wide stream, under the setting sun, the poets had planted beautiful islands, where Achilles and brave Diomed dwelt with heroes and demigods, and where, as Pindar expresses it, "the ocean breezes breathe around the abode of the happy, and golden flowers are blazing." Their knowledge of geology was confined to the belief that the caves of Sicily and Campania were frightful entrances to Hades, — a dark realm in the hollow earth, peopled, in its

* The Sanson family published a very imperfect map of the world in 1651. De Lisle, the real founder of geographical science, published his map in 1699, guided by the directions of Cassini, and by observations for determining longitude by the immersions of Jupiter's satellites.

two grand divisions of Elysium and Tartarus, with the spirits of brave men and cowards. In respect to botany,* they tell us little more than that Proserpina once gathered flowers in the meadows of Enna, and,

> "Herself a fairer flower, by gloomy Dis
> Was gathered."

Many of the elements of zoölogy † are so obvious to the most careless eye, that an acquaintance with the subject in some of its branches could hardly be avoided. Herodotus, therefore, one of the most patient and accurate observers, speaks, with characteristic exaggeration, of a certain kind of sheep in Arabia of the usual bodily size, but endowed with caudal appendages five feet long, — so long, indeed, that they always trailed on the ground, and were consequently liable to be damaged by rude contact with the rough earth. To obviate this inconvenience, he assures us that the shepherds were accustomed to fasten little wagons to the latter end of the unfortunate animals for the special support and conveyance of their tails. ‡ The observations of the ancient ornithologists led them to suppose that the bird of paradise was destitute of legs, and therefore always on the wing. Where she made her nest, and how she hatched her young, we are not informed. Upon how minute and careful an examination the naturalists of Rome had constructed the science of ichthyology may be inferred from the fact that Pliny gravely tells us of a fish whose various members were so widely extended in the Mediterranean that it could not pass the Straits of Gibralter. A superstitious reverence for the bodies of the dead left the

* Tournefort first established a uniform and consistent system of classification of plants. Grew discovered the sexual system in plants, and, together with Malpighi, founded the science of vegetable physiology.

† John Ray first gave to zoölogy the name of a science, by a natural classification of animals, and by using the aid of comparative anatomy.

‡ *Vide* Koran, Chap. VI., note, p. 114, Sale's translation.

disciples of Æsculapius in the grossest ignorance of the plainest facts and most important principles of physiology. The difference between the heart and liver was not recognized, and the same functions were, by different writers, ascribed to both. The arteries, so far from being suspected of having any connection with the circulation of the blood, were thought to contain, as their name implies, only *air*.

Mathematics, the foundation and superstructure of all modern science, was pursued by Euclid and Thales, not for the purpose of applying it to mechanics and natural philosophy, but merely to withdraw the mind from the concrete to the abstract, and enable it to luxuriate in the beauty of truth. Plato,* in enumerating the branches of study which should occupy the young in his imaginary Republic, specifies in particular arithmetic and geometry; but he is careful to say that they should not be studied, as he expresses it, with a view to operation and practice, not to acquire a facility in buying and selling as anxious merchants and retailers, not to degrade them to a vulgar utility by turning their principles to account in building machines of wonderful power, like those of Archytas, but to compel the soul to use pure intelligence in the search after pure truth, and thus to enable it to rise above the sensible and evanescent to a contemplation of the τὸ ὄν, the true and absolute being, the eternal essence of things, in distinction from their changing substance. When we read the discussions of Plato, clothed though they be in all the splendors of a glorious language, yet always impatient of contact with human affairs, and therefore ever hurrying from the beaten paths of common life, until they baffle all pursuit by their own complication, or are lost in the thin upper air, we are not disposed to quarrel with the author of Hyperion, when he tells us that "speculations in philosophy, literature, and religion resemble those roads in our Western forests, which,

* Republic, Book VII. chap. 9.

though broad and pleasant at first, and lying beneath the shadow of green branches, finally dwindle to a squirrel-path and run up a tree." If this be true of Plato, the favorite pupil of Socrates, and the most brilliant genius in the whole history of the past, we need not be disappointed overmuch at the barrenness and poverty of the hundred other philosophers, Roman and mediæval as well as Greek, whose teachings and systems have been transmitted to us. Aside from the eloquent and wellnigh Christian teachings of Socrates and Cicero, of whom the old world was not worthy, and certain mathematical principles clearly demonstrated, but never applied by themselves and never intended to be applied by anybody else, a *sterile exuberance of words* * constitutes the sole fruit of all the toil of all the wise men of sixty generations. Their philosophy, we are forced to say, with Bacon,† "was neither a vineyard nor an olive-ground, but an intricate wood of briers and thistles, from which those who lost themselves in it brought back many scratches and no food." The great minds which illumined the centuries immediately preceding and following the commencement of the Christian era were employed, not in enlightening the ignorant, not in healing the wounds of a bruised humanity, not in multiplying the conveniences of humble life, but in unavailing endeavors to answer the ever-recurring questions, What is the highest good? Is pain an evil? Can a wise man be unhappy? Are all things fated? Can we be certain of anything? Can we be certain that we are certain of nothing? However antagonistic the schools of rival sects might be, the combatants all agreed in despising everything which was so vulgar as to be useful.

It was not until the Reformation that the sceptre of Aristotle was broken, and the dominions of a dreamy specu-

* "Sunt *voces* prætereaque nihil." — Ovid.

† Novum Organum, Aph. 73.

lation were invaded by the heavy-armed cohorts of a living faith. The controversy in which Luther engaged was not about words, but about things. He despised the schoolmen and all their verbal subtilties. With the same feelings he looked upon the discussions of the Church and priesthood of the Middle Ages. The disputes of Duns Scotus and Thomas Aquinas, the queries about the immaculate conception, the theories of the real presence, the question whether an angel could go from one point to another without passing through the intermediate space,— these were all alike, to his practical mind, puerile and contemptible. The subjects which he treated took hold of the popular heart and lay within the range of the popular thought. The discovery of Faust and Gutenberg had scattered the best thoughts of the best thinkers among the people. The manuscripts of the Gospels, which it had taken the German monks long years to copy and illuminate, were now reproduced in days, so that the credulous multitude believed that the second edition of the Bible was the work of magic or of the Devil. Books were no longer chained to the shelves of monasteries, or enclosed in gold and jewelled cases in the palaces of princes, but were read and pondered around the cottage hearth-stone. The warnings of the great Apostle against "philosophy" had influenced a thousand communities besides that of the Colossians. Christianity, though, as Macaulay asserts, "the rights of the Pantheon had passed into her worship and the subtilties of the Academy into her creed,"* was nevertheless in her spirit favorable to independent thought, and her champions, Zuingle, Bucer, Peter Martyr, and Calvin, were tireless and fearless in their hostility to the overshadowing

* The Pagan mysteries were commenced with a proclamation, "Procul este profani"; and, according to Bishop Warburton (Divine Legation, II. 258), it was at one time customary to begin the celebration of the Eucharist with the similar proclamation, "Omnes catechumeni foras discredite, omnes possessi, omnes non initiati."

system of the Stagirite. Men began to think for themselves; great names had lost the spell of their power; reverence for authority was growing weak; there was no terror in the prescriptions of a hoary antiquity. In a word, the proud fabric of the ancient scholastic philosophy was tottering on its shattered foundations.

But it was left for BACON, the great English Chancellor, to complete the overthrow of a dynasty which had reigned for ages. He was fortunately endowed with all those various qualities and attributes which fitted him to be the interpreter of nature, and the founder of a new system upon the ruins of the old. His temperament was delicately susceptible to every outward influence; his imagination bore fruit as well as flowers; his understanding has been compared to the "tent which the fairy Paribanon gave to Prince Ahmed: fold it, and it seemed a toy for a lady's hand; spread it, and the armies of powerful sultans might repose beneath its shade." There was nothing too minute for his scrutiny; nothing too high for his telescopic vision; nothing too broad and diversified for the grasp of his comprehensive intellect. Whether stuffing a hen with snow,* — in which experiment he lost his life, — or giving counsel to a capricious sovereign, or reforming the civil law of the realm, or describing the riches of Solomon's House in the New Atlantis, or investigating the abstrusest problems in nature, he was always the same patient, earnest, luminous inquirer after truth. "Discover" and "Improve" were the two watchwords of his philosophy. He was a thinker; but he thought not for the sake of the exercise, but for the accomplishment of an end. He performed his experiments, not for his own amusement, but to establish principles and obtain useful results. He had no respect for an intellectual cultivation which yielded no harvest. His researches all tended to some practical good. He had no time to revel

* Montague's Life of Bacon, p. 112.

amid the beatitudes of the gods, or to gloat over the golden visions of an imaginary state; but he mingled with men, — imperfect and erring men, — and he strove to subserve their human interests.* In his belief, "nothing could be too insignificant for the wisest, which was not too insignificant to give pleasure or pain to the meanest." He did not attempt to elevate mere mortals above common wants, but he studied to supply these wants. He did not teach them how to bear pain with indifference, but how to remedy or prevent it. Man, in his view, was not made for philosophy, but philosophy for man. Metaphysics and moral science were useful only as they could be made serviceable in modifying the character and curing the diseases and perturbations of the mind. To enrich human life with new discoveries and possessions † was, as he affirmed, the real and legitimate goal of all knowledge. He began, therefore, with observing phenomena, and ended with the arts. Locke, Newton, Paley, Kepler, La Place, and Franklin, with their numerous disciples, all followed the inductive methods of their illustrious predecessor, and each, in his own sphere, enlarged beyond all precedent the boundaries of human knowledge and human happiness.‡

It is said by sneering essayists, that this is an age of utilitarian materialism. If this charge were true, in its literal sense and widest scope, it would undoubtedly be a truth to be deplored. But *that* is a material age in which gross matter is sovereign, overshadowing and hindering in its development the intellectual life. In such an age the sea is an untraversed and fearful expanse, separating the

* "Commodis humanis inservire." — *De Aug.*, Lib. VII. c. 1.

† "Dotare vitam humanam novis inventis et copiis." — *Novum Organum*, Aph. 81.

‡ Upon the noble foundation of Bacon's experimental philosophy three institutions were established, the last two of which still continue the perennial fountains of science, — the Academy del Cimento at Florence, the Royal Society of London, and the Academy of Sciences at Paris.

nations, and reigning alone in its own unsubdued majesty. Mountains and rivers form the impassable barriers between tribes and peoples. The stubborn earth yields scanty sustenance to toiling men. The mere wants of the physical being engross the time, and absorb and degrade all the faculties of the soul.

But the reverse of this picture is true of the present age. We use rather the empire of the mind, the service of the body.* The giant tossing hopelessly beneath the mountain no longer symbolizes the overlaid and crushed spirit. Matter, in all its multitudinous forms, is not a burden to oppress, but an instrument for use. Mind pervades and moves the mass.† The slender wires, stretching like a network over continents, thrill with thought and feeling like the living nerves. Fire, air, and water are our ministers, and hasten to execute our commands. The energies inherent in the fossil earth serve us with an efficiency which puts to the blush our vaunted strength. A good Cornish engine evolves as much power, during the combustion of five tons of coal, as would be equal to the continued labor of an able-bodied Helot or Saxon for twenty years, at the rate of eight hours per day.‡ A material age, forsooth, when a ton of Lehigh or Anthracite, which may be bought for ten dollars, and burnt in as many hours, may be substituted for four years of unremitting human toil!

But this subjection of matter to the dominion of an intelligent will, this rendering of latent forces subservient to the comfort and convenience of man, is seen only in those countries where the governments do not interrupt the connection between the thought of the thinker and the activities of the out-door world. We do not find it, of course,

* "Animi imperio, corporis servitio magis utimur." — Sallustii *Bellum Catilinarium*, Sec. 1.

† "Mens agitat molem." — *Æneid.*

‡ Prof. Henry's experiment.

among any people whose enterprise is quenched and spirit broken by a civil or ecclesiastical despotism. A contrast of the sluggish imbecility, the uncontriving helplessness of many of the countries of the Old World, with the mental activity manifest in every relation of our material life, might lead us to a higher appreciation of the influence of free thought when quickened and electrified by free institutions.

If we were to designate the grand characteristic of the present age, — a characteristic impressed upon it by its thinkers, — we should say at once, and in a single word, *analysis*. We analyze everything, from the soil of our onion-beds up to the Copernican system of the universe. If we find a strange flower in our summer walks, we analyze it, and assign it to a place among the hard names of Wood and Gray. If a person dies with mysterious suddenness, we analyze the contents of his stomach, and detect the presence of the slightest trace of arsenic or strychnine. If we stumble over a long word or complicated sentence in Greek or German, we analyze it, and determine its nicest shade of meaning by its component parts. If we find in spherics or the calculus a knotty problem, we subject it to the rack of an unpitying analysis, and torture it, as the old Romans did their slaves, until it consents to disclose the secret which it was attempting to conceal from us. We analyze the atmosphere; and we do not breathe air, like our fathers, but a gaseous mixture of nitrogen and oxygen in exact proportions, with more or less of carbonic acid. We analyze our fountains; and we drink no longer water, but the oxide of hydrogen. We analyze our fruits; and we do not eat apples, as of old, but a scientific compound, made up of potash, soda, phosphoric acid, sulphuric acid, lime, magnesia, chlorine, silica, phosphate of iron, malic acid, sugar, and other organic materials. There is nothing too high, nothing too low, nothing too grand, nothing too minute, nothing too beautiful, nothing too sacred, for this all-pervading spirit of analysis. It is equally at home in the laboratory, at the bar, in the pulpit, and in the study. Its method is an "obstinate questioning," its law is progress.

It is a singular fact, that an Encyclopædia, embracing a compendium of the "seven liberal arts," — grammar, logic, rhetoric, arithmetic, geometry, astronomy, and music, — written by Marcianus Capella, an *African*, and appearing at Rome in 470, actually remained for more than *one thousand years* the common text-book throughout the schools of Europe. The human mind, during all this period, pursued the same dull round, like a horse in a bark-mill, leaving off in the end, jaded and dispirited, at the same point where it began. Our school-books, on the other hand, under the influence of the analytic propensity of the times, have been rapidly changing in their character, until they, together with the modes of teaching from them, have become not merely reformed, but entirely transformed. The student cannot longer be imposed upon by a formidable array of names and authorities. He is not satisfied when told, as Aristotle told his disciples, that the stone falls and vapor rises because "it is natural," but he must go back to the universal law of gravitation, and see how, in its equal operations, it causes both alike. He looks for reasons, not for methods. It is not enough for him to solve the problem by the *rule*, but the rule itself must be solved. He asks not what the answer is, but why it is as it is. The caption is deemed of little worth, unless followed by its demonstration. He feeds his mind, not with arbitrary prescriptions, but with unchanging principles, and therefore it is that

> "Now good digestion waits on appetite,
> And health on both."

The smallest and most unpretending specimen of Young America feels that the fee-simple of his personal being is vested in himself, and he is ready to say of his head, as

Touchstone said of Audrey, his wife, "An ill-favored thing, sir, but *mine own*." There is coming to be more individuality and less gregariousness in the community. Men do not care to know what the scribes and Pharisees believe, but what is in itself worthy of belief. Religious sects and political parties, which have nothing to recommend them but their gray hairs and respectable ancestry, are left to lean totteringly on their staves, or are warned to "look out for the engine when the bell rings." New theories in science, as well as old dogmas in theology, supernatural revelations, miraculous interpositions, ghostly visitants, are all alike subjected to the crucible, and they must stand the fire or vanish into thin air.

It is easy to see, that the thinker, by exciting this spirit of careful and earnest inquiry among all classes of society, has done much, and is destined to do still more, towards freeing the world from the dominion of a debasing and tyrannical superstition.

The twofold nature of man, soul and body, and his consequent relation, according to almost all systems of faith, to a future existence as well as to the present, have rendered him, in all ages and conditions, liable to superstitions, more or less absurd, in respect to the agency of spirits, angels, and demons in the affairs of this world. Of these superstitions there are some which do not strike their roots down into the intellectual being, but merely float, like phantoms, in the airy realms of a speculative faith or poetic imagination. With these the thinker wages no war. They do not necessarily dwarf and degrade the mind, nor interpose any obstacles to the progress of science. We meet them, without a sense of humiliation, in our every-day walks in the living world, or find allusions to them in the records of our literature; and, in our severest moods, we can only smile at their harmless folly, or wonder, perchance, at the comfort which their victims gather from them. Byron, in describing the Turks who had fallen in the siege of Corinth, says of them:

> "Crimson and green were the shawls of their wear,
> And each scalp had a single long tuft of hair."

The Mussulman, as we know, when he shaves his head, is always careful to save one tuft or long lock, that Mahomet may draw him into Paradise by it. Milton tells us of "airy tongues that syllable men's names." The belief to which the poet here refers, that the souls of the dead inhabit the forms of *birds*, has not been an uncommon one. The Duchess of Kendall had no doubt that George the First, who had died some time before, flew into her window in the shape of a crow. A wealthy lady of Worcester, England, believing her daughter, long since buried, to exist in the form of a canary, literally furnished her pew in the cathedral with cages full of these little unpaid singers. A bird of dark plumage and soft note bears to the Brazilian a message from a departed friend, and, as its wild, mournful strain is borne on the night-air, he welcomes the invisible messenger, and asks for news from the loved and lost.

> "Thou art come from the spirit-land, thou bird!
> Thou art come from the spirit-land;
> Let thy voice through the dark pine-grove be heard,
> And tell of the shadowy band."

One of our own most gifted poets, whose genius

> "Flamed in the forehead of our morning sky,"

but was extinguished long before its noontide, avails himself of this superstition in his famous lyric, "The Raven." He recognizes, in the ungainly bird perched upon the bust of Pallas over his chamber-door, a visitant from the Plutonian realm, and he therefore adjures it,

> "By that heaven that bends above us, by that God we both adore,
> Tell this soul with sorrow laden, if within the distant Aden
> It shall clasp a sainted maiden, whom the angels name Lenore!"

But birds are not the only or necessary media of communication between this world and the "dark unknown." The Irish mother sees, in the smile upon the lips of her sleeping infant, the token of an angel's presence, and, in her joy at the thought, she sings in exultant voice,

> "I know that the angels are whispering with thee!"

The followers of Swedenborg, in the belief that their deceased friends still retain an affectionate interest in their earthly associations and companionships, keep their chair at the fireside and the table unoccupied, and, in the midst of the employments of daily life, welcome the familiar rustle of their wings, and listen to the low words which they speak. The Greeks knew no solitude in nature. Their groves were haunted with Dryads; their fountains were filled from the pure urns of the Naiads; the coralline chambers of their ocean echoed to the soft tread of dancing Nereids; their heavens were lighted up with the smiles of departed heroes.

But in more modern times, and under a Christian civilization, it is not an unusual thing to meet with intelligent men whose writings, as well as personal character, are tainted with superstition. Marvellous stories, told on winter evenings, by ignorant nurses, in the ear of listening childhood, cast their shadows down the whole lengthening pathway of life. We see this truth illustrated in the productions of Walter Scott, Hugh Miller, and others of not less note. Des Cartes, though the method of his philosophical inquiries was undermining the whole edifice of the national religion, was all the while obsequious in his devotions to the Holy Mother and the True Cross. Luther, although the bellowings of Papal Bulls had no more terrors for him than the plaintive lowings of hungry calves outside their paddock, yet was sorely exercised, while translating the Bible, by assaults from infernal spirits, and the black spot is still shown, on the wall of his room at the Wartburg, where the inkstand hit which he flung at the head of the Devil. Dr. Johnson, though despising the scruples of the Puritans, and ridiculing, as it deserved, their horror of mince-pies and dancing bears, has, nevertheless, gravely recorded in his diary, with tears in his eyes, that he once committed the grievous sin of drinking coffee on Good Friday. Talking with fanatical sectaries as if he were imbued with the divine philosophy of the New Testament, he at the same time showed by his conduct that he firmly believed his salvation would have been imperilled, if he had celebrated the close of Lent with sugar in his tea or butter on his bunns. Possessing a keen insight into human nature, at least that of London, and less liable than almost any other man to be imposed upon by a parade of outward forms, yet he did not always assign the profoundest reasons for the estimate which he made of the religious character of his friends. "Campbell," says he, "is a good man, a pious man. I am afraid, however, that he has not been inside of a church for many years; but he never passes a church without pulling off his hat: this shows that he has good principles." But while the mind of the great lexicographer was disfigured, to some extent, by these blemishes, still it had too much native vigor and disciplined strength to become the passive victim of supernatural delusions and superstitious follies. The influence of early impressions and a diseased physical system could only refract the rays of his enlightened reason; they could not disperse them. On the other hand, let superstition once take root in the soil of an imaginative, but uneducated mind, and it will grow until it overshadows the whole being. Thoughts, opinions, feelings, are all absorbed by it, and become a part of its substance. It holds its place and thrives by what it feeds on. It is like the watchman's wife in the tower of Warblingen, of whom Longfellow tells us, who grew to such a size that she could not get down the narrow staircase ; and when her husband died, his successor was forced to marry the fat widow in the tower.

The proposition, that ignorance is the prolific mother of superstition, is demonstrated by the facts of to-day as well as by the history of the race.

The fourth Council of Carthage, in 395, prohibited the Bishops from reading secular books. Jerome, one of the most distinguished of the Latin Fathers, condemns the study of them, except for pious ends. All physical science, especially, was held in avowed contempt, as inconsistent with revealed truth. As a natural consequence, a large proportion of the clerical members of the subsequent Councils of Ephesus and Chalcedon could not write their names. With the best scholars among the highest dignitaries of the Church, a knowledge of sacred music passed for literature; an ability to sing a psalm-tune was an extraordinary attainment in the fine arts. Of the laymen, from Gurth, the swineherd, born thrall of Cedric the Saxon, who tended pigs in the woods and got on holidays some parings of the pork, all the way up to Philip, the mighty king of France, not one, except some rare prodigy of genius, could either read or write. Deeds and charters, until the use of seals became common, were subscribed with the mark of the cross. It is asserted by the highest authority, that there was, in the last of the tenth century, scarcely a single person to be found in Rome, once the home of poets and orators and philosophers, who knew the first elements of letters. The whole race of thinkers had died out, and all the learning of the world was tied up in a few hundred parchment rolls, most of which, fortunately, was guarded with watchful care by obscure but reverent monks. In the midst of this universal ignorance, a thousand superstitions, like foul animals of night, were propagated and nourished. The footprints of the odious brood, whether Scandinavian or Etrurian, Celtic or Saxon, were visible alike on the fairest and the most forbidding fields of Europe. The opinion now entertained by the disciples of Miller and Dr. Cummings was everywhere the prevalent religious belief. "As the world is now drawing to its close," was the introductory clause to all their legal instruments. The present talk about the midnight cry, the signs of the stars, the four great kingdoms, the serpent, the beast, the cleansing of the sanctuary at the end of the 2300 days, and the final consummation on the tenth day of the seventh month, is all a mere rehash,— a warming over of the cold victuals left by the ignorant fanatics of the darkest period in the Dark Ages. Judicial combats supplanted all the forms of legal trial, and left the question at issue between the parties to the decision of the sword and the justice of Heaven. Ordeals, which required the accused to prove his innocence by travelling barefoot and blindfolded over red-hot ploughshares, or by plunging his naked arm into boiling water, or by swallowing a piece of consecrated bread, which a perfidious priest might have poisoned, left the victim at the mercy of the ministers of church and state. Haggard religious enthusiasts, clothed in white, passed, like sheeted ghosts, from province to province and from city to city, crying out "Misericordia," or singing in solemn strains the "Stabat Mater Dolorosa." Eloquent hermits, wrought to madness by the outrages which they had witnessed in their pilgrimages to the Holy City, harangued excited multitudes, until millions, in successive crusades, rushed to rescue from the hands of the infidels the sacred sepulchre, and left their bones to bleach on the plains of the Levant or before the walls of Acre.

Superstition has attained its highest power in those countries and periods of the past in which a few men of genius and learning, like the priests of Egypt, did all the thinking and monopolized all knowledge for their private ends, while the servile, wondering masses grovelled in utter darkness. The people of Rome were not more affected by the admixture of a Tuscan blood, than was their civilization by the pervading influence of Tuscan superstition. The city of Romulus, by its original inauguration, was also a temple: its walls and gates were holy; its soil was consecrated by the aruspices; its government was a ritual, borrowed from the dark and mysterious priests of Etruria. The sacredness of property in the land was shadowed forth in the reverence paid to the god Terminus, and the inviolability of contracts was secured by an apotheosis of Faith. The religion of the old Roman followed his conquering eagles, and its gorgeous pomps and mummeries became systematized and prevalent in all the tribes and states of Italy. The fact that the word "ceremony" is derived from Cære, one of its principal cities, sufficiently attests the formal and punctilious stateliness of its worship. The appearance of the heavens, the lightning's flash, the glare of meteors, the mutterings of the thunder, the monstrous prodigies of the volcanic nature about them, were all narrowly watched as intimations from the gods, and permitted to control the weightiest matters of the government and the people. In the bowels of animals, and in the flight, the feeding, and the voices of birds, they found signs for the future, whose hidden meaning the mystic priest could easily interpret to them. A ship might be manned for some important and pressing enterprise, its anchors weighed, its sails set, its stern crowned with garlands, the trumpet might have sounded the signal for its departure, and yet the alighting of a swallow on the rigging, or an unfortunate sneeze of a sailor "over the left," would stop the whole proceedings. Let the sacred chickens show an appetite less vigorous than usual, and a gloom settled at once upon all the seven hills of the Eternal City; but let them, on the contrary, eat their dough with an alderman-like relish, and joy pervaded and illumined all ranks and conditions of men, from the humblest plebeian up to the haughtiest consul.

In a community where the sickly imagination sits an incubus on the prostrate judgment, and visions of insanity are reckoned as realities, it is easy for a few master-spirits to subdue the million by working on their fancies and their fears. Those who know nothing of natural causes are always ready to attribute all startling phenomena to the agency of the imaginary beings with whom they people the elements, and whose wrath they are anxious to turn aside. In this fact lies the origin of all forms of Demonolatry. But as it is difficult for the untrained mind to retain its conception of a spiritual essence, some visible representation is attempted, and Idolatry, in all its grotesque and multiform hideousness, from the Moloch of Gehenna down to the Brahma of the Hindoos, is the natural product. Idols are fashioned so as to correspond with the evils which they are supposed able to inflict, or with the emotions which they are designed to excite. Horrible shapes, whose hybrid features are borrowed from all that is terrible in the world of imagination as well as that of sense, are called into existence. Dragons, centaurs, furies, gorgons, griffins, harpies, hydras, hippogriffs, minotaurs, satyrs, sphinxes, and other unearthly combinations of the human body with that of beasts, birds, fishes, reptiles, and demons, — all, in their uncouth ugliness, attest the ingenuity of their sacred inventors. But to give the highest efficiency to these fiendish creations, active qualities must be communicated to them. Some of them, therefore, in the earlier or middle ages, were made to move their heads and arms; others, like the picture of the Virgin, of which Cardinal Bedini wrote a few years ago, winked with one eye or both; and others still, spoke, groaned, smiled, or perspired, just as they happened to feel. The hierophantic magicians who accomplished these results were men of intelligence, far in advance of their times, adepts in mechanical philosophy and chemistry, as well as master-players on the human passions. Claiming kindred with heaven, and living apart in the secret recesses of the temples, they rendered their superior knowledge available in maintaining their ascendency over the multitude. They knew how to move gods to compassion by wires, or rouse them to anger by explosive compounds. The experiments in their subterranean laboratories were performed, not, as now, to elucidate principles of science and promote human comfort, but for the purpose of crushing out from men their manhood, and reducing them to trembling and imbecile slaves.

The highest achievement of these sacerdotal mechanics was the *Æolipile*, or Fire-Blower, — a hollow god of semi-human form, in whose capacious abdomen inflammable liquids and chemical preparations were concealed, and from whose mouth and nose and eyes streams and jets of many-colored flames issued forth, to the consternation of the astonished beholders. Sometimes these gods, or steam idols, of immense size, carefully charged with fiery mixtures ready to be ignited at the right moment, were mounted upon wheels and followed by their favorite priests to the battle-fields. With what horror and dismay the troops of a superstitious enemy would flee before beings of supernatural form, rushing upon them in chariots of smoke and a whirlwind of fire, may be easily conceived. Ewbank, I have no doubt, is right in affirming that the Old Testament writers repeatedly allude to these Æolipiles, the silence of the commentators to the contrary notwithstanding. Eliphaz, the Temanite, has one of them in his eye, when he says of the wicked: "By the blast of God they perish, and by the breath of his nostrils are they consumed." If David had never seen one of them on its war-car in the full tide of successful experiment, we never should have had the splendid, though terrible imagery of the eighteenth Psalm: "There went up a smoke out of his nostrils, and fire out of his mouth devoured; coals were kindled by it. . . . . . And he rode upon a cherub, and did fly; yea, he did fly upon the wings of the wind. . . . . . At the brightness that was before him his thick clouds passed, hail-stones and coals of fire. . . . . . Yea, he sent out his arrows, and scattered them; and he shot out lightnings, and discomfited them." The visible properties of these Æolipilic Deities of the heathen were naturally enough ascribed by the Hebrew Prophets, with some modifications and embellishments, to their own Elohim. If a familiarity with the expressions had not blunted their force, we should hardly recognize, in the God of a more enlightened age, the Being who, in the Oriental imagery of the Jewish sacred writers, sent fire from his mouth and smoke from his nostrils, whose anger waxed hot and burned, and whose breath like a stream of brimstone kindled the wood of the valley of Hinnom.

But Æolipiles, with their kindred prodigies, the Typhons, Chimeras, and Cerberi of a mythological age, have passed away forever. Monsters are well represented in the fable as the children of Night. It is certain that they retire as civilization advances, and it may be said of them, as of spectres, that they flutter with the dawn and vanish with the sunrise.

There is nothing for which our country, in particular, is more distinguished, than for the rapid progress it has made in popular education. Our thinkers, whether teachers or preachers, have vied with each other in their efforts to elevate the common people above the murky fogs of ignorance to the clear atmosphere of positive knowledge. The superstitions which the first settlers of this continent brought with them from the Old World find, among the books and school-houses and newspapers which are now sending their benign light down to the lowest valleys of life, no resting-place for the "sole of their unblest feet." It is true, there are among us yet men born out of due time. They belong to a past age, — an age of signs and wonders. They listen with patient anxiety to the oracular responses of Pythian girls and inspired tables; or run wild in reading the mathematical prophecies of William Miller, and in staring with fear-stricken awe at the painted menagerie of those remarkable beasts which John saw in the Revelation of Patmos. There still exist in some of our rural neighborhoods elderly matrons, who can tell any young lady, just budding into her teens, whether the matrimonial visions which begin to flit before her imagination shall become splendid realities, or fade like an "insubstantial pageant." It is only necessary to look at the lines which traverse the palms of the hand, or to scrutinize the grains of an exhausted tea-cup. It is worthy of notice, that the destiny revealed by the modern sorceress, like that of the threadbare fortune-teller of the deceitful Circus Maximus, is brilliant just in proportion to the ability of the inquirer to pay.

But these follies are noticeable, because they are exceptional. They are not common to whole communities; they do not enter into the constitution of society, intruding into the school-room, ascending the pulpit-stairs, modifying the faith and moulding the character of the great masses. In this fact lies the evidence of our progress. With our fathers, less than two centuries ago, superstitious credulity, more especially in relation to every department of our spiritual nature, was the order of the day. Those extraordinary trials for witchcraft in a New England city, only one hundred and sixty-five years ago, seem to us like the grotesque myths of a remote antiquity; but to Governor Stoughton and the people of Massachusetts, as well as to Cotton Mather and his immediate followers, they were stern and grim realities. To them there was more truth than poetry in Milton's couplet:

"Millions of spiritual creatures walk the earth
Unseen, both when we wake and when we sleep."

If we may believe Cotton Mather, the most famous clergyman of his day in New England, one of these "spiritual creatures," in particular, was a source of no small inconvenience to our Puritan ancestors and the rest of mankind. "The Divil," says he,* "even like a dragon keeping guard upon such fruits as would refresh a languishing world, has hindered mankind, for many ages, from hitting upon those useful inventions, which yet were so obvious and facile, that it is everybody's wonder they were no sooner hit upon. The bemisted world must jog on for thousands of years without the knowledge of the lodestone, till a Neapolitan stumbled upon it about three hundred years ago. Nor must the world be blest with such a matchless engine of learning and virtue as that of printing, till about the middle of the fifteenth century. Nor could one old man all over the face of the whole earth have the benefit of such a little, though most needful thing, as a pair of spectacles, till a Dutchman a little while ago accommodated us."

But it would seem, from the same learned divine, that his cloven-footed majesty not only stood in the way of all useful inventions, but he managed also, from his familiar knowledge of chemistry and natural philosophy, to exert a more positive and mischievous influence upon men. "'T is the Destroyer, or Divil," says our author, "that scatters plagues about the world; pestilential and contagious diseases, 't is he who does oftentimes invade us with them. 'T is no uneasy thing for him to impregnate the air about us with such malignant salts, as, uniting with the salt of our microcosm, shall immediately cast us into that state of fermentation and putrefaction which shall utterly dissolve all

* "Observations upon the Nature, the Number, and Operations of the Devils."

the vital ties within us ; even as an aqua-fortis, made with a conjunction of nitre and vitriol, corrodes what it seizes upon. And when the Divil has raised those arsenical fumes, which become venomous quivers full of terrible arrows, how easily can he shoot the deleterious miasms into those juices or bowels of men's bodies, which will soon inflame them with a mortal fire!"

"Once more," continues our learned doctor, "why may not storms be reckoned among those woes with which the Divil does disturb us? It is not improbable that natural storms on the world are often of his raising. We are told in Job, that the Divil made a storm, which hurricanoed the house of Job upon the heads of them that were feasting in it. Paracelsus could have informed the Divil, if he had not been informed, as be sure he was before, that if much aluminous matter, with saltpetre not thoroughly prepared, be mixed, they will send up a cloud of smoke, which will come down in rain."

But amidst the multiplicity of his out-door employments, the Devil seems to have found time to inaugurate in New England an order of witches, whose diabolical practices were as much his own delight as they were the terror and confusion of all good people.

The Pilgrims, it should be remembered, had gone forth from their homes in the mother country to "wrestle against principalities, against powers, against the rulers of the darkness of this world, against wicked spirits in high places." They brought with them to these shores the opinions and sentiments of the communities in which they had dwelt; for it was as true then as when Horace wrote his Epistle to Bullatius, that "they who cross the sea change the climate, not the mind." Their only text-book in philosophy was the English Bible, and their rules of exegesis required the most literal interpretation. The injunction, "He that hath a familiar spirit must die," was full of significance to them.

The eminent divine* who drew the first abstract of the civil and criminal code which afterwards formed the basis of the statute law of Massachusetts, was careful to copy that provision of Moses which made death the penalty of witchcraft. Besides, the wild and solitary scenes of nature, which surrounded the Puritans, wrought upon their imagination, and quickened their faith into an unquestioning credulity. Behind them was the sea, rendered more awful to them by their recent experience of its dangers. Before them frowned the dark and mysterious woods, whose primeval silence had never been broken by the voice of civilized man, and whose grand old cathedral aisles had been trodden only by prowling beasts and painted savages. The great idea of free schools had been conceived, but their elevating influence had hardly begun to be felt. Their rudimental text-books were ordinarily worse than none, and their "schoole-masters" were, in most instances, inferior to their text-books. Not a single newspaper,† the great educator of modern times, had been published on the continent. Their life was one fierce struggle with the reluctant soil and hostile Indians, and, more than all, with imaginary demons.

But a change has come over the scene, transcending the magic of the most wondrous fairy tales. The Aladdin's lamp which has wrought it is *free thought*, — free thought in its multitudinous applications to every department of human industry, as well as to the nature and wants of the soul. There is nothing, from a brimstone match up to hoary theological creeds, which has not felt its transforming power. It determines the revolutions of the most erratic comet, and, with the same mathematical exactness, traces the curve of a ship's keel and gives shape to the mould-board of a plough. It not only guides the rich ar-

* John Cotton.

† The first newspaper published in this country was the "Boston News-Letter." Its first number was issued on a half-sheet, in 1704.

gosies of the merchant over pathless seas, wings the flying shuttles of the manufacturer, reveals to the farmer the hidden resources of his wasted acres, and, in the twinkling of an eye, girdles the earth with the flash of intelligence, but it is also, in the exercise of that reformatory benevolence which is always the attribute of profound thought, striving to free society from every debasing superstition, and to purify governments and laws from their follies and oppressions. The energy of the Anglo-Saxon mind, under the genial influence of our political system, is asserting its dominion over the land and over the sea. The ports of trade on our Pacific coast, and the railroads which shall erelong unite our distant oceans, will bring the commerce of the nations under the control of our race. "The empire of our language will follow that of our commerce; the empire of our institutions that of our language." It has been truly said, therefore, that "the man who writes successfully for America will yet speak to all the world."

It is the glory of this country, that *its thinkers are doers*, and *its doers men of thought*. The toil-worn and weary, quickened into a higher life, are beginning to be able to appreciate the productions of genius, to understand the dark responses of the priests of science, and to catch that strain of upper music which floats on the song of the poet. Truth, in relation to whatever subject, is not now, as of old, a mere torch-flame, casting a partial splendor over the sparry incrustations of a cavern, but it is a holy and universal sunlight, gladdening and making beautiful all the wild and varied workings of external nature. The humblest dwellers in the shadows of the mountains rejoice in its warm radiance, while the powers of evil, which once haunted the imagination, have fled with the darkness, leaving their broken sceptre at the feet of Redeemer and redeemed.

EDUCATED LABOR.*

[North American Review, October, 1859.]

IT was the king of Brobdignag who avowed the opinion, "that whoever could make two ears of corn or two blades of grass to grow upon a spot of ground where only one grew before, would deserve better of mankind and do more essential service to his country than the whole race of politicians put together." Whatever may be said of politicians, there can be no doubt that the scientific farmer is a public benefactor. Government-tinkers and place-hunters may be, like Cardinal Wolsey, men of "unbounded stomach"; but, aside from the "home market" which they furnish in their own persons, they are of very small account in "this working-day world." They are mere consumers. The agriculturist, on the other hand, is the chief, if not the only, food-producer, or, more properly, food-manufacturer for the

* Farm Drainage. The Principles, Processes, and Effects of draining Land with Stones, Wood, Ploughs, and open Ditches, and especially with Tiles; including Tables of Rain-Fall, Evaporation, Filtration, Excavation, Capacity of Pipes, Cost and Number to the Acre of Tiles, &c., &c., and more than One Hundred Illustrations. By Henry F. French. New York: A. O. Moore & Co. 1859. pp. 384.

Elementary Treatise on the Drainage of Districts and Lands. By G. D. Dempsey, C. E. With Illustrations. London: John Weale.

Practical Landscape Gardening, with Reference to the Improvement of Rural Residences, giving the General Principles of the Art; with full Directions for planting Shade-Trees, Shrubbery, and Flowers, and laying out Grounds. By G. M. Kern. Second edition. Cincinnati: Moore, Wilstach, Keys, & Co. 1855.

nation. He it is who turns Peruvian guano and superphosphate of lime into wheat, bones from the Pampas into esculent roots, Russian oil-cake and Syrian locust-pods into beef and mutton. But to do all this he must be intelligent, — acquainted with something more than the manipulations of the spade and the wheelbarrow, with something higher than the vulgar traditions of an ignorant ancestry. It is only under the hand of such men as Robert Bakewell, Jonas Webb, and Josiah Parkes, that long-legged, slab-sided, ill-bred oxen are metamorphosed into small-boned, quick-fattening Devons and elephantine Durhams; that lean, hurdle-backed Norfolk rams become beautiful "firkin-bodied" South Downs; that drifting sand-plains are converted into corn-fields, and shaking fens, from which benighted travellers were once warned by beacon-lights, are transformed into English gardens and apple-orchards.

Every book, therefore, which sheds new light upon the principles and processes of agriculture in any of its departments, we welcome as a contribution to the public welfare. Such is the work whose title we have placed first at the head of this article. Elaborate in its explanation of methods, and lucid in its philosophical statements, it leaves little to be said by others on altogether the most important branch of American husbandry. It is tastefully printed and illustrated; and, if read at every farmer's fireside morning and evening, "with judicious care," it would soon renovate the face of the country, clothing the exhausted fields at the East with fresh verdure, and turning the ocean-like prairies of the West, now to a large extent too wet for tillage or for health, into the very garden of the world. The author is one of those versatile, open-eyed men, whose constant and careful observation of minute and disconnected facts is happily accompanied by a rare power of analysis and generalization. He presents a pleasant combination of scholarly culture and practical energy, and is equally at home at the forum and in the field, discharging with singular tact the twofold function of an accomplished jurist and a skilful tiller of the soil. He seems to receive from frequent contact with the earth fresh vigor for wrestling with hard questions of law. For many years associate editor of the New England Farmer, and special contributor to other similar journals, he has devoted the leisure wrung from a laborious profession to the study and practice of agriculture. His articles and addresses are not the mere speculations of a white-handed theorist, but they all have the flavor of fresh-ploughed fields and new-mown hay. As a racy and instructive writer upon the various topics connected with the garden, the orchard, and the farm, he has no superior and few equals in this country. He has the faculty of making all his resources, of whatever nature, contribute to the illustration of the particular subject in hand, no matter what that subject may be. The necessity of "gratings at the outlet of drains," in order to keep out all sorts of vermin, is not a very promising topic for pleasant rhetoric, and yet the pages occupied by him in its discussion sparkle with flashes from Virgil and Shakespeare, Coleridge and Matthew Prior.

"There are," he says, "many species of vermin, both creeping things and 'slimy things that crawl with legs,' which seem to imagine that drains are constructed for their especial accommodation. In dry times it is a favorite amusement of moles and mice and snakes, to explore the devious passages thus fitted up for them; and entering at the capacious, open front-door, they never suspect that the spacious corridors lead to no apartments, that their accommodations, as they progress, grow 'fine by degrees and beautifully less,' and that these are houses with no back-doors, or even convenient places for turning about for a retreat. Unlike the road to Hades, the descent to which is easy, here the ascent is inviting; though, alike in both cases, '*Revocare gradum, hoc opus, hic labor est.*' They persevere upward and onward, till they come, in more senses than one, to an 'untimely end.' Perhaps, stuck fast in a small pipe tile, they die a nightmare death; or perhaps, overtaken by a shower, of the effect of which, in their ignorance of the scientific principles of drainage, they had no conception, they are drowned before they have time for deliverance from the strait in which they find themselves, and so are left, as the poet strikingly expresses it, 'to lie in cold *obstruction*, and to rot.' In cold weather, water from the drains is warmer than the open ditch, and the poor frogs, reluctant to submit to the law of nature, which requires them to seek refuge in mud and oblivious sleep in winter, gather round the outfalls, as they do about springs, to bask in the warmth of the running water. If the flow is small, they leap up into the pipe, and follow its course upward. In summer, the drains furnish for them a cool and shady retreat from the midday sun, and they may be seen in single file by scores, at the approach of an intruding footstep, scrambling up the pipe. Dying in this way affects these creatures as 'sighing and grief' did Falstaff, — it 'blows them up like a bladder.'"

In the summer of 1857, Judge French visited Europe for the purpose of acquainting himself with the superior modes of husbandry in the Old World. The few months spent among the intelligent farmers of England confirmed him in his previous impression, that the first duty in American agriculture is systematic and thorough drainage; and the value of the volume before us, treating of "the principles, processes, and effects of draining land," is not a little enhanced by the writer's careful attention to the working, in the mother country, of the various systems of Elkington, Smith of Deanston, Josiah Parkes, and Lord Wharncliffe.

The sixty million acres of swamp lands, given away as worthless by our general government to the new States in which they lie, constitute but a very small portion of the territory in these United States which might, by judicious drainage, be transformed from unsightly, pestilential "bog-holes" into waving grass and grain fields of exhaustless fertility. If Great Britain, a country of less area than our youngest State, is justified in loaning $ 40,000,000 to companies engaged in the drainage and improvement of her highlands, certainly the subject so ably discussed by our author cannot be unworthy of the earnest consideration of the American public. It is to be remembered that the agricultural districts of this country are lower and flatter than those of England, and that they receive *double the amount of rain-fall* per annum. We have no doubt that the value of the prairie lands in Illinois, Indiana, Iowa, and Missouri might be at least trebled by a proper distribution of drain-tiles, four feet under ground. The face of the country might in this way be entirely changed. Corn, instead of being dropped into sub-aqueous drills from a raft, in June, with poor prospect of a harvest, might be planted on dry ground, early in May, with an assurance of reaping a hundred-fold. Wheat, no longer frozen out of the clayey soil every winter, might yield, not twelve, but, like John Hudson's on his Castle Acre farm, "forty-eight bushels to the acre." The farmers themselves, now shaking with intermittent chills amidst the noxious miasmata that rest like a pall upon coarse sedge and miry pools, might riot in fragrant clover and luxuriant health.

The present great need in this country is, first, a more thorough investigation of the principles of agriculture by scientific men, and, secondly, a more ready application of these principles to the processes of agriculture by working-men. A better understanding between these two classes would be an advantage to both. It is a pleasant indication of progress in the right direction, that professional men are beginning to take a more active interest in the material affairs of the field and the workshop; that the toil-hardened hand and weather-stained face are now regarded by none, except patent-leather, tape-selling cockneys, as marks of dishonor, but rather as the heraldic emblems, the armorial insignia of

Nature's noblemen. Emerson is right when he says: "The first farmer was the first man, and all nobility rests on the possession and use of land." If, as Hebrew scholars tell us, Adam, the parent of all living men, means, etymologically speaking, "dark loam," then are the bonds of relationship between us and this teeming earth fixed in nature, and strong as the ties of blood. We are fed literally from the same maternal bosom, and the theory of a human brotherhood is something more than a dream of philanthropy. It was the boast of the Athenians that they were *αὐτόχθονες*, — children of the soil; that, in the olden time, they, like their olive-trees, sprang out of the ground. Attica, with its vine-clad hills and fertile valleys, was to them, therefore, not merely a territorial possession, but it was, as Thucydides expresses it, "a father and mother land." Every rood of it was consecrated in their affections; and the foreign foe who ventured within its borders was sternly encountered, as an invader of the privacy and sanctity of home; while the citizen who should raise his hand against it was treated, not as a traitor only, but as a parricide. The old Roman, though contemning the subtilties of the poetic Greek, yet, like him, recognized his relationship to the soil. It is a noteworthy fact, that the words *ground* and *man* have, in the Latin language, a common root.

But, leaving to scholars the niceties of philological discussion, one thing we may affirm as certain: A nation is strong only when, like the fabled Libyan giant, it rests its feet upon the solid earth. Land is the basis of our power; the everlasting hills are the pillars of our imperial sovereignty. Men in successive generations may give themselves up in mad frenzy to slaughter and extermination; dynasties may follow dynasties in lengthening cycles of misrule and oppression; the refluent wave of barbarism may dash against the broken arches of a former civilization; palaces, temples, capitols, all the trophies of art, may pass away in the ages like the ephemera of a summer morning; but Nature is eternal, and the husbandman is her minister, and should be her interpreter. In dealing with her mysteries he is dealing with the principles and laws which regulate the growth and determine the destiny of a people. The stewardship of our nationality is vested in the men who till the soil; for it depends on them whether our fields shall be yellow with corn, and a wide-spread commerce relieve our bursting granaries, or whether we shall return to the want and savagism of a past age, and worship again the "sacred oak," — *sacred* because it feeds us with acorns. It becomes a question, therefore, of the highest moment, how these men shall be awakened to a consciousness of their position, and furnished thoroughly for the discharge of their weighty responsibilities. How shall agricultural and mechanical labor, tasking as it does the energies of three fourths of the working male population of these United States, be elevated to its highest dignity and efficiency? The answer is as obvious as it is emphatic: By making the man of action a man of thought. Muscle must not be divorced from mind. It was said of Lord Bacon, that he never used one of the hundred hands of Briareus until he had opened all of the hundred eyes of Argus. There never was a great act, whose pedigree might not be traced back to some great thought as its ancestor.

We propose, in the further consideration of Judge French's book, to expatiate a little upon the subject of Educated Labor, incidentally treated by him; and if our readers do not discover a tile-drain running through our article, it will be either because our tiles are laid so deep as to be invisible, or because our discussion, as we proceed, may seem to us so dry as not to need draining.

There are counties in England in which, not long since, according to governmental statistics, only one person in ten could read; and at a little earlier period, if we may believe pleasant Arthur Young, "not one farmer in five thousand did read anything at all." In these same districts the old Roman plough and harrow still belabored the patient soil, and the cattle were cured or killed by enchantment. The peasants wore charms for the ague; nailed horseshoes on the threshold to keep out the witches; carried around in their pockets pieces of a coffin to ward off the cramp; and tied red strings around the tails of their new-milch cows to prevent the fairies from stealing the butter. In Italy, as we are told in some recent reminiscences of travel, the farmer breaks up his land, not with a double-eagle plough, but with the root of a tree, attached by a grape-vine to his two cows. This remarkable style of tillage, however, is altogether outdone in Egypt, where Stephens assures us that the insulted ground is vexed by a grotesque thing, ycleped a plough, constructed in some pre-Adamitic era, and actually drawn in the furrow by an old woman and a jackass harnessed together. We shrewdly suspect that the modern traveller had been reading Pliny, who made the same extraordinary statement some eighteen hundred years ago.

There are among ourselves not a few whose brawny strength is turned to weakness by their ignorance, and whose stalwart manliness is dwarfed by the hereditary taint of a thousand shrivelling superstitions. They tremble and turn pale at the breaking of a looking-glass, or at the upsetting of a salt-cellar, or at the ticking of a little harmless insect which they have named the death-watch. They would no sooner engage in any important enterprise on Friday, than an old Roman general would go into battle when the sacred chickens refused to eat their dough with the proper relish. They never look at the new moon "over the left" without an indefinable apprehension of evil; nor pass in the evening a retired churchyard without encountering some unhappy ghost, or haunting devil. They will not wean their calves when the sign is in the stomach, for fear the poor animals may pine away over their meal and clover; and the pig whose tail unluckily curls to the left is, they are sure, scarcely worth the raising. They could not be persuaded to plant their potatoes on the increase of the moon, lest they all run to tops; nor to kill their swine on the decrease of the moon, lest the pork boil away in the pot. If an ill-fed or sick ox have nothing in his second stomach to be pumped up for rumination, they are certain he has "lost his cud," and will die, of course, unless they can manufacture a new one for him. If an unfortunate cow, from exposure to storm or cold, should, in the first flow of her milk, have a swollen bag, they thrust a butcher-knife through her dewlap, and insert a garget-root, or else saw off one of her horns.

It is a matter of congratulation that the common school and the agricultural journal are fast driving this whole brood of party-colored superstitions and follies, like spectres of night, to the mountain-caverns and forests on the outer rim of civilization. Let scientific men do their duty to the community, and the time is not far distant when no place shall be found among us for the "sole of their unblest feet." Every profound thought lifts a shadow from the earth. Every good book, whether it treat of "Farm Drainage" or "Celestial Mechanics," helps forward the millennium.

The advantages of intellectual culture are as obvious in those pursuits involving manual labor, as in the learned professions, so called. A good education is of some consequence to the lawyer and the physician; it is of not less consequence to the mechanic and the farmer. We have known professional men who could make a little learning go a great way with the wondering multitude; but such poor tricks cannot be played off upon the hidden forces of nature. It is the finger of Intelligence alone which can touch the secret springs that set the mountain streams to the music of machinery, and clothe the naked fields with waving grain. It is a maxim in New England factories, where a fluctuating and often hostile tariff has taught a wise economy, that they cannot afford to hire cheap, ignorant labor. Not many years ago a factory in Lowell imported a large number of workmen from England. But it turned out that these persons, though paid but half the wages of better-educated operatives at home, were nevertheless an expensive luxury to their employers. They could not earn their living, and, in a few weeks, they were all, with three or four exceptions, dismissed. A partner in one of the most respectable mercantile houses in Boston, having the principal direction of extensve cotton-mills, stated, a few years ago, in reply to the interrogatories of a Congressional Committee, that, of the twelve hundred operatives annually employed by him, forty-five only were unable to write their names; and that the difference between the average wages of these forty-five and of the remaining eleven hundred and fifty-five was just twenty-seven per cent in favor of the latter. There were also in the same mills a hundred and fifty girls, who had been engaged in teaching school. The wages of these school-mistresses was seventeen and three fourths per cent above the general average, and more than forty per cent above the wages of those who were obliged to make their mark. It is safe to affirm, that there is not a cotton-mill in the country, with operatives, whether native or foreign, too ignorant to read and write, which could be made to yield a profit in the best times. The fabrics would be inferior in quality and in quantity; the machinery would be misused and prematurely worn out; and the stockholders would be soon brought to a realizing sense of the difference between dividends and assessments.

We are not of those who entertain a prejudice against foreigners as such. We care not what may be a person's origin, name, or complexion.

> "Tros, Tyriusque mihi nullo discrimine agetur";—

a verse unconsciously, though happily, rendered by Robert Burns in his democratic song:

> "A man's a man for a' that."

But still, though revering as we do the splendid names in Irish history, we cannot conceal from ourselves the obvious fact that the introduction of uneducated Irish "help" in the field is working the same mischief to our sons which its introduction in the kitchen has already wrought to our daughters. It is making labor dishonorable by associating it with ignorance, and is therefore driving our young men away from the old homesteads,—some into mercantile pursuits, some into the over-crowded professions, some into the wild hazards of stock-speculation, or into the still wilder hazards of gold-digging at some far-off Pike's Peak or Fraser River. In this way our farms in the older states, instead of being divided and subdivided, as they ought to be, are growing larger and more unmanageable. The tendency of the times is unquestionably towards immense estates, like those in England, each with a manorial mansion in the centre, and a dependent tenantry crouching in its shadow. We need not say that this is not "a consummation devoutly to be wished." If there is anything which we as patriots should deprecate and struggle against with sternest resolution, it is the gradual division of our people into the two classes of landholders and tenants,—an educated nobility and an ignorant peasantry,— the wealthy few and the poverty-stricken, grovelling many. The immigration into this country of intelligent foreigners, who, like very many of the Germans and a very few of the Irish, appreciate and admire the freedom of our republican government as intensely as they hate the tyrannies, civil or ecclesiastical, of the Old World, is a matter, not of anxious solicitude, but of national felicitation. But the extraordinary influx of men, bringing with them little wealth and less intelligence, trained to unthinking, servile toil, and accustomed to look with helpless awe upon the glittering pageantry of monarchical institutions, is threatening, as its legitimate result, the gradual transformation of American society. The change, of course, is noiseless in its progress, but, unless arrested, it will be palpable enough in its effects. The laws of social chemistry are as fixed and inexorable as those which regulate the combinations of the laboratory. Athens, though her natural position and unequalled harbor, as well as the character of her native-born citizens, seemed to indicate that she was preordained to be the mistress of the world, yet was not able to withstand the deteriorating influence of vast hordes of unlettered "barbarians," pouring continuously into her streets from petty despotisms or conquered provinces, supplying the Bema and the Academy with the gross amusements and empty shows of the amphitheatre, and degrading a cheerful industry to the reluctant toil of enslaved Helots. If we allow labor on the soil, north or south, to be surrounded with menial associations, we should not be surprised that the Anglo-Saxon, rather than stoop to it, chooses to live by his wits, or to die like a fool in some ill-omened expedition of piratical filibusters.

We can remember, young as we are, when the farmer's daughter deemed it no disgrace to her to "work out" as "help" for any respectable man, whose son, perchance, in process of time, deemed it no disgrace to him to take her as his wedded wife, if he could get her. But now he would be a bold man who should venture within any farm-house in New England, and attempt to secure, at any price, the services, as cook or chamber-maid, of either one of the half-dozen young ladies working worsted at the front windows, or reading the last orange-tinted novel on the tear-besprinkled sofa. In all probability Bridget would be called from the kitchen, and the rash and unromantic intruder unceremoniously and ignominiously swept out like a muddy boot-track, or mopped up like an unlucky slop. These things ought not to be. Far be it from us to say aught in disparagement of the highest personal accomplishments and the amplest literary leisure. But these, so far from being inconsistent with the industrial pursuits of life, are its most appropriate embellishments. The kitchen and the field alike should be, in fact and in public estimation, laboratories of science, in which the speculations of theorists are daily tested and authoritatively pronounced either wise or worthless, as the result may prove them to be. Labor, to be respected, must be respectable; to be lucrative, it must be intelligent.

Cotton cloth was first made in Hindostan, centuries ago, and its manufacture is still continued there in all its original simplicity. But to-day one Yankee in Lowell or Manchester can spin with the mule as much cotton as three thousand Hindoos can spin with any machinery of their contrivance. In the sleepy sunshine of that Southern clime, the red brawn of the people lacks the electrifying influence of genius. The inert organism, called a body, is interpenetrated with barely thought enough to "save the expense of salt." The truth is, in every department of human labor, he succeeds best who brings to his work, not the greatest physical strength, but the keenest intellect.

The agriculturist, dealing not merely with inanimate matter, but with the vital forces of nature, needs, most of all things and most of all men, intellectual culture in the broadest and deepest significance of the term. We shall have, however, space only to indicate, in a general way, two departments of knowledge, to which every farmer should give especial attention ; — first, he should know how to make his fields in the highest degree productive ; and, secondly, how to render his home beautiful. In other words, he should be familiar with the conditions of vegetable growth, and with the principles of good taste in their application to rural embellishments. Let us briefly consider each of these desiderata.

All vegetables, whether grain or grass, trees or turnips, corn or cotton, require, as absolutely indispensable to their growth and maturity, at least six things ; namely, heat, air, moisture, food, light, and protection from destructive insects. Of these, we shall see as we proceed, that the first and most important four can be made available to a majority of the farmers in this country only by subjecting their lands to a system of thorough drainage.

No plant can germinate without a certain degree of *heat*. Each plant, however, has its own peculiar range of temperature. Wheat will not germinate when the soil is below 45° Fahrenheit, or above 95°. Corn requires 10° more heat than wheat. Should it be planted, therefore, when the soil does not indicate 55° at least, its starchy portions, if the weather continue wet and cold for a week or two, will be decomposed and diffused, wholly or in part, through the soil, so that when the warmth becomes sufficient to quicken the germ into activity, the plumule, failing to find the proper nourishment at its root, does not appear at all, or comes up a puny starveling, and, after living a few weeks "at a poor dying rate," expires, like the wretched Cardinal, and "makes no sign." This principle is universal in its application to the germinating processes of the vegetable kingdom. The man, therefore, who puts his seed into the ground without any reference to its temperature, is liable both to lose his time and to "beg in harvest."

But heat is quite as important to the growth of the plant as to its germination. It is a very remarkable mathematical law, recently ascertained in M. Quetelet's researches upon the climate of Belgium, that *the increase of growth is as the square of the increase of the temperature of the soil.* If a corn-plant, when the earth in which it grows is 20° above the freezing point, adds to its weight three grains in one day, it will in the same period add twelve grains, or four times as much, when the thermometer is twice as high, or at 40° above freezing. It is obviously, then, of some consequence, in our higher latitudes, to supply by our skill any natural deficiency of heat in the soil. There are three methods of doing this, — two partial, and one general. We may, in accordance with a well-known political principle, select for our premium crop a piece of land, which, like a candidate for some high office in the nation, has a southern exposure, and which will, therefore, receive a greater number of solar rays on a given area than a northern slope or a horizontal level; we may blacken the surface of our soil with charcoal-dust and meadow-muck, and thus increase indefinitely its power of absorbing heat; or we may gain at least a fortnight every spring, and secure a warmer soil through the season, (maturing our potatoes and corn before the rot and frost strike them,) by thorough under-draining, drawing off the superabundant waters, which, by their evaporation, chill the ground, until its "sensible warm motion becomes a kneaded clod," and the root-fibres in their paralysis are unable to supply the plant with its currents of life. It has been found by accurate experiment, that the vaporization of water requires one thousand times as much heat as would be sufficient to raise its temperature a single degree. We should not be surprised, therefore, that the evaporation of one pound of water from one hundred pounds of saturated earth causes a loss of ten degrees of heat; or, as Judge French enunciates the principle, that "the evaporation of every gallon of water requires as much heat as would raise five and a half gallons from the freezing to the boiling point." We say nothing of the familiar fact, that heat cannot be propagated downward in liquids. Every one knows that a cord of the best hickory would not be sufficient to make one small tea-kettle boil, if the wood should be burned above the kettle rather than below it. The surface of a "water-logged bog" may be burned and "shrivelled like a parched scroll," while the saturated sub-soil is as cold as in mid-winter. The warm spring rains run off from the surface of a soil saturated with snow-water, but penetrate a well-drained soil, imparting to it a portion of their own warmth, and enriching it with various elements of fertility. This point, in connection with the laws of heat-propagation in fluids, is thoroughly discussed and happily illustrated by our author in his fifteenth chapter, to which we commend our philosophic readers.

But stagnant surface water, in addition to its chilling effects, hardens and packs the soil so closely as to render it impervious to the *air*, thus preventing the second condition of vegetable growth. If the air be exhausted from a bell-glass, in which any common house-plant has been placed, the plant will die in a few minutes beyond the reach of recovery. If the air be shut out from the roots of the thriftiest fruit-tree in our garden by overspreading the ground for some ten feet from its trunk with a puddling of impermeable clay, the tree will sicken and eventually die for want of breath. On the same principle, cattle, standing in considerable numbers during the hot season under some favorite shade-tree in the pasture, not unfrequently cause its death. Its roots are suffocated under the hard earthen crust which covers them.

The fertility of a field is wonderfully increased by the oxidation or decay of the organic matter existing in the soil. But oxygen is indispensable to oxidation, and the process, therefore, can be carried on only by the presence and frequent renewal of the air. Our success in preserving fruits in glass jars or tin cans, is measured by our success in excluding the oxygen of the air. Without such exclusion, our tomatoes and berries undergo the very process to which we should like to subject them in the ground, but which does not heighten their excellence for the table, — they oxidate, or, in familiar language, they rot. We see, in the light of these and kindred facts, the philosophy of thorough tillage. Draining, by relieving the soil of its excessive moisture, secures its proper aeration, and thus, while facilitating important putrefactive processes, which are checked by the presence of cold water, it furnishes also to the plant-roots the carbonic acid and ammonia always indispensable in "intensive culture." The destruction of weeds among our corn and potatoes is not the highest use of the hoe and cultivator, — their chief function is to render the soil porous and permeable to the air.

The third condition of vegetable growth is a sufficiency of *moisture*. In many countries this can be effected only by artificial irrigation. In Scripture phrase, "the rivers of water are turned" into the fields, or the same thing is accomplished by means of "pots," suspended from a sort of yoke across the shoulders of slaves. This last method is referred to by the writer of the eighty-first Psalm, and a picture of it was made the significant emblem of Aquarius, the eleventh sign of the zodiac. The definition of Oriental agriculture is "valuable machinery for raising water." This definition will answer for New England to-day as well as for Egypt three thousand years ago. But with us the only machinery necessary is, first, an Irish spade, with an Irishman thrown in as a "dative of accompaniment," and, secondly, a Michigan plough, with a good team of horses or oxen at one end, and a skilful ploughman at the other. Let there be a deep and thorough pulverization of the soil and sub-soil, and, except in extraordinary cases, capillary attraction will raise an adequate amount of moisture. Besides this, when the rain fails to come in its season, the warm air, saturated with vapor, will permeate the well-tilled, porous soil, and, coming in contact with the cooler plant-roots, will deposit with them its dewy treasures, just as it does with the cabbage-leaf in the garden, or with the outer surface of a pitcher of iced water on a hot day, or with a frosty axe when held near the fire. The principle is perfectly simple. The capacity of air for moisture is diminished by cooling it; and whenever, therefore, in a state of saturation, it meets a colder body, whether above ground or below, the water is squeezed out of it just as we squeeze with the hand a juicy lemon or a wet sponge. The amount of dew deposited in the soil or on it has been estimated by Dr. Dalton to be equal, in England, to five inches' depth of water in a year. In this country, where the nights are clearer, there must be more, — as much at least as would be equivalent to "one quarter of our rain-fall during the six summer months."

Under-drains are not merely useful in carrying off the floods in a rainy season; they also greatly mitigate the severity of our scorching droughts. They do this in three ways. First, a deep-drained, thoroughly pulverized soil is in just the right condition, as we have seen, to absorb moisture from the air; secondly, it has a greater power both of drawing up water from the lower strata, through its countless capillary tubules, and of holding it when thus drawn up; and, thirdly, it invites the plants to extend their researches to unexplored depths. Wheat, which, like Mr. Denton's, has roots nine feet long; parsnips, which, like Sheriff Mechi's, run down "thirteen feet and six inches"; and lucern, which, like Mr. Cobbett's, "sends its roots thirty feet into a dry bottom," — certainly need have no apprehensions, though a "hot and copper sky" distil no rain upon the earth for a few months.

The fourth and most important condition of vegetable

growth is an abundant supply of suitable *food.* It is a fundamental proposition in agriculture, that all plants live by eating, — grow by what they feed on. From the delicate moss, which clings to the hard rock, up to the "high-haired oak," of which Homer sings, every green thing, if it does not, like some human vegetables, live to eat, must eat to live.

The whole outward fabric of nature, whether vegetable, animal, or mineral, is built up of some sixty elements, of which not more than one fourth enter into the composition of our ordinary edible plants. From these dozen or fifteen articles of diet, each particular plant, whether rose or ruta-baga, chooses those adapted to its constitution as carefully as an epicure at a *table d'hôte* makes his selection from a bill of fare. Unlike the epicure, however, the plant seeks no variety, but is satisfied with its one course of soup, morning, noon, and night, from infancy to old age, only varying the relative proportion of the ingredients in different periods of its growth. Its food, aside from certain invisible gases absorbed by its leaves, is always liquid, and is sucked up by its rootlets or spongioles, not exactly as a "fast" youth sucks mint-juleps through a straw, but by a law of *osmotic diffusion*, classically defined *endosmose* and *exosmose.*

What we call manure is known in the Ionic dialect of science as food for growing crops. There are two general divisions of manure, organic and inorganic; — the former consisting of decayed matter, or *humus*, which had once been organized into some form of vegetable or animal life; and the latter being the dust or *detritus* worn off from rocks, partly by friction, but chiefly by frost, heat, and the play of chemical affinities. Of these elements the most important are four gases, oxygen, hydrogen, nitrogen, and chlorine; five metals, potassium, sodium, calcium, magnesium, and aluminum; and four metalloids, carbon, silicon, phosphorus, and sulphur. These are seldom found simple, but in various combinations among themselves, and with other substances, such as iron and manganese. Water is a union of oxygen and hydrogen; air, of oxygen and nitrogen; ammonia, of hydrogen and nitrogen; carbonic acid, of oxygen and carbon; sulphate of lime (gypsum), of oxygen, sulphur, and calcium; carbonate of potassa (potash), of oxygen, carbon, and potassium; and so of all the rest. These unions of acids and bases constitute the various neutral salts, which Nature, like an enthusiastic chemist, is constantly forming, decomposing, and re-forming, for her own amusement, in her two laboratories, the soil and the plant. The combinations of greatest interest to the agriculturist are potassa, lime, soda, magnesia, alumina, silica, carbonic, sulphuric, phosphoric, and hydrochloric acids, and the oxides of iron. Of these, potash is supplied in great abundance by recent ashes and by the disintegration of granite, about fifteen per cent of whose felspar, when *orthose*, is potash. Soda, magnesia, and chlorine abound in common salt, and exist also, together with lime, the silicates, and sesquioxide of iron, in ashes, leached or unleached. Alumina is the basis of all the clays, and though no trace of it has yet been detected in any plant, its mechanical value, as a retainer of moisture and of useful gases in the soil, can hardly be over-estimated. Silica is extracted from rock-crystal and the quartz of our granite, by the action of the weather and the more effective action of the plough and harrow. Sulphuric acid is furnished in gypsum and in all the sulphates. Phosphoric acid constitutes nearly one fourth of the bones of Mammalia and of birds, and is found largely in guano. Carbonic acid, as well as ammonia, is the universal product of the putrefactive processes of vegetables and animals. It is the result, too, of combustion both of burning wood and of burning food. Whether discharged from the chimney-top or from breathing lungs, it is brought back from the atmosphere down to the earth in every fall of rain and snow. To intelligent farmers, the application of facts like the foregoing is obvious. If the ashes of potatoes consist chiefly, as in fact they do, of potash, sulphuric acid, phosphoric acid, lime, magnesia, silex, and iron, it is perfectly plain that these ingredients must be in the soil, or there will be no potatoes. A brick house cannot be made without bricks. It was an axiom with the old philosophers, as enunciated by Lucretius, "*De nihilo nihil*,"— that is, we cannot create something out of nothing, whether that something be a potato or a planet.

There is one noteworthy peculiarity in plants, as distinguished from animals. They require absolutely and unconditionally certain kinds of food, which cannot be replaced by any substitute. The amount of any one specific kind may be extremely small, — discernible in its infinitesimal minuteness only to the eye of the chemist; but unless that is supplied, the functions of life and growth will not be carried on. The kernel of wheat cannot be developed without phosphoric acid and ammonia; the stalk, in common with that of all kinds of grains, must have silex, or the rapidly ascending sap will burst the feeble tissues, and the promising harvest, in popular phrase, will be "struck with the rust." An eminent lawyer of Maryland, by a liberal application of phosphate of lime to his worn-out lands, under the advice of a book farmer, increased his yield of wheat from one peck to twenty-nine bushels per acre. Clover, peas, and beans, as well as tobacco, that

> "Indian weed,
> Which from the Devil did proceed,"

are all fond of lime, and should, therefore, be fed with gypsum. Raspberries and blackberries have a hungry appetency for potash, and so they cling to crumbling stone walls, and spring up, as by enchantment, on burnt ground.

But we need not pursue this topic further. If our young farmers would spend their rainy days and winter evenings in the careful reading and study of books on chemistry, instead of hunting in the mud for the patten-tracks of their great-grandfathers, the knowledge easily acquired, in spite of the hard names, would shed upon their daily work a light more cheerful than that of the sun. They might not become Liebigs or Boussingaults, but they could learn enough to protect themselves from the imposition of scientific mountebanks, and to conduct properly to their legitimate issue experiments on their farms, whose results might be of incalculable advantage to the agricultural community. Bacon lost his life in stuffing a hen with snow, in order to ascertain the effect of cold in the preservation of meat; but upon the foundation of his experimental philosophy two institutions were established, which still continue perennial fountains of knowledge, — the Royal Society of London, and the Academy of Sciences of Paris.

The relation of "Farm Drainage" to this topic of plant-food is patent enough when we consider that, in much the larger portion of our arable territory, draining is an indispensable prerequisite to an increased depth of soil; and the deeper the soil, the richer and more extensive the feeding-ground for the plant-roots. A horse fastened to a post in a clover-field, by a rope a hundred feet long, would be more likely to "wax fat and kick," than if tied to the same post by a rope of half that length. Just so, a hill of corn, whose roots can expatiate in a soil four feet deep, ranging at will among "fat things full of marrow," will, in the autumn, bristle on all sides with full-grown ears; while one whose roots are compelled, by "hard pan" or stagnant water, to spread like spiders' legs over the exhausted surface of the ground, will wear a "lean and hungry look" through the summer, and finally will yield to the granary a puny handful of cobs.

Another condition of vegetable growth is *light*. All plants are, in the strict Greek sense of the word, *heliotropes;* they turn to the sun. The potato-vine in the cellar crawls like a serpent towards a crevice in the wall, through which the light streams in once a day, and the blossoming tree inclines its thousand tinted corols to catch the first ray from the sun in his rising. One of the most important functions in the vegetable economy — the absorption of carbonic acid from the atmosphere, and the exhalation of its oxygen, by means of the leaves — is performed only in the daylight. Dumas, the French chemist, says, that plants absorb carbonic acid with so much avidity, that the air blown with a bellows over a branch of fresh foliage placed in a glass globe loses, in its rapid passage over the leaves, every particle of its carbonic acid, provided the sun shine on the process. In darkness this action does not take place. Flowering plants in our houses are, of course, healthful in the day-time, but do no good in the night. If a jar be filled, half with chlorine and half with oxygen, there is no union so long as they are kept in a dark place; but when exposed to the direct rays of the sun, they instantaneously unite, with a violent detonation, and a probable shivering of the glass to atoms. It is the solar ray alone which decomposes the watery sap in the upper surface of the leaf. Without its chemical power, there would be no carbon to form, by various affinities, the starch, sugar, gum, and woody fibre necessary to the development of the plant. The intelligent farmer, therefore, whether cultivating corn-fields or apple-orchards, will do well to remember that he always "stands in his own light," when, from any carelessness of arrangement or any unwise economy of space, he fails to secure to his growing crops an abundance of the blessed sunshine. Never inappropriate for him is Milton's august invocation: —

> "Hail, holy Light! offspring of Heaven first-born,
> Bright effluence of bright essence increate!"

The sixth and last condition of success in vegetable cultivation, to which, though, like the preceding condition, it has no relation to drainage, allusion should be made in this discussion, is the *protection* of our growing crops *from destructive insects.* Every farmer should know, that in the insect world he has his friends as well as his foes; he should know, too, how to discriminate between them. Without stopping to speak of the familiar fact, that insects, besides their chrysalid or intermediate state, have two forms of active existence, the larva and the winged form, we will specify briefly two or three classes whose services deserve our kindly regard.

The Carabidæ are ugly-looking, dark-colored, fast-running bugs, of different sizes, having wings concealed under stiff, horny cases, and living under loose stones or pieces of board. They are hatched from eggs deposited in the ground, and both in the larva and in the perfect state they are fierce destroyers of cut-worms and of the slate-colored grubs, which sometimes lay waste our gardens.

The Cicindaladæ, or tiger-beetles, which we see, in sunny summer days, running and flying before us in the trodden paths, embellished with handsome spotted and striped wing-cases, are as carnivorous as the Fejee-Islanders. Not an insect, which once comes within the reach of their mandibles, ever has another opportunity to eat leaf of tree or stalk of corn.

The mason-wasps are pitiless insect murderers. They lay their eggs at the bottom of little clay cells, which they plaster to our attic ceilings, or fashion in the ground, and then fill them with immense quantities of spiders, caterpillars, or canker-worms, that their young, when hatched, may eat their way up through successive layers of fresh meat until their wings are ready for the upper air. Levi W. Leonard, D. D., who contributed to the late Dr. Harris, his classmate, not a few of the most important facts in his published works, and who is undoubtedly at this time the best entomologist in his State, recently told us, that he once found, in the six or eight cells belonging to one of these wasps, seventy-nine spiders, not really killed, but so stung and benumbed as to lie still and wait to be eaten, with the glorious indifference of stoics or martyrs.

The Aphides, or plant-lice, which exhaust the juices from the tender growth of apple-trees and the young leaves of peach-trees, are swallowed by the larvæ of the beautiful lady-bug in as great numbers, and with as much relish, as succulent oysters are gulped down by hungry aldermen — when the city pays the bill.

The dragon-flies, or darning-needles, are a predaceous race; and, besides other small insects, they consume such clouds of those summer-evening pests, the mosquitos, as to have won for themselves the significant title of mosquito-hawks.

Certain flies, bearing some resemblance to the common wasp, and called ichneumon-flies, from their practice of destroying insects in the egg, just as their namesake, on the banks of the Nile, destroys the eggs of the crocodile, are most terrible enemies to the maggot of the weevil and the wheat-fly, and especially to the apple-tree caterpillar, in whose back they lay their eggs. "When these are hatched," says Dr. Leonard, who has carefully watched their operations, "the young ichneumons feed upon the fat of their living victims till fully grown, touching in the mean time no vital part, but finally causing their unlamented death."

But without proceeding further in this specification, and without enlarging upon the manifold virtues of the slandered mole and toad, it is pertinent to say, that by far the most efficient allies to the farmer, in his war against destructive insects, are the birds,— the beautiful singing-birds. It has been proved by actual count, that two sparrows, during a single hour, have carried to their nest forty caterpillars. The number of apple-moths, and millers prolific in hurtful larvæ, consumed in a season, by a swallow on the wing, is beyond the reach of computation. The grubs of various kinds slaughtered by a common robin, in the months of May and June, while tending her young, would far outnumber all the Philistines slain by David in his whole life. Even the much-abused crow, about which the wise Solons of our State Legislatures waste their harmless ammunition every year, digests at least five hundred grubs to one kernel of corn. The lordly raven does not condescend to a vegetable diet when there is any fresh meat to be had. In a word, there is not one of the singing-birds of our fields, woods, and gardens, whether thrush or jay, cat-bird or black-bird, king-bird or blue-bird, wren or pewit, martin or bobolink, — not one in the whole range, from the humble ground-sparrow up to that "feathered lyric," the aspiring skylark, which does not deserve the profoundest gratitude and most painstaking protection of the husbandman. And yet, though rendering us valiant and voluntary service in our insect warfare, though gladdening our eyes in this dusty, sin-blighted world with forms and hues of beauty, though making our trees as divinely vocal as the oaks of Dodona, and flooding the air with their joyous music, like a vernal shower, they are stupidly, meanly, wickedly shot and robbed of their young by idle boys and empty-headed men.

We said, in the early part of this article, that the farmer should be a proficient in two grand departments of agricultural knowledge; that he should know how to impart to his fields a maximum fertility, and how to clothe his home with beauty. We have occupied so much space in the discussion of the first topic, that we have little left for the second, and, in this country, even more important one. We join, therefore, in Carlyle's prayer: "O for the power of condensation!"

How shall we render our homes more pleasant and attractive? Some one has said that the three most beautiful words in the English language are Mother, Home, and Heaven. They naturally go together, either of them implying the other two. The great error in Plato's Republic is his subversion of the family. No mere "community," whether foreshadowed by a Grecian philosopher or organized by a French Socialist, can develop in men the deepest sympathies and highest energies of their nature. Sunder the ties which unite them in family groups, and the incentive to labor is gone. The distinguished traveller, De Laborde, attributes the utter hopelessness of all attempts to elevate the character of the Bedouin Arabs, and to bring back to the land of Mohammed the social cultivation and national glory of its earlier history, to their indifference to their household gods. The sweet charities and beautiful amenities which spring up and flourish in the magic circle of home, cannot take root by the wayside of a nomadic life. They require "a local habitation." Family and property are correlative terms; the love of the one creates a desire for the other. The incentives which impel men to the drudgery of the shop or field lie in the fact that they "have given hostages to fortune"; that they can in reality, or in prospect, enjoy the fruits of their industry around some warm domestic hearth-stone. The poet appreciated, if he never experienced, the reward of daily toil, as well as the motive to it, when he says:

> "'T is sweet to hear the watch-dog's honest bark
> Bay deep-mouthed welcome as we draw near home;
> 'T is sweet to know there is an eye will mark
> Our coming, and look brighter when we come."

There are many homesteads which are not homes. Philosophically speaking, a true home has an attractive outward seeming and a luminous inward life. To secure the former, there must be some architectural fitness about the buildings, and an exhibition of good taste in the grounds. To secure the latter, there must be, books, social and intellectual culture, and the hallowing influence of every Christian virtue. Human beings may exist in a habitation whose uncouth ugliness, concealed by no overshadowing tree or climbing vine, is a pain to the eye. They may accustom themselves to its shapeless deformity; to the rude inconveniences, which fruitlessly exhaust their time and strength; to the "ear-piercing fife" of half-starved squealing brutes, looking wistfully from hollow eyes, like animated "anatomies of melancholy," or wallowing in impassable mud before the kitchen door; to the stercoraceous stenches, which, exhaled from contiguous manure-heaps, do not "waste their sweetness on the desert air," but pour through the broken windows, checked by no intervention of "shocking bad hats," and neutralized by no fragrant breath of flowers. Such a place is not a home, but rather a lair for wild beasts; and the children who come forth from it will carry its taint and its barbarism to the grave.

A fine-looking house, on the other hand, like a fine-looking woman, cannot but exert a cheerful and elevating influence upon the community. There is a renovating power in every object of beauty and of worth on which the eye of man can rest. Steele was not extravagant when he said of a certain lady, whom the poet Congreve had admired and celebrated, that "to have loved her was a liberal education." We always grow into the likeness and catch the spirit of our surroundings. Our characters, like chameleons, take their hue from the objects with which they come in contact. But while we are thus material beings, in a material world which is sure to affect us for good or evil, we must not forget that the subtile spiritual nature with which we are endowed was not meant to be simply a passive recipient of accidental influences. It is a positive entity, and aspires to feed on ambrosia and drink nectar with the gods. It is not all of life to live. There are other and higher functions of the human organism than the digestion of beef and bread. The gastric juice is not the universal solvent, vainly sought amid smoke and toil in the laboratories of the old alchemists. We have hearts as well as a digestive apparatus; heads as well as hands. If the stomach of the last Lord Orford did survive the rest of his person, it was a phenomenon not likely to be repeated. For ourselves and our children, the primal duty is intellectual and moral culture. Our sons should be thoroughly trained to some business or profession, so that they may be intelligent and useful members of the community, and not, in the grand epic of life, mere parentheses, which, in the language of the spelling-books, might be omitted without injuring the sense or construction of society. Our daughters should be taught that a genuine woman cannot be made wholly of cotton and crinoline; that the small head, which surmounts her vast circumference, should be radiant with thought, — the dome of a pure and broad-visioned soul; that her heart, striving, perhaps vainly, to beat beneath her encircling zone, was intended for something more than to flutter with hope under the smiling glance of a city exquisite, or to tremble with fear at sight of a spider or a *cow;* that it is her divine right, not only

> " to sing, to dance,
> To dress and troll the tongue and roll the eye,"

but to develop every faculty of the mental and moral nature, to such an extent and completeness that she may always be a sunshine in the shady places of life, the light and joy of home; that it is her sphere " to study household good," to keep the vestal fires undimmed, to elevate the tone of social intercourse, and purify the currents of life at their fountain; that it is her mission, not to be fondled like a passive, painted doll, but to think and act like a living intelligence, conscious of its power and its responsibility.

When each member of the family is thus educated, our homes will glow with a new lustre, because we shall see in them, not merely the embellishments of a cultivated taste, but also the reflection of a beauty first radiated from our own spirits. "We need not then visit the Como Lake or the Madeira Islands." The alluring cry of the gold-hunter and the rifle-crack of the adventurous pioneer will have no power in that "good time coming"; but, laboring with quickened energies and a higher intelligence, we shall illustrate, on the wasted acres where our fathers toiled, the prophecy of the inspired seer, "There shall be a handful of corn in the tops of the mountains, and the fruit thereof shall shake like Lebanon," and, at the same time, we shall make the spot, which our "young barbarians all at play" call their home, attractive for its artistic beauty, and, in its moral influence, the nursery of every manly excellence and womanly virtue.

PROGRESS IN POPULAR EDUCATION.*

THE Bollandists, a society of Jesuits at Antwerp, in their "Acta Sanctorum," have related, among other veracious legends, the story of seven Ephesian youths, whom, in the bloody persecution of the Christians, the Emperor Decius barbarously shut up in a cave, into which they had fled for refuge. The persecuted youths, we are told, immediately fell into a profound sleep, from which they did not awake until the reign of Theodosius the Younger, one hundred and eighty-seven years after. Under the impression that they had been aroused from an ordinary night's slumber, they were, like Geoffrey Crayon's famous Dutchman, not a little puzzled and surprised at the strange appearance of things in their native city. The events which had taken place in the Roman Empire, during the two centuries in which they had slept, though not startling in themselves, as they occurred one by one, had nevertheless gradually changed the whole face of society. The seat of government had been removed from Rome to Byzantium; the ensigns of imperial splendor and power had been transferred from the banks of the Tiber to the shores of the Thracian Bosphorus; the throne of the persecuting pagan was filled by a Christian prince; the altars of Diana

* An Address delivered before the Rockingham Teachers' Institute, Exeter, N. H., the Massachusetts Teachers' State Association, New Bedford, Mass., the American Institute, Bath, Me., and in other places. 1852 – 55.

and the shouts of a heathen multitude had been exchanged for the chantings of devout worshippers in lofty cathedrals; the Roman Empire, dissevered and belligerent, had lost its power, and the golden eagles, which had looked down upon a thousand victorious battle-fields, were trailing their wings in the dust; the genius which had embellished the court of Augustus was shining with a dim and uncertain light amid gathering darkness; Scythian hordes, pouring from the frozen North, had crushed the invincible legions of the Cæsars, and, now in the undisturbed possession of the fairest provinces of Europe, were gazing with a strange wonder upon the pictures and statues which embalmed the beauty of divine women and the valor of brave men, or were prying with excited curiosity into the parchment rolls which contained the breathing words and burning thoughts of Cicero and Horace and Livy. Here were, undoubtedly, changes striking enough when taken in the aggregate; and that these changes, however adverse to human improvement some of them might at first glance appear, were yet really reformatory in their character, is sufficiently obvious to the thoughtful student in history. Into the bloated and heated life of Rome was infused the colder and purer blood of the hardy tribes of the North. On the one hand, luxurious, effeminate beauty was wedded to brawning strength; on the other, the feeble sons of the old Romans were allied to the energetic daughters of their rude conquerors. In this intermarriage, there was a reciprocal advantage, and a new race sprung into being, combining to some extent the culture of Italy and Greece with the strength of the Huns and Visigoths.

Numerous periods in the history of the world might be selected, of much briefer duration than two centuries, in which the progress of society has been far more rapid than that which astonished the Seven Sleepers. We are not to forget, however, that no one age can be taken as a type of all the ages. There are lulls in the ocean of human thought and being, and then again the face of the great deep is lashed into fury by the storms of excited passion. There are times when the current of human events seems to eddy in narrow circles, and times when it rolls on in an ever-widening, ever-deepening, faster-flowing stream. In discussing the question of human progress, therefore, in any of its relations, we must not limit our view to any one people or to any one epoch. In determining the direction and rapidity of the Gulf Stream, the navigator does not confine his observations to a single point, but makes them in all latitudes, in storm as well as sunshine.

It is not to be denied, that some things were done, in the centuries gone by, which surpass the highest power of modern art, when employing similar instruments in a similar direction. No combination of the five mechanical powers known to us could raise the massive stones of the pyramids; no skill of modern labor could, with copper tools, polish the faces of these stones so that the keenest eye can scarcely detect their joints; no ingenuity of modern artist can fix in stucco or on stone colors which shall last for ages, or stain glass so that the dye shall strike with uniform and permanent clearness through the entire mass, formed as a species of mosaic and fused so as to defy detection. A beautiful lecture has been written by one of the most eloquent speakers of the present day, on "The Lost Arts." But there is not, in my apprehension, much reason to suppose that a single invention in the arts, of any *importance* to man, has ever been lost. There is but little evidence that any scientific truth, which was fitted to benefit the race, has ever been obliterated from the human mind and forgotten. Of what profit to the world, in any point of view, were it now to spend centuries and exhaust the labor of a nation in piling up vast and unsightly pyramids, or obelisks, or sphinxes? A modern steam-engine, managed by a skilful engineer, carries with it an efficiency which would have astonished the one hundred thousand workmen of Cheops. What advantage to the living or the dead to people our mountain caverns, like the catacombs of the Upper Nile, with medicated mummies? One ounce of chloric ether, disarming the surgeon's knife of its terror, is worth more to the race than all the saline compounds which, in successive generations, pickled for immortality the whole line of disembowelled Ptolemies and Cleopatras. What use in knowing the composition of the famous Greek Fire, when we do know the composition of gunpowder, — a far more efficient and terrific agent for good or evil? The arts which were lost, were lost because they were not worth preserving, and they have never been found because they were not worth finding. Much as we may regret the wanton acts of barbaric ignorance and superstitious fanaticism, it is by no means certain that much which was really valuable or practically useful in *literature*, any more than in *science*, has perished from the world. It is true, that Omar, the Saracen Caliph, consigned to the flames the Alexandrian library. It is true, that the baths of the city were heated for the space of six months with the burning manuscripts and rolls, which it had taken centuries to accumulate. It is true, too, that the monks of the Middle Ages, having discovered a way of erasing the ancient writings from parchment, may have substituted the legend of a saint for a book of Livy. But so far as the researches of modern labor afford any means of judging of the character of those old tomes, they were not deserving of the lamentations which have been made by scholars and antiquaries over their destruction. According to Lyell,* of four hundred volumes of papyrus recovered from Herculaneum, all are "unimportant works, chiefly relating to music, rhetoric, and *cookery*." This last topic seems to have been prominent in

* Lyell's Geology, new edition, p. 393.

the discussions of the learned men of that day. *Carving* was an art regularly taught in institutions of the Greeks and Romans, established especially for that purpose. The carvers were applauded for their skill, and, at large entertainments, they cut the meat to the sound of music; keeping time with their knives, as dancers with their feet. Two young Athenians were deemed worthy of the honor of knighthood on account of the excellent salt-fish sold by their father. A household receipt, published as late as 1660, shows that the subject of good eating still commended itself to the business and bosoms of men. "Take," says the receipt, "a goose, or duck, or some such lively creature; pull off all her feathers, only sparing her head and neck; make a fire round about her so that the smoke may not choke her too soon; when she roasteth and consumeth inwardly, moisten her head with a wet sponge, and when you see her giddy with running and begin to stumble, she is roasted enough. Then take her up and set her before guests; and she will cry as you cut any part off from her, and will be almost eaten up before she be dead, — a sight mighty pleasant to behold." If the books of the Alexandrian library were fraught with information as vitally important as this specimen, we may, without a smile of contempt, assent to the logic of the bigoted old Arab who burnt them: "If these books accord with the Koran, they are unnecessary; if not, they ought to be burned."

But the grand difference between the past and the present is not between the writings or the great men of the two periods; but it is between the masses of the people. It may, perhaps, admit of some doubt, whether Egyptian priests and Grecian philosophers have been excelled in their several departments, so far as abstract knowledge is concerned, by any men of modern times. But while Plato and Aristotle shed a light and a glory upon the high places of antiquity, still there is more practical wisdom in a single New England school-house than there ever was in the whole valley of the Nile, or peninsula of the Peloponnesus. It is in the universality of our systems of education, as well as in the subjects and objects of study, that we are most unlike the nations which have flourished and fallen. It is in this direction that we shall find the most satisfactory evidences of human progress. With our common schools and churches, the ancient republics might have continued to this day; without them, they lacked the only elements of stability, and therefore perished. In arbitrary governments the education of the people is deemed a matter of small importance. Unreasoning obedience is their first duty and highest virtue. The laws of the statute-book, as well as the prescriptions of society, are on this point not unlike the directions of the great English Admiral to his midshipmen. "There are three things," says Lord Nelson, "that you are to bear constantly in mind. First, you must always obey orders implicitly, without attempting to form any opinion of your own respecting their propriety. Secondly, you must consider every man your enemy who speaks ill of the king. Thirdly, you must hate a Frenchman as you do the Devil." But in this land of universal suffrage the people are sovereign, and every beardless boy is a prince of royal blood, and liable to reach the Presidential throne. The government is but the organic expression of the popular virtue and intelligence. Whether it shall be beneficent or oppressive, permanent or tottering to its fall, depends entirely upon the character of the multitudinous individuals who constitute it.

Such being the importance of mental and moral discipline to the masses in a country like our own, — the permanence of free institutions and the consequent elevation of the race being so obviously and intimately connected with the success of our common-school system, — it seems not inappropriate to an occasion like this to find if we can our latitude and departure, and to determine, with what accuracy we may, whether the cause of popular education has, in spite of the adverse influences of avarice and parsimony and pride, borne up against the stream, or whether its friends have rested on their oars, and left it, like Virgil's boat,* to drift down with the current and the tide.

Believing, as I do, not only that progress has been made in every department of learning, but that our free schools have been the pioneers of improvement in all the relations of life, the advanced guard in the march of civilization, it will be my purpose, in the further continuance of this discussion, to try to encourage our hopes, and to strengthen our faith in the certainty of the "good time coming," by suggesting two or three of the indications of progress in popular education.

In the first place, then, progress is indicated by the higher appreciation of the utility of the *mathematical*, or *exact sciences*. It has come to be understood that the mathematics have an objective relation to society, as well as a subjective relation to the human mind. The distinguishing characteristic of the present age is the *practical application of mathematical science to the business and comfort of life*. Men, before the time of Bacon and Galileo, never attempted to deduce general principles of action from the facts in science which had been amassed. Books were studied in the most enlightened periods of the ancient world, not for the purpose of benefiting society in any of its common, every-day interests, but merely for the sake of embellishing the dreamy abstractions of the student. Euclid had no regard to the practical utility of his investigations, but only made them

* "Non aliter quam qui adverso vix flumine lembum
Remigiis subigit; si brachia forte remisit,
Atque illum in præceps prono rapit alveus amni."
Georgics, Lib. I. v. 201 - 203.

to discover the beauty of truth. Plato, when asked what would be the employment of heaven, immediately answered, "The study of geometry." It was with this conception of the ethereal nature and mission of mathematical study, that he inveighed with great indignation against Archytas and Eudoxus for having debased geometry by suggesting its application to mechanical pursuits, and thus, as he maintained, "bringing it down from incorporeal and intellectual to sensible things, and disgracing it by contact with matter, which requires manual labor, and is the object of servile trades." Seneca, in his ninetieth Epistle, vehemently declaims against Posidonius, a distinguished writer contemporary with Cicero, because he had ventured to enumerate among the humbler blessings which mankind owed to science, the discovery of the arch and the introduction of the use of metals. Science, he says, has nothing to do with material substances or mechanical contrivances. It is not her office to teach men how to use their hands. The purpose of her lessons is to form the soul. It seems to have been a leading object with the ancient philosophers, of whatever sect, to elevate their contemplations above the world of sense to the world of ideas; to conceal from the vulgar herd all the results of their researches by wrapping them in mystical figures; to teach men, not the means of increasing their physical comfort, but the duty of bearing physical pain with indifference or equanimity. It is true, therefore, as has been said, that "the ancient philosophy was a tread-mill, not a path. It was a contrivance for having much exertion and no progress. The mind, accordingly, instead of marching, marked time." Entertaining these opinions as to the ultimate objects of science, it is easy to understand why so few scientific improvements are found in the most polished nations of antiquity. There is not among all the huge, grotesque piles of Egypt, the mother of learning and civilization, a single structure which required in its erection the solution of complicated problems in art, or the exercise of high scientific powers. Strabo, in speaking of one of the grand hypostyle halls of Memphis, says: *Οὔδεν, ἔχει χάριεν οὐδὲ γραφικὸν ἀλλὰ μεταιοπονίαν ἐμφαίνει μᾶλλον.* In Greece, during the whole period of its national existence, the employment of water to turn a mill was never attempted at all, nor, indeed, at Rome until near the Christian era. Grinding was accomplished by animal strength. Hence it is that the same word, *ὄνος*, in the Greek language, means both an ass and an upper millstone, so inseparably connected were the two. The boards and lumber which were used in the construction of the Parthenon and the Temple of Jupiter were all sawed with the human hand. The coarse cloth which covered the Spartan soldier, and the delicate fabric which lent a grace to Athenian beauty, were alike the product of unaided female skill and industry. The aqueducts of Rome and other ancient cities, while they are wonderful exhibitions of unlimited wealth and power, do not indicate a very profound knowledge of the laws of hydrostatics. There is more science in one modern hydraulic ram, than in all the magnificent water-works of antiquity. In the science of medicine, intimately connected as it is with human health and life, little was done by the physicians of the Old World, except what is involved in a few irregular, unsystematic attempts to ward off disease by the herbs of the sorceress or the incantations of the priest. There was no knowledge of the laws of health, and no intelligent effort made to restore the sick. Indeed Plato, in the third book of his Republic, expressly declares that "a life protracted by medical skill is a lingering death; that the best thing which can happen to men with bad constitutions is to die at once, — the sooner the better." The dissection of the human system was a thing never attempted prior to the fourteenth century. The bodies of the dead were considered sacred, and any efforts to learn of their internal structure and mechanism, by means of the scalpel of the anatomist, would have been deemed sacrilegious. But at the present day, the community, so far from being satisfied with superficial examinations, expect the medical student to explore the most hidden mysteries of our physical being. The study of anatomy has now become a passion, and the place of every muscle and nerve and bloodvessel, as well as the functions which they severally perform in the animal economy, is distinctly understood. The enthusiastic naturalist, Buffon, could be reconciled to the loss of a wife, to whom he was devotedly attached, only by the pleasure which he anticipated in dissecting her.

Many of our most indispensable articles of household furniture, as well as our most useful implements of husbandry, were entirely unknown to the ancients. Neither knives nor forks were used at the tables of the Egyptians. The refined and cultivated Greeks and Romans took their food in their fingers. Hence the advice of the poet, Ovid:

> " Your meat genteelly with your fingers raise ;
> And, as in eating there 's a certain grace,
> Beware, with greasy hands, lest you besmear your face."

There were four utensils, however, which were known to the most remote nations of antiquity. The origin of the plough, the yoke, the axe, and the distaff could never be discovered, and so they were supposed to have fallen bodily from heaven. But a comparison of one of these heaven-descended ploughs, as described by Virgil, with one of Ruggles, Nourse, & Mason's, as we have seen it, would not greatly redound to the credit of celestial science or workmanship. A distinct impression of the progress of the human race could be obtained, perhaps, in no better way than by contrasting the rude inconvenience of the agricultural tools of past ages with the mathematical adaptedness and scientific beauty of the implements with which the farmers of the present day cultivate the earth. We are now, in every department of human labor, availing ourselves of the results of human thought. Every principle in science becomes at once a rule of art. Every invention of genius is deemed valuable only as it may be made serviceable in the material affairs of life. *Cui bono?* — for good to whom? — is the one grand question of the practical Present, — a question which the dreamy Past would have scorned to answer. Abstract speculation has given place to intelligent action; the vagaries of the poet, to the demonstrations of the mathematician; brute force and servile toil, to labor-*saving*, or rather labor-*doing* machinery. The Commissioner of Patents reveals some facts on this subject which are not unworthy of notice. The free-school system, it should be premised, is peculiar to the Free States. Common schools, from the nature of the case, cannot exist amid the magnificent distances which intervene between the plantations of the Slave States. Now the fact which deserves our attention is this: of the 16,685 patents issued to the several States of the Union from 1790 to January 1, 1850, 14,359, or more than six sevenths of the whole, were issued to the Free States, and only 2,326, or less than one seventh, to the Slave States. New York received patents for 5,245 inventions, while Virginia, the self-gratulating mother of states and of statesmen, received 568. The number issued to old Massachusetts alone is 2,171, or only 155 less than the number issued to all the Slave States put together.

These very remarkable facts are not of course the result of any natural superiority on the part of the citizens of one section of the country over those of another, but they grow primarily out of the quickening influence of our district-school system, — out of the mathematical training to which our children are subjected, not only in our colleges, but in those little seminaries which are scattered along every road-side, and which have been called the people's universities. Scientific truth is no longer allowed to "lie bed-ridden in the dormitory of the soul," but is taken out and aired. Philosophers think, as of old; but now ships and factories and steam-engines are the garb which their thoughts put on. The student to-day devotes himself to mathematical studies with a zeal unknown to the pupils of Thales or Euclid, because he finds in these studies not only "the beauty of truth," but also the germs of all human improvement. The heavens above and the earth beneath are, as he sees, replete with the results of mathematical science. There is nothing too high for its far-reaching glance, nothing too deep for its analysis, nothing too minute for its scrutiny. Le Verrier observes certain irregularities in the motions of Uranus. He predicts the existence of a disturbing body, and sits down in his chamber to verify his prediction. With his curtains drawn, alone amid figures and diagrams, he demonstrates the existence of an unknown world, determines its magnitude, and assigns its exact place in the heavens. The astronomer is told just where to look for the new globule of light. Telescopes from a hundred observatories are pointed to the spot, and the new planet Neptune is revealed to the astonished gaze of night-watchers all over the world. James Watt turns the acumen of a mathematical mind to the investigation of the properties and applications of steam. The tea-kettle of the indignant Mrs. Muirhead expands into the steam-engine; and now the fire-winged car, as Carlyle expresses it, "is flying from far cities to far cities, weaving them together like a monstrous shuttle." It is in the facilities for rapid locomotion that science has made its most wonderful achievements and accomplished its most beneficent results for society. A little more than three fourths of a century ago, a stage-coach that pretended to go from Philadelphia to New York in three days was advertised in the newspapers as "a *flying* machine."

Now the same distance is travelled in less than three hours. The passage across the ocean to a foreign country is less difficult and formidable to us to-day, than was the annual visit of our fathers to their adventurous relatives "down East." Out of this rapidity of intercommunication — this more intimate nearness of the nations — there grows, it is easy to see, that intense commercial activity which is enabling England and this country, in particular, not only to enrich themselves with "the wealth of Ormus and of Ind," but also to exert an immense moral and political influence upon the nations of the earth. Steamships pass and repass each other on every sea, and visit every port. Anglo-Saxon energy and enterprise, and Anglo-Saxon customs and principles, are finding their way among every people and modifying every government. The "Celestial Empire" is awaking to a consciousness of the power and importance of the "outside barbarians." The most distant island of the ocean is introduced into the community and brotherhood of nations. American ingenuity is building railroads for the Russian Czar; American curiosity is prying into the harems of the Turkish Sultan; American indifference to danger is whittling on Mount Vesuvius; American thrift is hawking wooden clocks in the streets of Canton, and selling bass-wood hams to the "chosen people" in Judæa; American adventure is searching for relics of Sir John Franklin among polar icebergs, and for Lot's wife along the shores of the Dead Sea; American piety is establishing religious institutions in the Sandwich Islands, and teaching the Christian faith to Caffres and Hottentots. It was true, when Cowper said it, that

> "Lands intersected by a narrow frith
> Abhor each other. Mountains interposed
> Make enemies of nations, which had else,
> Like kindred drops, been mingled into one."

But its truth will soon become a voice from the Past, which

can find no echo in the Present. Friths are bridged, like a Hellespont, with steamboats, and mountains melt away before a mightier power than that which levelled Athos. There comes, with this annihilation of distance, an approximation to a greater harmony of interests, and a consequent assurance of a golden age of universal peace.

Let us not forget the silent, unobtrusive cause of the superiority of the age in which we live over every period of past history. Steam-engines, mule-jennies, miners' lamps, magnetic telegraphs, chloric ether, reaping-machines, water-rams, — what are they all but the outward vestments of mathematical science? Logic in theology, precision in law, analysis in chemistry, profound reasoning on any subject,— what are these but the fruits of mathematical training and discipline? The history of mathematics, if it should ever be written, will be found to be the history of intellectual growth and development, — of social improvements and international amity, — the history, in a word, of human progress.

In the next place, a striking indication of progress in popular education is seen in the increasing importance attached to *female instruction.* A school for the higher education of *girls* was never heard of, even in the most cultivated of the ancient nations. Of course the idea of *woman as a teacher* was never entertained in their theories of education. With the exception of the talented and ill-fated Hypatia, who sat like a queen among nobles at the head of the Platonic school at Alexandria, in the fourth century, and Maria Agnesi, the gifted daughter of Italy, who was appointed Professor of Mathematics in the famous old University of Bologna, I think of no females, in the history of the past, who have sustained the office of teacher in the schools.

It was not until the age of chivalry that woman began to assume her proper place and importance in the affairs of the world. With the spread of the principles and faith of the Teutonic-Christian tribes of Germany, there sprung up all over Europe a higher appreciation of the female character, and a higher reverence for female worth and genius. So far as she is concerned, the age of chivalry is *not* passed, Burke's epigrammatic assertion to the contrary notwithstanding. John Knox, in the zeal of Reform, may denounce "the Monstrous Regimen of Women." Milton, after one of his three wives had run away from him, may, in the recollection of wounded pride, cry out:

> "O why did God,
> Creator wise, that peopled highest heaven
> With spirits masculine, create at last
> This novelty on earth, this fair defect
> Of nature, and not fill this world at once
> With men as angels, without feminine?"

But these voices, whether of contempt or complaint, are unheeded in the willing homage which is now everywhere in Christendom accorded to virtuous and intelligent womanhood. It is true, that we do occasionally, in these latter days, amuse ourselves with learned discussions about the relative intellectual superiority of the sexes. But a recollection of the simple principle in arithmetic, that a ratio can subsist only between like quantities, would save us from all this harmless folly. We might as well ask, Which is superior, Swedish iron or the paintings of Michael Angelo? as to ask, Which is superior, the male or female mind? The things compared are unlike, and the question, therefore, in its very nature, admits of no answer. Still, as Shelley expresses it,

> "We, — are we not formed as notes of music are,
> For one another, though dissimilar?"

One thing, at least, is undoubtedly true: women, whatever atrabilious defamers may say of their heads, have certainly softer hearts than men, — a greater wealth of affection, a quicker insight into duty, a firmer faith where we cannot walk by sight, a more ready tact in emergencies, more enduring patience under trial, a livelier interest in children, a higher-toned and purer morality. These are traits of character now valued everywhere above price, as constituent elements in the composition of a teacher. And so it has come to pass, that, while antediluvian fogies in the political, and seven-by-nine luminaries in the moral world, make themselves merry with coarse jests about woman's sphere and woman's rights, there is one place which it is agreed on all hands she may occupy, and be in her sphere, — one office which she may hold in the republic, and not intrench on the province of the masculine gender, or break the charmed spell of her own mysterious power. That place is none other than the school-room; that office, none other than the instruction of the young.

Nature never intended that men should reckon among their prerogatives the care of children. They are unsuited to the duties which it imposes. The boy despises the doll; the girl has no fondness for guns and boats. Man loves the variety and activity of the out-door world; woman is happy in the quiet and seclusion of home. Man is eager to mingle in the strugglings and conflicts of mature minds; woman is content to assist the unfledged younglings in their first attempts to fly. It is obvious, therefore, that a man in a primary school is out of his place; that this realm belongs to woman alone. To train boys and girls to gentle dispositions, a respectful demeanor, and unquestioning obedience; to inspire them with an enthusiastic love and invariable practice of the truth, though the heavens fall; to secure from them the greatest amount of study and discipline, without hazarding their health or hindering their physical development; to control the ardent impulses of young hearts, and direct them to all high and holy aspirations; to fashion anew the bad manners and soften the harsh and self-willed perverseness of neglected children; to begin with patience every new day, with no perceptible advance on the previous day; to look with hope into rayless pewter eyes where "there is no speculation"; to wait and watch with an unfaltering faith for light to dawn in faces where there is no day-star nor promise of morning; to follow with prompt and kindly sympathies the idle and the vicious in their wanderings, and win them back to industry and virtue by the power of love; — to do all these things, and more, requires in the teacher a variety and union of qualities seldom if ever found in the male sex, and to be sought, if sought at all, among females, "in whose own hearts," as has been well said, "love, hope, and patience have first kept school."

We would not be supposed, in anything which we have said, to entertain the opinion that woman should be limited to the primary departments of human instruction. We believe that a large majority of the *Grammar* Schools in this State would be better taught and better *governed* by educated and accomplished women than by men. They have a power peculiar to their sex, interpreting the paradox that weakness is strength, and enabling them to control those stubborn and imbruted natures which laugh to scorn mere physical force. There is something in the gentleness of shrinking maidenhood more terrible to Young America than the bludgeon of the sternest man, though he be bearded like the pard. Byron had in mind the power to which we refer, when, in painting a storm on the Alps, he exclaims:

"O night,
And storm, and darkness, ye are wondrous strong,
Yet lovely in your strength, as is *the light*
Of a dark eye in woman!"

There is a magic in female beauty and refinement more potent than Aaron's rod, or the rod of anybody else. Wild, rough-hewn boys, who "neither fear God nor regard man," yet have a remarkable respect for woman. This simple fact is beginning to be recognized and applied in our methods of instruction. In the State of Massachusetts — whose common-school system is unquestionably the most perfect one in the Union — the whole number of teachers for the year 1857, according to the Report of the able Secretary of the Board of Education, was 7,153, of whom 5,385, or more than three fourths of the whole, were females. Other States are following her example. Out of this acknowledged adaptation of the female mind and heart to the business of teaching have grown the means and appliances for the education of girls which characterize the present age. Woman, to teach, it is understood, must first herself be taught. Hence Female Seminaries, Teachers' Institutes, and Normal Schools have sprung into being. In all the agencies of the present day, which are elevating the female character and introducing into our school-rooms and nurseries a greater amount of enlightened female instruction, we recognize the indispensable elements of progress in popular education, and the efficient means of renovating, to some extent, our fallen humanity.

In the next place, we may discover indications of progress in popular education in the introduction of *music* into our schools. On this topic we shall say but a word. It is urged by some, that most persons are so constituted by nature as to be utterly unable to learn to sing, and that therefore the time spent upon this exercise in school is lost to a majority of the pupils. Petrarch mentions an individual of his acquaintance who was less charmed by a concert of nightingales than by a serenade of frogs; and we have all known persons who were apparently so insensible to the finest musical strains, that they felt no more pleasure in listening to the best adapted tones of melody, than in hearing the jar of a poker on a pair of tongs. But all such cases as these are rare, — mere exceptions interspersed among men at remote intervals, like rests in a staff of music. A child, it is true, may be totally unmoved by the "linked sweetness long drawn out" of an Italian concerto, and yet turn a delighted ear to the grinding of a barrel-organ. Now if there were in him no elements of music, he would have no preference for one kind of sound to another. All alike would be an indifferent or annoying vibration of the tympanum. But the fact that he knows "Yankee Doodle" from "Old Hundred," and prefers one to the other, is indubitable evidence that he has in him materials to work upon. While, therefore, it cannot be denied that some few persons are destitute of a very *discriminating* love for "sweet sounds and harmonies," it may nevertheless be safely affirmed that much of every one's relish for the niceties of musical composition is the result of cultivation and practice, and the great difference in respect to musical ear is a difference in degree rather than kind. In relation to

> "The man that hath *no* music in himself,"

it is as true now as in the days of Shakespeare, that

> "The motions of his spirit are dull as night,
> And his affections dark as Erebus."

We have ourselves visited more than once a primary school of nearly one hundred scholars, in which every child could sing. If there was any cold and unimpassioned nature among them, yet, in the glow of excitement and sympathy, the frozen tunes thawed out of him, as they did out of the coachman's horn, hung up by the fireplace, in the story-book. They began young, and sung together every day, — in these two facts lay the secret of their success. The time and effort spent in accomplishing this result, so far from making injurious drafts upon other branches, seemed to facilitate the progress of the pupils in their regular and prescribed studies.

Considered, then, either as an intellectual or moral discipline, either as an elevated science or as a means of humanizing harsh and stubborn natures, we regard the practice of singing in our common schools as one of the happiest innovations of the present day. Music is indeed in itself as dignified and practical a branch of study as geography or history. But it is a recreation as well as a science. It breaks up the dull monotony of tedious recitations, gives variety and entertainment to all the exercises, soothes the petty animosities of children, quiets the excited nerves of teachers, growing neuralgic and dangerous, and makes the school-room pleasant to everybody. Its influence as a species of moral suasion in government is of the highest importance. Lorenzo was right, when he said to Jessica:

> "There 's naught so stockish, hard, and full of rage,
> But *music* for the time doth change his nature."

Cleinias, when moved to anger, would strike his lute and say, "I am in search of serenity." We are firm believers in Solomon, and think that, when lectures on obedience are uniformly disregarded and despised, they may very properly be enforced and illustrated by means of *wood-cuts*. At the same time, we have no doubt that, as a general truth, a fiddle is far better than a ferule in a school-room, and that a song well sung may often save a strapping well laid on.

The last indication of progress in popular education to which I shall refer, is seen in a higher regard to the *moral influence of beauty*, — beauty of architecture and beauty of natural scenery. A sketch of our school-houses as they were is hardly necessary. We may each, probably, recollect one specimen, at least, as it lay on the landscape, in our childhood, like a blotch on the face of nature, — in its outward seeming, an uncouth and hideous shape,

> "If shape it might be called that shape had none,"

and in its inward arrangement gloomy, mutilated, inconvenient, spine-distorting, as full of cramps as Stephano in "The Tempest," and all bedimmed and befogged with a hot and fetid air, as "thick and slab" as the hell-broth which boiled and bubbled in the witches' caldron. Those of us who, in our younger days, worshipped in one of those Temples of Apollo and the Muses, can easily credit the descriptions given by a Parliamentary Committee, some years ago, of the schools in the mother country. In respect to one of them, the committee say: "In a garret up three pairs of dark, broken stairs, was a common day-school, with forty children, in a compass of ten feet by nine. On a perch forming a triangle with a corner of the room sat a cock and two hens; under a stump-bed immediately beneath was a dog-kennel in the occupation of three black terriers, whose barking, added to the noise of the children and the cackling of the fowls at the approach of strangers, was almost deafening. There was only one small window, at which sat the master, obstructing three fourths of the light." The labors of the first Secretary of the Massachusetts Board of Education, in representing to the public eye the unmitigated deformity and ugliness of the pens in which our children were crowded like prisoners in a Calcutta "Black-hole," prepared the way for the valuable and popular work of Henry Barnard, — a work which is gradually renovating the public taste, and accomplishing for our school architecture what the writings of the lamented Downing are accomplishing for our "Country Houses and Cottage Residences." Some of the school edifices in this State are now models of beauty, — finished in their exterior with some appreciation of the rules of art, and within with some regard to the laws of health. But this, though much, is not all. They are not, when built, left to stand like the Pyramids on a leafless plain, under "a hot and copper sky," but they are surrounded and sheltered with *trees*. It is remembered that in their *grounds*, as well as halls, the children of the community obtain their earliest and strongest impressions, — impressions which the longest and busiest life cannot efface. The youngest school-boy, not less than the banished Duke in Shakespeare, can, if he have the chance,

> "Find tongues in trees, books in the running brooks,
> Sermons in stones, and good in everything."

Nature has a thousand dialects, but none which the human heart cannot read and understand. I can pardon the ancient Epirotes, who heard the voice of the gods in the "speaking oaks" of Dodona. I do not wonder at the reverence which the old Celtic Druids had for trees. There is something in their graceful form, their living beauty, their overshadowing protection, their answering whisper to every questioning wind, which seems to endow them, not only with the physical attributes, but with the intelligence of an exalted humanity. There have been worse heretics in the world than the old Manichæans. "Whoso plucks the fruit or the leaves from trees is guilty of homicide," say they, "for in each case he expels a soul from its body." * Whether bending under the green luxuriance of summer, or decked in the crimson glory of autumn, or defying in their naked strength the wintry tempest, they are among the most majestic objects of nature. The most beautiful word employed in Holy Writ, as descriptive of heaven, is the word Paradise, — *a garden full of trees.* There is no spot on earth which may not be made more attractive through the help of trees. They gather around themselves a thousand associations, — associations connected with all that is delightful in our recollections of childhood and innocence and parental love. Every sapling which we plant on the naked street before our dwellings makes, with every expanding leaf and spreading limb, home pleasanter, and

* Augustine, De Morib. Manichæ., Lib. II. cap. 17.

our attachments to it stronger. The saddest thing in the sad lament of Eve, when she was driven by the angel from Eden, was her apostrophe to the trees and flowers, which she had reared "from the first opening bud," — trees and flowers

"That never would in other climate grow."

If the child is always to feel that, under the influence of a "manifest destiny," he must leave the home of his father, we can at least so surround this home with beauty that he shall go away more and more reluctantly, and his heart, in whatever distant land it beats, shall, like the sea-shell far from its native ocean, retain some faint whispers of its early dwelling-place. Whether planted in our yards, or on the streets, or in our public squares, or in our school grounds, trees always and everywhere exert a controlling moral influence. That natural scenery possesses a power over human hearts and human life every attentive observer of men and things must have seen. The quiet and phlegmatic Dutchman is a natural product of the level, monotonous Netherlands. The Switzer, with his bold, adventurous, and unconquerable spirit, is, in his character, a legible transcript — a daguerrotype — of the peaks and glaciers and rugged beauty of the Alps. We may not be able to tell how this influence is exerted, but the fact we know and feel in our daily life and experience. How often does it happen that a falling leaf, a faded flower, or a blooming landscape has changed the whole current of our thoughts and our being! There is often more of divinity and divine instruction in the "still, small voices" of nature, than in the articulate teachings of men. The hardened and the vicious may turn away their ear from the warnings of the fireside, and from the expostulations of the pulpit, but they cannot thus easily escape from the preaching of nature. Some strain of music from this overarching cathedral, or some breath of incense from its thousand altars of worship, will reach them in their wanderings. Not a thing, animate or inanimate, is presented to the eye of the young, but enstamps itself upon their minds and hearts. Their every thought takes its hue and coloring from the objects which surround them. It has come, therefore, to be regarded as a matter of no small importance, in a moral point of view, that our school grounds should be something besides naked, glaring sand-banks, diversified, if diversified at all, with shapes of ugliness. If, as somebody somewhere says, a man's progress in holiness of heart and life depends somewhat on the *binding* of the Bible and prayer-book from which he reads, how important is it that the leaves of the great volume of nature, which our children read, not morning and evening, but always, should be pure on every page; that no blurred or blotted text should hide the meaning of the Author; that no gross or hideous picture should defile the imagination of the reader! We are material beings, and live in a material world, which is certain to affect us for good or ill, whether we will or not. The author of "Yeast" utters a true sentiment when he says: "The spiritual cannot be intended to be perfected by ignoring or crushing the physical, unless God is a deceiver and his universe a self-contradiction." The moral which this truth teaches, and which is beginning to be understood and applied, is nothing more nor less than this: while we are beautifying our own dwellings with trees, we should remember the school-house, and not "lay down the shovel and the hoe" until we have made the play-grounds for our children there such in themselves and in all their associations as shall inevitably tend to elevate and purify and ennoble human character.

I have thus brought before you, very imperfectly, some of the indications of progress in popular education. Other topics in this connection will suggest themselves to my audience. I have said nothing of the higher and more intelligent regard now paid to physical health, as shown particularly in the modern methods of school-house ventilation; nothing of the influence of Normal Schools and Teachers' Institutes in elevating the instructor from an artisan to an artist, and his business from a wood-hewing and water-drawing servitude to a dignified and honorable profession; nothing of the tendency of Educational Festivals, to give concert to action and to crown labor with success; nothing of the deeper interest of the people in the mental and moral illumination of the young, as indicated by more ample appropriaions of money for schools and a more careful personal supervision; nothing of the higher appreciation of the value of indefatigable and enlightened instruction, as shown by the more liberal salaries now paid to competent teachers, — salaries which actually enable them to eat the food convenient for them and to cast a shadow.

If, in conclusion, I might, after clerical fashion, be indulged with two very brief reflections, I would remind you, in the first place, that, next to the mother by the cradle, the common-school teacher is the most important element in the national greatness. We may say of his profession, as Dr. Boteler said of strawberries: "Doubtless God could have made a better berry, but doubtless he never did." Without any of the pinchbeck emblazonry which glitters alike on the shield of the warrior and on the forehead of the politician, the teacher lays his hand upon the central forces of our common nature, and "wields at will the fierce democratie" of untamed passions, and wins to high and worthy objects grovelling affections.

My last reflection is this, and it may not be inappropriate to the younger portion of my audience: Thorough, luminous instruction in school-room and nursery, costly libraries in every neighborhood, magnificent school edifices, surrounded with grounds as beautiful as the gardens of Alcinoüs, — these, and such as these, can never be made to serve as substitutes for unremitting, self-reliant, individual exertion. There is no way, as a modern writer has intimated, of developing character in a young man by putting guano in his shoes, or training him like a tropical shrub against a south wall. Splendidly bound volumes of classic lore on our shelves, with their gilded leaves unthumbed, will not impart to us the elegant scholarship of a Felton or a Woolsey. There is no key but labor which can unlock to us the mysteries of mathematics, and make ill-looking symbols and distorted diagrams beautiful with meaning and intelligence. It is as true now as when Hesiod sung it:

> *Τῆς δ' ἀρετῆς ἱδρῶτα θεοὶ προπάροιθεν ἔθηκαν*
> *'Αθάνατοι.*

"The gods have placed sweat in the pathway to excellence."

> "The heights by great men reached and kept
> Were not attained by sudden flight;
> But they, while their companions slept,
> Were toiling upward in the night."

If we would see the glory which encircles the great truths that lie beyond the vision of dim-eyed men, we must see it in the light of our own enkindled intellects. If we would assure ourselves of the future progress of popular education, we must be ourselves the common multipliers in the ascending progression. If we would be true patriots, we must listen to our country, as from her thousand mountain heights she calls us to *labor*, as the cry of the muezzin calls to prayer. If, in a word, we would make the most of life, we must remember that "he most lives who thinks most, feels the noblest, acts the best."

PERCY BYSSHE SHELLEY.*

[Now first printed.]

PERHAPS there are no efforts of human industry so little heeded, no productions of the human mind so little valued, as those of the poet. The reason is obvious. The poet acts not in the outward, but in the inner world; not upon substance, but upon spirit. Let genius be employed upon inert matter, and the result is at once apparent in the living marble or speaking canvas; let it be employed in making the mind a "mansion for all lovely forms," the "memory a dwelling-place for all sweet sounds and harmonies," and it requires an inward-seeing eye to appreciate its effects. All men acknowledge and applaud the genius of Watt and Fulton, because they see the steam-vessel riding like a sea-god over the ocean, and the fire-winged locomotive flying over the land. But Shakespeare and Dante are, in the apprehension of most men, nothing but empty names. They, forsooth, never constructed a railroad nor built a hospital; they never commanded an army, nor made a stump-speech in a political campaign. But yet it is not difficult for one who looks beneath the surface of things to understand that the influence of the great poet is far more powerful and permanent than that of artisan or warrior, statesman or orator. We may not be able to define the elements of poetry, nor explain the method in which they act. "The wind bloweth where it

* The Poetical Works of Percy Bysshe Shelley, edited by Mrs. Shelley. With a Memoir. In Three Volumes. Boston: Little, Brown, & Co.

listeth, and we hear the sound thereof, but cannot tell whence it cometh nor whither it goeth." Who can express in words the effect which music exerts? And yet every one has felt its power. The often-quoted remark of the Scottish statesman, "Let me write the songs for a nation, and I care not who makes the laws," is founded upon a deep and accurate knowledge of human nature. The simple notes of the *Ranz des Vaches*, played rudely in strange lands upon the Alpen-horn, seldom fail to suffuse a whole regiment of Swiss veterans in tears. The Marseilles Hymn, sung in the streets of the cities of France, effected more in enkindling the patriotism and arousing the indignation of the French people, than all the feudal and ecclesiastical tyrannies which had crushed them during the despotic reign of Louis XVI.

Poetry is as universal as nature. Its tones are heard in the glad voices of children; in the passionate appeals of the orator; in the death-song of the savage; in the whisper of love. Its spirit looks out from the star and smiles in the flower. An old Greek has called the world the *Poem of God*. Few have read this "Poem of God," or listened to its solemn music as chanted by a thousand voices from hill and forest, air and ocean. We are often told by persons of the utilitarian school, that poetry is a mere effeminate luxury, — a suitable aliment for weak and sickly minds, but by no means fit for men. They forget that it has nourished and inspired the most masculine intellects. They forget that Homer's Iliad was the daily and nightly companion of Alexander in his conquest of the world. They forget that the shadowy pages of Ossian enkindled the enthusiasm of Bonaparte before the battles of Austerlitz and Jena. They forget that Galileo outwatched the stars in reading the great epic of Ariosto. They forget that Chatham, the first orator of England, made the Greek poets the study of his life; and that Burke owed his superiority over the other distinguished statesmen of his age to the power and brilliancy of a cultivated imagination. In a word, they forget that man is endowed with passion as well as reason, and that his feelings, not less than his intellect, have their wants and their capabilities. The elements of poetry, therefore, may be found in all men,—even in those who are most prose-like in their exterior, and who, under some circumstances, exhibit the most unpoetic qualities. The author of Lear and Macbeth, we are assured, was at one time a deer-poacher in the parks of Warwickshire; at another, a link-boy in the streets of London; and, as tradition hath it, unfortunately terminated his career by an over-dose of home-brewed humming ale! But that he is nevertheless a poet—nay, *the* poet—will not be questioned so long as the wavering ambition of Macbeth, the shattered greatness of Lear, the filial affection of Cordelia, the deadly malice of Iago, the proud jealousy of the Moor, and the pure love of Desdemona shall find an echo and an interpretation in the human heart. Carlyle has said, that "all are poets who can *read* a poem well." That all are mathematicians who can read the *Mécanique Céleste*, is a truth not more obvious. "The imagination that shudders at Dante's Hell" is the same, though weaker in degree, as Dante's own. The peasant who is a worshipper of nature, though his faith may not be so strong, nor his devotion so deep, yet kneels at the same altar with Wordsworth. One after another rises up, at long intervals, who is able to "wreak his thoughts upon expression": the rest, the multitude, can only *feel* a response, or simply say amen. Theirs is the unwritten poetry of the heart.

Of those who have left us the records of their genius, we regard with especial interest the gifted, though unfortunate and misguided SHELLEY. We are drawn to him, not for his prominence in the world of letters, but for his unappreciated, intrinsic worth; not because his poetry is faultless, or his character a model, in many of its features, for imitation, but because his good qualities shine with peculiar lustre, and of his faults we may say, with King Henry, that

> "There is some soul of goodness in things evil,
> Would men observingly distil it out."

We shall speak of him as we would of Burns, in terms neither of unqualified eulogy, nor of indiscriminate censure. The independence of his philosophical investigations, his disregard of many of the established forms of society, his hostility to old customs, the boldness of his innovations, and his reckless contempt for the religious dogmas which had come down to him hoary with age and sanctified by time, — these have cut him off from the sympathies of men, and left him in the world, as he says of himself,

> "neglected and apart,
> A herd-abandoned deer, struck by the hunter's dart."

Some have ventured to extenuate his faults; few have had the courage to extol his virtues. His poetry has been garbled and condemned by hireling critics; his character calumniated and his name anathematized by the "overmuch righteous"; and even the publication of his works was not long since, in spite of Talfourd's eloquent defence, adjudged a crime by the Court of Queen's Bench. Still the productions of his pen are bound up in the same volume with Coleridge and Keats; they lie on our centre-tables, or stand in the goodly company of authors on our shelves, and are beginning to be read, for good or evil, by the whole literary world. Such being the position which Shelley now occupies, a discussion of his character as a man and his claims as a poet seems not inappropriate.

It has been said that a poet's life is one of his poetical works. Shelley's life was a *tragic* poem. Born near the close of the eighteenth century, he entered upon the stage with Byron, Coleridge, and Wordsworth as fellow-actors and rivals. The connection of his family with that of Sir

Philip Sidney, one of the most illustrious names in English history, secured to him a favorable introduction to the world. At the age of thirteen he was sent to Eton, where he foolishly distinguished himself for his neglect of the prescribed studies of the school, and for the publication, in the fifteenth year of his age, of two novels, "The Rosicrucian" and "Zastrozzi." This was the first act in the drama. At the age of sixteen he was removed to Oxford, where, becoming imbued with the elements of logic, he ventured to apply them to the investigation of hypotheses which it had been prudent not to question. Adopting as his motto the first maxim of the Cartesian philosophy, — "Disbelieve everything till it is proved," — he began to inquire into the reason of things, and to resist what he could neither demonstrate as true, nor reconcile to his own notions of right. The result was the shipwreck of his faith, his expulsion from college, and the curse of his father. This was the second act in the drama. Soon after his expulsion, he married a beautiful girl much younger than himself, who, by her birth and education, was utterly unfit for companionship with a poet. The consequence of this ill-assorted marriage was the unhappiness of both, until their final separation, in a few years, by mutual consent. His two children, at the instigation of his own father, were wrested from him by a decree of Lord Chancellor Eldon, because, forsooth, he was not within the pale of a healthy religious organization, and he was cast forth upon the world again alone. This was the third act in the drama. Soon after the death of his first wife, he married Mary Wolstonecraft Godwin, daughter of the noted author of "Political Justice," and of the no less noted authoress of "The Rights of Women." With her he left England for Italy, where he resided alternately at Venice and Pisa. Here, in connection with Byron and Leigh Hunt, he had just commenced the publication of a periodical miscellany, entitled "The

Liberal," when the curtain fell on the fourth act of the drama. In the summer of 1822, while returning from Leghorn to his house on the Gulf of Lerici, the boat in which he set sail was lost in a violent storm, and all on board perished. More than a week had elapsed, when he was found with a volume of the latest poems of Keats still open in his hand. His body was placed by his friends on the shore of the Tuscan Sea, where, with the ancient accompaniment of myrrh and frankincense, it was burned to ashes, — all but his heart, which would not consume. This was the last act of the drama. Shelley was less than thirty years old at his death. The eccentricities of his youth had just given place to the better judgment and maturity of manhood. He died in the midst of unaccomplished purposes, of magnificent beginnings. "We doubt," says Macaulay, "whether any modern poet has possessed, in an equal degree, all the highest qualities of the great masters. Had he lived to the full age of man, he would undoubtedly have given to the world some great poem of the very highest rank both in design and execution."

Without stopping to dwell upon the splendor of his talents, the variety and extent of his acquirements, the kindness and generosity of his disposition, the integrity and purity of his character, or the mistaken efforts of his life, it will be sufficient in this place to say, in the language of another, that "he was a singular illustration of the force of natural genius breaking the bonds of birth and habit and the conventional ties of the circle in which he was born, and soaring high under the direction of his own spirit, chartless and alone." It is not improbable that, if his first errors had been treated with more lenity or less attention, his hostility to the established religion and social institutions of his country would not have been so bitter nor so lasting. If the learned Faculty of Oxford, instead of visiting their indignation upon the first Dissertation of

Shelley, had passed it over with the silent contempt which it deserved, the subject would have lost all interest in his own eyes and been forgotten, or remembered only with mortification, as one of the follies of his youth. If his first poem had been permitted to rest in obscurity until the spirit of love had brooded over it, its atoms of chaotic thought might have subsided into shapes of symmetry and beauty, and its "wild and whirling words" might have assumed a high and harmonious meaning. As it was, he lost all confidence in the clemency and justice of the world. His conduct, therefore, was regulated entirely by his own ideas of right, and, as a matter of course, he was in constant warfare with the usages and ceremonies of society. His portrait, accompanying his published works, is strikingly indicative of his character. Like that of Dante, as Carlyle has described it, his face is the mournfullest that was ever painted from reality. There is in it the softness and gentle affection of a child, the purity and intelligence of an angel; but all is overshadowed with a proud, and silent, and hopeless pain. It is the face of one wholly in protest, and life-long, unsurrendering battle against the world.

It may be well at this point, before discussing the claims of Shelley's poetry, to notice some of the graver charges which have been brought against his philosophy. In the first place, it is said by some, that he was an *atheist*. If this charge were true, as it probably was at one period of his life, we should hesitate in pronouncing over his *works* our unqualified "anathema maranatha." If we should stop to curse all whose belief is not in unison with our own, how little time were left to bless! Milton was a believer in the pre-existence and eternity of matter, — the ὕλη of Plato; in the materiality of the human soul; in the lawfulness of polygamy; in the entire abolition of the Mosaic code, — Decalogue and all; in the competency of any person, without form or ceremony, to act as an ordinary minister, to perform the rite of baptism, and dispense the elements of the Sacramental Supper to an indiscriminate congregation, disciples or infidels. Now, shall we, because one or all of these articles in Milton's creed are utterly at variance with our own notions of what is true and right, denounce him as a miserable heretic, and hasten to do God service by burning his "Paradise Lost"? We may detest Shelley's stern and barren philosophy, but we need not, in our wide-sweeping wrath, consign his character and his poetry, as well as his metaphysics, to perdition. We may deplore the unhappy consequences of his belief to himself, but we may not despise him. We may wonder at his rashness, as we see him blotting, one by one, the stars from his sky, and converting his future into the darkness of a rayless, hopeless night, but we may not question the earnest sincerity of his investigations, we need not adopt his "most lame and impotent conclusions." In our honest admiration of Shelley's good qualities, far be it from us to apologize for atheism in any form. We pity the man who can discover in this beautiful and breathing world no traces of God's handiwork. We pity still more the man who would attempt to measure moral worth or poetic genius by the number or length of the articles in his creed. It is a melancholy fact, that there are but few productions in the world of letters in which some things may not be found that deserve our reprehension. Even our standard works — those which have received the seal of public approbation — must be read with caution as well as admiration. There is the subtile scepticism of Hume; the insidious infidelity of Gibbon, where more is meant than meets the ear; the vulgarity of the old dramatists, from Congreve down to Shakespeare; the cold rationalism of the German mind, — of Goethe and Schiller, of Lessing and Wieland. Yet he would hardly deserve the name of scholar who, for these faults, would blot from the firmament of literature these its most brilliant lights.

There is one precaution of paramount importance, which should always be observed in determining the moral character of any author. We should be careful to distinguish between those opinions which are truly *his own*, and those which are expressed simply on account of their *dramatic propriety*. It would assuredly be most unjust to accuse Milton of impiety on the ground that Satan and Beelzebub, in his "Paradise Lost," denounce Omnipotence, and declare eternal war against the *tyranny of Heaven*. It would be no less unjust to charge Shelley with atheism or irreverence, because his Ahasuerus, the scoffing Jew, rails at an "Almighty Fiend." It is in a poem called "Queen Mab" that the arguments in support of this charge are mainly found. This poem, it may be well to premise, was written at the age of eighteen years, when his opinions on all subjects, and especially on the mysteries of spiritual existence, were immature and chaotic. It was printed for private circulation only, but was fraudulently obtained and published to the world long after the writer had altered and openly disclaimed many of the sentiments which it avowed. The poem itself is a strange compound of wild chimeras, wayward fancies, and intellectual beauty. In entering upon it you seem to enter an ice-grotto: all is hung around with grotesque and beautiful shapes, but they are frost-work, and the light that falls upon them is the light of a wintry moon. Still there is in the poem a life and affection. It breathes throughout a spirit of uncompromising hostility to every form of oppression, civil and ecclesiastical, and a passionate, if mistaken, devotion to human happiness. It must be acknowledged that, in speaking of a Supreme Being, he was not always sufficiently explicit. In his animadversions, he was not uniformly careful to discriminate between the essence of Deity and the image set up by men for worship. The commonly received notions of God it is certain that he treated with contempt. Nor is this altogether unaccountable, when we consider the manner in which the character and attributes of Deity were too often portrayed, even in his enlightened age, by mitred bigotry and ignorance. Religion was a thing of legislative enactment, — the creature of civil and political power. It was in view of this cold formality and intolerance which he saw pervading a Christian nation, that Shelley turned away in disgust from its religious systems, and panted after those olden times when the presence of Divinity was felt in earth and ocean, and worshipped in simplicity as the "Soul of Nature." It was for the same reason that Wordsworth dared to ejaculate a wish for those old and palpable Divinities of Grecian mythology, when he exclaims:

"Great God! I'd rather be
A pagan, suckled in a creed outworn;
So might I, standing on some pleasant lea,
Have glimpses which may make me less forlorn;
Have sight of Proteus coming from the sea,
Or hear old Triton blow his wreathèd horn."

Superstition, which, Bacon says, "erecteth itself into a tyranny over the understanding of men, destroying reason, philosophy, natural piety, laws, reputation, and everything that can serve to conduct to virtue," Shelley hated almost to insanity. The grotesque absurdities and pompous pretensions of Catholicism, its sacred relics and pictured saints, its mummeries and its miracles, its indulgences and its intolerance, were all alike his utter abomination. The rigid sternness of Calvin and John Knox, which Burns could ridicule, he shuddered at as repulsive to all that is true and trustful in human nature. Though, as a climax to his youthful folly, he dared, in the Album of Mont Auvert, to subscribe himself *Atheos*, still he clung with all the pertinacity of a poetic faith to the idea of some "Great Spirit of Intellectual Beauty," pervading, animating, ennobling all things. The truth is, Shelley, like his models, the poets of classic Greece, was, to all intents and purposes, a Pantheist. To him everything was God, and God was everything. Every place was peopled with forms of beauty and animated with living intelligences. Hills and valleys, forests and fountains, were each thronged with presiding deities,—bright effluences from the Divinity that stirred within and shone above the whole. For this faith, however poetic it may be, we have in this age no excuse to offer in his behalf. Pantheism, though sometimes preached from Christian pulpits, is not Christianity.

Shelley had an excess of fancy, —"enough," as Moore says of him in his Life of Byron, "for a whole generation of poets." Through this, as an alembic, his facts as well as his theories were too often distilled. While, therefore, the foundations of his philosophy were laid in the deductions of enlightened reason, the superstructure was the air-chateau of a creative imagination. The temple which he built was beautiful without and adorned within, but it contained no "ark of the covenant," nor "golden candlestick," and its altar bore the Athenian inscription, "To the unknown God." He had little faith in the authenticity of the Sacred Scriptures as a record from Heaven; and yet, in his inconsistency, he read and studied the book of nature published under the same sanction, with all the eagerness and docility of a true disciple. If he denied the existence of the God of the Jews, yet he worshipped the God of universal being "in spirit and in truth." Following Queen Mab to her palace in the centre of the universe, he exclaims, while suns and systems circle round him:—

"Spirit of Nature! here,
In this interminable wilderness
Of worlds, at whose immensity
Even soaring Fancy staggers,
Here is thy fitting temple.
Yet not the lightest leaf
That quivers to the passing breeze
Is less instinct with Thee;

Yet not the meanest worm
That lurks in graves and fattens on the dead
Less shares thy eternal breath."

Now, while we admire the simple, unpoetic doctrines of our Puritan fathers, yet it seems to us that, if we should blend our worship with that which goes up like incense from every true poet's heart, the tendency would be neither to mutilate our faith nor quench our devotion. The religious fervor of no sane man was ever cooled, the religious principle of no sane man was ever shaken, by reading Shelley's poetry. We expect from the poet not so much a castle of strength as a landscape of beauty; not so much a theory of divinity as a dwelling-place in his ideal paradise; not so much a trusting faith as a soaring imagination; not so much the psalms and hymns of Dr. Watts as the inspiration of Shakespeare.

A second charge brought against the philosophy of Shelley is, that it denies the existence of a future state of being. A sufficient refutation of this charge may be found on every page of his poetry. No one can read his Adonais, a poem written in memory of the author of Endymion and Lamia, who died at Rome a few years before his own untimely death, without finding the doctrine of the soul's immortality taught in the most explicit terms.

"Peace! peace! he is not dead, he doth not sleep.
He hath awakened from the dream of life;
'T is we, who, lost in stormy visions, keep
With phantoms an unprofitable strife,
And in mad trance strike with our spirit's knife
Invulnerable nothings."

The last charge brought against Shelley's philosophy which we shall notice has reference not so much to the world of spirits as to this more tangible world of men and women. We mean the subject of marriage. His theory on this point is briefly this: Love is inevitably consequent upon the perception of loveliness. It withers under restraint; its very essence is liberty. A husband and wife, therefore, ought to continue so long united as they love each other, and any law which should bind them together after the decay of their affection would be a most intolerable despotism. The conviction that wedlock is indissoluble holds out the strongest of temptations to the perverse; they indulge without restraint in all the little tyrannies of domestic life, when they know that their victim is without appeal.

There is, undoubtedly, some little truth in this view of the matter; but its general fallacy is too obvious to warrant its discussion, though it has been supported in its main features by a writer of no less celebrity than John Milton. The melancholy suicide of Shelley's first wife, and his own consequent insanity for long and bitter months, is a sufficient commentary on the practical workings of his marriage system. While, therefore, it is admitted that his opinions of the conjugal relation are decidedly heterodox, yet it is certain that he appreciated, to the fullest extent, the power and influence of woman. His writings, unlike those of Milton, are all fragrant with the incense which he has offered to female worth and beauty. Near the opening of his "Episychidion," an overwrought poem, intended, probably, as introductory to another, he thus, in the fulness of his adoration, apostrophizes woman: —

"Seraph of Heaven! too gentle to be human,
Veiling beneath the radiant form of Woman
All that is insupportable in thee
Of light, and love, and immortality!
Sweet Benediction in the eternal Curse!
Veiled glory of this lampless Universe!
Thou Moon beyond the clouds! thou living Form
Among the dead! thou Star above the Storm!
Thou Wonder and thou Beauty and thou Terror!
Thou harmony of nature's art! thou mirror
In whom, as in the splendor of the Sun,
All shapes look glorious which thou gazest on!"

Whether this eulogium of woman be just or extravagant, we will leave it, without note or comment, for the "better half" of our readers to decide.

We come now to speak of the *poetry* of Shelley.

The word *poetry* is derived from a Greek word signifying *creation.* These ideal "creations" have their origin in the longings of the human soul for something higher and holier than can be found in a material universe. Surrounded by deformity and sin, we aspire to the beautiful and pure. Sick of the meanness and littleness of men, we create to ourselves a new world, and people it with angels. It is in this dissatisfaction with what is false and fading, and in this ceaseless longing after the true and ever-during, that we find, aside from Revelation, the strongest evidence of our immortality.

The ancient Romans attributed to the poet not so much *creative* as *prophetic* power. Hence, in the Latin language, the same word, *vates*, is used indiscriminately either for poet or prophet. Sometimes both of these endowments are found in the same individual. Such was the case, in an eminent degree, with the old Hebrew prophets, — with Isaiah, and Hosea, and Ezekiel, — those "trumpets filled with the voice of God." Coming unbidden from the depths of the wilderness, or from caves in the shadows of Sinai and Horeb, their stern words of inspired warning were always fringed on their terrible edges with poetry.

Extended definitions have been given to poetry, and patient analyses made of its elements, but with a success like that of the ancient anatomists searching for the seat of the soul, — while the matter was scrutinized, the essence escaped. Simonides says, "A poem is a speaking picture, and a picture is a silent poem." Not unlike this is the definition of Macaulay. "By poetry," says he, "we mean the art of doing by means of words what the painter does by means of colors." In this view of the matter, poetry is not, as some suppose, confined to any particular species of writing, but is seen in everything, however familiar and commonplace, which the imagination has painted for the eye to rest on. There is poetry in the answer of the poor mute, who, when asked for a definition of *forgiveness*, wrote on his slate, "Forgiveness is the fragrance which a bruised flower yields to him who tramples on it." There is poetry, too, in the explanation which some one has given of the simple Christian precept, "Love your enemies." He who loves his enemies is like "the sandal-tree, which sheds a perfume on the axe that fells it." There is poetry in the Table-Talk of Coleridge, not less than in the stately verse of Milton; in the Book of Job, as well as in the play of Hamlet. But after all these explanations, it must be felt to be understood; and to be felt, there must be a soul alive to every noble impulse and strong emotion.

> "Divine it is, a light, a love,
> A spirit which like wind doth blow,
> As it listeth, to and fro,—
> A dew rained down from God above."

He who is endowed with a poetic temperament is alone in harmony with all things. It is said that, if a certain note in music be struck, this note will be answered by a precisely corresponding tone from a viol, or any stringed instrument, which may be standing in another part of the room. Just so the varied tones which come to the poet from sky and earth find ready responses in the harp-strings of his own heart. Let the sun rise in brightness, and they make melody sweet as that of Memnon. Let it set in storms, and they vibrate to the rainy winds in sad Æolian music. "I am always," says Byron, "most religious on a sunshiny day; as if there was some association between an internal approach to greater light and purity, and the kindler of this dark-lantern of our external existence." But notwithstanding this sympathy between nature and the poet, we are by no means to believe that poetic genius is dependent on the outward world for its inspiration and development. The light and beauty which the shifting scenes of nature may fling upon the spirit of the poet are not radiant, but reflected. They were first shed from his own being. The soul impresses its own forms upon matter, and gives it its own hue and coloring. In the language of our own Dana: —

"The rill is tuneless to his ear who feels
No harmony *within*; the south-wind steals
As silent as unseen among the leaves.
Who has no inward beauty, none perceives."

To give those not already acquainted with him even a faint idea of Shelley as a poet, in the space left to us, were no easy task. David Hume has said, that "criticism is nearly useless, unless the critic quotes innumerable examples." To do this, in the present instance, is impossible, and to attempt to make a fair exhibition of the genius of Shelley by merely an extract or two from his poetry, would be to imitate the well-known Scholasticus, with his specimen brick. Perhaps there is no better way of accomplishing our purpose than by considering him in connection with two other poets with whom every intelligent person is supposed to be familiar. We remember that a reviewer, many years ago, made Byron, Shelley, and Wordsworth, in the order of their names, a synonyme with the progress of poesy. Without stopping to question the justice of this arrangement, we will compare them briefly with each other in some particulars.

Byron is the favorite poet of impassioned youth; Shelley, of intellectual manhood; Wordsworth, of infancy and old age. The genius of Byron flashes forth in the fitful splendor of the Aurora Borealis; that of Shelley burns with the clear and constant flame of the Roman vestal; Wordsworth sheds upon you the quiet light of the harvest-moon, or rather the fading glory of the western sky.

While reading Byron you seem to sit in an old castle, among whose gray ruins autumn winds are wailing, and through whose widening crevices and painted windows streams the light of a golden sunset. Shelley transports you to some far-distant "Hall of Spells," where spirits live and dream, — where all that is sweet in sound or pure in vision floats on the air or passes dimly before the sight. Wordsworth takes you by the hand, and leads you forth from the busy haunts of men to green pastures and by still waters.

In the selection of *subjects*, Byron has restricted himself to the world of *passion*. Voluptuousness and misanthropy are his never-failing themes; — hate your neighbor and love your neighbor's wife, it is truly said, are the two great commands of his decalogue. His poetry, like the harem of an Eastern prince, is full of beauties; but while you approach to admire, the fierce scowl of their keeper is upon you. It is only when portraying the darker features of the human heart that he is in his sphere. His sky is always sunless and starless. The earth is to him "a weary land, without the shadow of a great rock,"— a desert, without fountain or oasis. He seems to feel that "every man's hand is against him," and, like a true son of Ishmael, "he turns his hand against every man." Life is a burden to which he clings only from the fear that his death may gratify his enemies. Hence he writes in a letter to Moore: "I should many a good day have blown my brains out, but for the recollection that it would give pleasure to my mother-in-law; and, even in that case, I would have done it, if I could have been sure to haunt her, and fling my shattered scalp in her frightful face." His poetry is a transcript of himself. The life which animates his heroes is an emanation from his own. His Cain, and Manfred, and Lara, and Harolde are nothing but the writer himself, in different countries, and clothed in different costumes.

His own proud and dissatisfied spirit pervades all his works. Like the ever-open eyes of some painted saint or sire, its cold glance will follow you whichever way you turn. It is related of Phidias, that, in constructing the ivory statue of Minerva at Athens, he so wrought *his own image* into the shield as to render its removal impossible without the destruction of the statue. So the features of Byron are wrought into the very structure and framework of his poetry; they are chiselled by his own dark genius for immortality.

Shelley, in his subjects, has little intercourse with the lower and darker passions of men. His sphere is the higher one of *Intellect*. In studying his poetry, you feel that those olden times have returned, when the "groves of philosophy were watered by the Ilissus of the Nine." In his earnestness to inculcate principles, he forgets himself. If you see him at all, he is but a dim, shadowy figure standing in the far background. He acts under the strong belief that the structure of society is fundamentally wrong; that the wheels of government, in their revolutions, crush the weak and helpless, while the minions of power ride over them in triumph and derision; that hoodwinked custom is binding in chains of ice all the warm and gushing feelings of our natures; that superstition is brooding, like night, over the spirits of men, enshrouding the light of reason and filling the imagination with spectres of darkness. He does not, in view of these things, envelop himself in a gloomy misanthropy, and rail at all human kind; but, with the strong purpose of a reformer, girds himself for conflict with the world. Yet every page of his poetry is warm with kindness, as well as luminous with thought. The melioration of society, the elevation of men to freedom of thought and equality of privilege, the expulsion of the demons of hate and discord and oppression by the power of love, — these are the objects of his ambition, and to the accomplishment of these he brings alike the treasures of learning and the enthusiasm of genius. Sick of the regal pomp and ecclesiastical tyranny of his own country, he longs for the liberty of the old democracies. Responding from his very heart to the sentiment of Burns, —

> "The rank is but the guinea-stamp,
> The man 's the gowd for a' that,"

he dreams of a "good time coming," when the shows and shams of a titled dignity shall be swept away before the might of a redeemed and disenthralled manhood; when the princes, powers, and potentates of the earth shall be but as chaff on the breath of an awakened, and intelligent, and free people. It is, therefore, with all the exultation of hope that he hails, in his "Revolt of Islam," the rising republic of America.

> "That land is like an eagle, whose young gaze
> Feeds on the noontide beam, whose golden plume
> Floats moveless on the storm, and in the blaze
> Of sunrise gleams when earth is wrapt in gloom."

Wordsworth, in the selection of his subjects, tells us himself that "low and rustic life was generally chosen, because in that condition the essential passions of the heart find a better soil in which they can attain their maturity, are less under restraint, and speak a plainer and more emphatic language." Acting upon this theory, he runs, as a matter of course, into a thousand absurdities. You are pained at every step with a palpable incongruity between his characters and the parts which they perform. The pedler of small wares, in his "Excursion," is made the organ of the soundest social and philosophical reflections. Gypsy women become oracles of wisdom; and shepherds, because they are most familiar with the varying scenes of the outward world, are inducted, without the "laying on of hands," into the high-priesthood of Nature. He seems to have forgotten that a familiarity with Nature often hardens the heart to her charms, even as water sometimes converts the leaf or limb over which it flows into stone. The traveller who, for the first time, looks forth from the icy summit of Mount Washington upon the world of hills around him, will, if he has a soul, feel an oppressive sense of his own littleness and insignificance amidst the sublimity and grandeur of nature. But his guide, who was born among those hills, and whose journeyings have been through mountain passes from boyhood to gray hairs, sees neither sublimity nor beauty, but wonders only in his heart that a man in his senses should go so far and spend so much money to see a great pile of rocks. Wordsworth constantly overlooks the fact, that, with the poor, life is often regarded as a necessary evil, and the world as a sort of vast Sahara. The necessity of incessant toil checks the flow of their finer feelings and blunts their keener sensibilities. They may, like the beautiful Alice, — one of the finest creations of Bulwer, — contain the germ of a higher nature, but it is enshrined in an impenetrable chrysalis. If a hope steals over them, it comes shadowed with despair, like a dream of future happiness to the Hebrew in a strange land, faint with watching for the Messiah. They have little sympathy with earth or its inhabitants, but rather look beyond, like the poor washerwoman, who longed to die, that she might exchange the tub and rubbing-board of earth for the white apron and psalm-book of heaven.

Byron, in his *style*, is impetuous and unstudied. You are hurried on in the full tide of some overpowering passion. His characters never sit in attitude till he has sketched them off, but all are up and in motion. His language, as would be supposed, is strong and glowing, abounding, in some of his poems, with all the gorgeous imagery and splendor of the East.

Shelley's style has all the conciseness of Sallust, blended with an Ionic elegance, which would scarcely lose by a comparison with Sophocles himself. There is in his classic verse a music, not wild and clarion-like, but deep and measured as the orchestral chantings of an old cathedral. No one better than he understood the capabilities of the English language, or was more competent to express high thoughts and impassioned feeling,

> "In notes with many a winding bout
> Of linked sweetness long drawn out;
> Untwisting all the chains that tie
> The hidden soul of harmony."

The style of Wordsworth is, in many of his productions at least, cumbered with verbiage. There is no correspondence between the multitude of his words and the paucity and meagreness of his thoughts. A passage from the third canto of his Wagoner, which has been criticised by Professor Wilson, illustrates this assertion: —

> "Now, heroes, for the true commotion,
> The triumph of your late devotion!
> Can aught on earth impede delight
> Still mounting to a higher height;
> And higher still, — a greedy flight!
> Can any low-born care pursue her,
> Can any mortal clog come to her?
> No notion have they, — not a thought
> That is from joyous regions brought!
> And while they coast the silent lake,
> Their inspiration I partake;
> Share their empyreal spirits, — yea,
> With their enraptured vision see —
> O fancy — what a jubilee!
> What shifting pictures clad in gleams
> Of color bright as feverish dreams!
> Earth, spangled sky, and lake serene,
> Involved and restless all, — a scene
> Pregnant with mutual exaltation,
> Rich change, and multiplied creation!"

Now under all this pomp and circumstance of diction, this Pelion-on-Ossa pile of words, the crushed and purple-faced thought looks out distressfully, and asks for help. A sailor and a wagoner, it seems, are reeling from a grog-shop late at night, along toward home, by the side of their team of eight horses and a donkey, until they come to the margin of a lake, when they stop to glorify the beauties of nature, and in a fit of drunken affection shake hands and hug each other till they fall asleep. There is a passage in an Icelandic poem, entitled "The Song of the Sun," which, for its striking similarity in some respects, deserves to be mentioned in this connection. The literal translation of the original is as follows: "I hang the round, beaten, gaping snake on the end of the bridge of the mountain-bird at the gallows of Odin's shield." For a solution of this wordy enigma, we are to learn that the "round, beaten, gaping snake" is a ring, — a snake with his tail received into his "gaping" mouth representing a circle. The "mountain-bird" is the falcon, and his "bridge" is the hand; that is, the part on which he is supported by the falconer. The end of the "bridge" or "hand" is the finger. The "gallows of Odin's shield" is the arm, — the limb on which the shield is *hung*. The passage, therefore, "I hang the round, beaten, gaping snake on the end of the bridge of the mountain-bird at the gallows of Odin's shield," when stripped of its muffled disguise, is found to contain a thought no bigger and no more beautiful than this: I put a ring on my finger.

Byron, in his efforts, and therefore in his productions, is irregular and uneven. The most brilliant stanzas are intermingled with the most puerile pratings. "Dirt and divinity" are blended in due proportions. This is especially evident in one of his latest and longest poems, — a poem written under the inspiring influence of hot gin-sling, — a beverage to which the noble Lord, it would seem, had no very particular aversion while engaged in some of his other works. The high powers with which he was endowed were not self-acting nor self-sustaining, but required the inspiriting influences of bad liquor or the lashings of the Scotch Reviewers.

Shelley depends on his own resources, and therefore never sinks below his own standard. There is a strength and Doric delicacy in his slightest as well as his more labored efforts. "He touches nothing which he does not adorn." From the visionary dreamings of his "Queen Mab" to the last offering to his Muse, every line is finished. Whether you sit amid the gloomy magnificence of "The Cenci," or gaze upon the glory-tinged expanses of the "Revolt of Islam," or watch the calm agony of the "Titan," you feel that you are in the presence of high and commanding genius. There are no spasmodic outbursts of passion, followed by an epilepsy of all thought and feeling; no striking beauties set off by a background of deformities; nothing dependent for its sublimity on a corresponding bathos. His imagination, though lofty in its flights, yet, like the famed Eastern bird, soars on a pinion which never tires nor rests. He has an eye for the harmonies of the outward world, but so far from depending on them, like Byron, for his inspiration, he turns from them as from shadows to listen to his own spirit: —

"The land of song within thee lies,
Watered by living springs:
The lids of Fancy's sleepless eyes
Are gates into this paradise;
Holy thoughts like stars arise,
Its clouds are angels' wings."

Things visible are regarded by him as unsubstantial and evanescent. Permanence is predicated only of what pertains to mind; or, in his own language,

"Thought
Alone, and its quick elements, — will, passion,
Reason, imagination, — cannot die."

His conceptions on this subject are beautifully expressed in a passage of Plato's Republic, in which the mistaken apprehensions of the human mind with respect to the material world are compared to those of a man, who, in a cave into which no light can enter but by a single opening, views upon the wall opposite to the entrance the shadows of external objects, and mistakes them for realities.

Wordsworth, in his productions, is still more uneven than Byron. You have every variety, from the highest and severest walks of poetry down to the lullabies of the nursery, — the melodies of "Mother Goose." Some parts of his "Excursion," though on the whole it is a tedious poem of nine books, show the skill and power of a master. His sonnets are second only to those of Milton. The address to his sister, in "Lines composed a few Miles above Tintern Abbey," is full of tenderness and beauty. His "Intimations of Immortality," though deeply imbued with the Platonic theory of the soul's pre-existence, has all the elegance and lyrical music of a Grecian chorus. But when we turn from these to such effusions as "Goody Blake" and "Peter Bell," we are ready to exclaim, with the prophet, "How art thou fallen, O Lucifer, son of the morning!" The gifted author of the majestic Sonnet to Milton sinks so low as to spin out a hundred doggerel stanzas about an idiot boy, — stanzas which the boy himself, in his brighter moods, would have been ashamed to write. The muse to whom he had been bound, as he assures us, for "fourteen years," is solemnly invoked to aid him in telling us how old Susan Gale is taken sick in the night, and Betty Foy, as a good neighbor should, lifts her idiot son Johnny upon a donkey, and sends him after the doctor. The night waxes late, and old Susan waxes worse, and Betty waxes anxious; or, as the poet himself expresses it, —

"And Susan 's growing worse and worse,
And Betty 's in a sad quandary;
And then there 's nobody to say,
If she must go, or she must stay!
She 's in a sad quandary."

At length the clock is on the stroke of one, and she, full of woful apprehensions, starts off after Johnny, who, it seems, in the proud enjoyment of his first ride, has forgotten to look after the doctor, but is amusing himself in listening to the screech-owls or staring at the moon. After wandering a weary while in dim lanes, through bush and brake, and indulging in a variety of speculations as to the fate of the object of her search, and inly cursing old Susan for being sick, and half resolving, in the extremity of maternal anguish, to drown herself in a pond, — at last, when hope is darkening into despair, she spies through an opening in the trees the pony and its rider. Her joy at this event the poet describes in these highly graphic stanzas: —

"And now she 's at the pony's tail,
And now is at the pony's head, —
On that side now, and now on this;
And, almost stifled with her bliss,
A few sad tears does Betty shed.

"She kisses o'er and o'er again
Him whom she loves, her idiot boy;
She 's happy here, is happy there,
She is uneasy everywhere;
Her limbs are all alive with joy.

"She pats the pony, where or when
She knows not, happy Betty Foy!
The little pony glad may be,
But he is milder far than she,
You hardly can perceive his joy."

It ought, perhaps, to be added, that old Susan recovered, and, so far as we know, is still alive and doing well.

With Byron and Shelley there is always a correspondence between the subject chosen and the language employed. A trifle is not invested with the dignity of the Epic Muse, nor is an elevated theme rendered trivial by clothing it in the language of children and idiots. The beggar is not tricked out in purple and fine linen, nor does the emperor grovel in dirt and rags.

Wordsworth, on the other hand, in not a few instances, adopts an entirely different method. The most lofty discussions are treated in the style of the nursery, while characters the most insignificant are made to strut in the buskin of Sophocles. In many of his earlier and minor poems, the "poetic diction," to say nothing of the laws of rhetoric, finds little favor at his hands. In respect to a band of Gypsies, whom he unexpectedly finds just where he had left them "twelve bounteous hours" before, he exclaims: —

"Behold the mighty moon! this way
She looks as if at them, but they
Regard not her! O better wrong and strife
(By nature transient) than such torpid life!
The silent heavens have *goings-on;*
The stars have tasks, but these have none."

He seems to have been so interested in the dress of one of the Gypsy women that he essays a description of it: —

"She had a tall man's height, or more;
No bonnet screened her from the heat;
A long drab-colored cloak she wore,
A mantle reaching to her feet;
What other dress she had I could not know,
Only she wore a cap that was as white as snow."

His appreciation of the "good points" in a certain young lady are beautifully set forth in the following stanza: —

"I met Louisa in the shade,
And having seen that lovely maid,
Why should I fear to say,
That, nymph-like, she is fleet and strong,
And down the rocks can leap along
Like rivulets in May?"

We have thus, as was proposed, compared Shelley with Byron and Wordsworth in several particulars; — in the adaptedness of their poetry to the different periods of human life; in the hue and strength of their imaginings; in the selection of their subjects; in the style of their execution; in the evenness of their efforts; and in the appropriateness of their diction. In all these respects there can be little hesitation in awarding the palm of superiority to Shelley. But still he is not without his faults. The splendor of his intellect is sometimes clouded by his metaphysical speculations; his faith in human perfectibility involves him at times in theories as visionary as the "Utopia" of Sir Thomas More; the brilliancy of his imagination leads him to color too highly some of the creations of his pen; the multiplied classical allusions in his poetry place it, like Milton's, above the appreciation of the many; but the paramount fault, which has been already noticed when speaking of his philosophy, is his manifest discredit of the authority of the sacred writings. It is true that he was an ardent admirer of their beauty and sublimity; but while his lyre caught its spirit-like tone from the harp of Judah, and his imagination its fire from the altars of the prophets, he failed to acknowledge the "inspiration of the Almighty." In searching for subjects and for characters in his dramas, he uniformly turns from Holy Writ to Grecian mythology. He gathers for his Muse the flowers of Parnassus rather than the roses of Sharon. But in all this Shelley, unfortunately, is by no means peculiar in the world of letters. Since the production of "Paradise Lost," Milman and Bailey in England, and Hillhouse in our own country, are the only poets worthy of mention who have exerted their genius upon Scriptural themes. It is a matter of no small surprise, that a record so hoary with age, so rich in incident, so thrilling in adventure, so glowing in descriptions of things visible and invisible, so fraught with the strange and miraculous, so hallowed by heart-felt associations, has found so little favor in the eyes of aspiring poets. If it boasts of no Jupiter shaking Olympus with his nod, yet it glories in a legislative Deity, beneath whose feet the tops of Sinai smoke and tremble; if it declares no responses from the golden Diana of Ephesus or the marble statue of the Parthenon, yet it utters the voice of Him "who spake and it was done"; if it tells us of no smouldering Ilium, yet it exhibits the ruins on Mount Moriah and the mournful desolation of Salem; if it describes no wanderings of Æneas or king of Ithaca, yet there is the scattering of the sons of Jacob to the ends of the earth; if it portrays the patriotic devotion of no Curtius ready to cast his life into the abyss to save his country, yet it speaks of One who sacrificed himself for a world. Shelley has shown in his "Prometheus Unbound," a magnificent drama, that, although he had but little respect for the theological distinction between ὁμουσία and ὁμοιουσία, or for any of the other subtile speculations about the nature of Christ, still he appreciated the moral beauty of his life and the sublimity of his death. It hardly need be said, that his eye is fixed on Calvary, and that he is watching the death-struggle of the Saviour, when, in the language appropriated to Prometheus, he cries out:

> "Remit the anguish of that lighted stare;
> Close those wan lips; let that thorn-wounded brow
> Stream not with blood; it mingles with thy tears.
> Fix, fix those tortured orbs in peace and death,
> So thy sick throes shake not that crucifix,
> So those pale fingers play not with thy gore!"

If the space would permit, it might not be an unpleasant task to analyze some of the principal poems of Shelley, — especially those on which his claims to celebrity most depend. A passing glance of recognition is, however, all that we shall now bestow upon them.

The "Revolt of Islam," his longest work, represents the conflict of man's uprising, free-born spirit with the crushing tyranny of custom, — the struggle of the soaring eagle with the serpent.

"The Cenci," a highly wrought and admirably sustained tragedy, second in thrilling interest to none in the English language, is founded upon the bloody and revolting history of an old Italian family, and is intended to show the horrid enormities which may be perpetrated with impunity by the minions of ecclesiastical power. The beautiful face of the heroine, Beatrice, made immortal by Guido, smiles upon us, through its tears, upon the wall of many a modern parlor; and her statue, chiselled by the skilful fingers of one who is an ornament as well to her sex as to her chosen profession, even now, through the delicate munificence of a noble-spirited patron of art and learning, graces the hall of the Mercantile Library in the city of St. Louis.

His "Adonais," one of his most finished and beautiful productions, is a tribute of affection, welling up from his heart of hearts amid the roofless recesses of the Pisan Hills, to the memory of the poet Keats, and in every essential respect deserves a higher place than either the Lycidas of Milton or the Elegies of Bion and Moschus.

The "Prometheus Unbound," a lyrical drama, suggested by a lost drama of Æschylus of the same name, written among the deserted and flower-grown ruins of Rome, depicts in glowing colors the high contest between the strong endurance of the champion of mankind, and the haughty despotism of their unrelenting, omnipotent oppressor.

His "Alastor; or, the Spirit of Solitude," paints the lofty aspirations of a young poet, and his fruitless search in the world of sense after the bright creatures of his own imagination, — a sad picture of his own strange life.

We might with great propriety refer to the briefer poems which are scattered throughout his works, and which, for melody of verse and spirituality of conception, we have no hesitation in saying, are unsurpassed and unequalled, except, perhaps, by Keats and Tennyson, in the whole range of English lyrics. There is "The Sensitive Plant," a fitting emblem of the poet himself, whose extreme delicacy of organization could

> "scarce uplift
> The weight of the superincumbent hour."

There, too, is the ode "To a Skylark," which, like the spirit-bird it celebrates, is full of "music sweet as love."

But, without specifiying further his several productions, we will only commend them to a discriminating perusal. Read them with the assurance that, if death had not prevented, he would have himself protested with a sad but earnest spirit against the scepticism and false philosophy which mar many of the productions of his earlier years. Read them as the history of a mind groping through the darkness which overshadows the earth, on toward the light which shines from heaven. Read them as the record of a man who died in the morning twilight of his intellectual and moral being.

He will not, like the gentle Cowper, welcome you to the repose of the "Sofa," but he will demand of you patient, vigorous, sleepless thought. He will not, like the pathetic Crabbe, depict man as he is in the "Parish Register" of Muston or the "Borough" of Suffolk; but he will endow him with the attributes of an ideal perfection, and exhibit him as he lives in the El Dorado of a poet's dreams. He will not, like the didactic Young, shrouded in the gloom of "Night Thoughts," assail you with "the pious violence of prayer"; but he will portray the spirit-land in all the reality and freshness and beauty of the "Isles of the Blest." He will not, like the moralizing Wordsworth, give unending lessons from the book of nature, as the only source of all that is fair and good; but he will unfold to you "a mythology rich with visions as glorious as the gods that live in the marble of Phidias, or the virgin saints that smile on us from the canvas of Murillo." He does not, like the majestic Milton, attempt to

> " assert Eternal Providence
> And justify the ways of God to men";

but he teaches us, with Prometheus in his conflict with Jupiter,

> "To suffer woes which Hope thinks infinite,
> To forgive wrongs darker than death or night,
> To defy Power which seems omnipotent,
> To love and bear; to hope till Hope creates
> From its own wreck the thing it contemplates:
> Neither to change, nor flatter, nor repent;
> This, like thy glory, Titan! is to be
> Good, great and joyous, beautiful and free;
> This is alone Life, Joy, Empire, and Victory!"

WEALTH IN SOME OF ITS RELATIONS TO A FREE GOVERNMENT.*

IN the nations of the Old World, the safety of the state is the principal problem; with us, the living man is considered of more consequence than a hoary abstraction. With them, the throne is set on the people; with us, the people sit on the throne. With them, the strength of the nation lies in its standing armies; with us, it is seen in the infantry of the primary school. With them, a partial legislation is intended to subserve the interests of favorite classes; with us, a democratic legislation is fitted to secure the inalienable rights of individuals. With them, the "insolent prerogative of primogeniture," as Gibbon denominates it, renders the oldest son a mere appendage to a freehold, and drives all the others into professions to which they are unsuited, or which are already full to overflowing; with us, there is no entailment to the few, but estates are divided as children are multiplied, and when this mathematical process has been carried far enough in any district, we turn our eyes to the untrodden West, and take up the chorus, "'Uncle Sam is rich enough to give us all a farm." With them, all property is deemed a gift or grant from the government, and therefore subject of right, and without reserve, to its disposal; with us, property is the reward of

* A Lecture delivered before the Lyceums of East Boston, Newburyport, and Chicopee, Mass., Biddeford and Lewiston, Me., Manchester and Milford, N. H., and in other places. 1853 - 55.

labor, and he whose industry has been most wisely directed occupies his broad acres "without leave asked" of kings. In a word, the grand characteristic of our national civilization — a characteristic impressed upon us by the peculiarity of our political system — is *the energy of individual life, the force of personal existence.*

When Demosthenes was asked what were the three grand requisites to an orator, he answered, "Action, action, action." The spirit of this answer is exhibited to-day in the life and enterprise of the American people. Action, ceaseless and tireless, is the attribute of our intellectual and physical being. The baby-jumper of the nursery and the panting engine of the machine-shop are simple outward manifestations of the energy that, from infancy to age, struggles within us. Under the stimulus of our free schools, alike the product and protection of our other free institutions, the mind of the masses has been awakened to an activity without precedent or parallel in the history of nations.

Let us, in the further discussion of our subject, consider this mental activity in some of its objective relations to the material world, and more especially in its connection with the accumulation of wealth. It is obvious that all intelligent action has some impelling motive; it tends toward some result. Children may exercise for the fun of it, but men work for an object. There is method in their industry; their energies are not poured out wastefully upon the surface of things, but they flow in one channel toward some end. In this country, where all the prizes of life are held out alike to the grasp of all, the most tempting, perhaps, is wealth, — tempting because of the advantages which it confers, both in itself and in its relation to the other great objects of human ambition.

The young man cannot fail, as he looks abroad on society, to see that money does give a person consideration and consequence among his fellow-men; that the doors to political preferment and to aristocratic pretension do swing open most easily when "on golden hinges turning." He has hardly left the school-room before he catches the spirit of the bustling worshippers of Mammon, and begins at once his life-struggle in the crowd who are making haste to be rich.

It cannot be denied that we are emphatically a money-loving and money-getting people. With us wealth is a virtue, and poverty a crime. We graduate everything, material and immaterial, on the scale of dollars and cents. We estimate a writer's merit, not by the depth of his thought and the brilliancy of his style, but by the number of books he makes and sells. We determine the character of the preacher, not by his talent and piety, but by the amount of his salary. We prize the chief works of the artist, not by their intrinsic excellence of design or execution, but by the extravagance of their cost. We recognize a true gentleman, not by that unbought grace, that indefinable charm of conversation and manner, which gives far stronger assurance of gentle blood than the longest line of princely ancestors, but by the length of his rent-roll. We judge of the wife-like qualifications of the maiden we woo, not by her beauty of mind or person, but by the number of her father's shares in the railroad or factory; for now, as in the days of Mistress Anne,

> "A world of vile, ill-favored faults
> Looks handsome in three hundred pounds a year."

The influence of money is felt in every department of our busy life, in every profession and handicraft. It sits in the front pews of gorgeous churches, modifies the tone of the pulpit, takes off the bandage from the eyes of Justice, is a power at the long end of the lever in our political action, looks over the shoulder of the writer, follows the laboring-man like his shadow to the field, and the shop, and over the sea. Even on the Sabbath, the time when, if ever, men are "from worldly cares set free," the same hurried air is observable; the same care-worn, calculating expression sits heavy on the countenance. There is many a man whose eye is turned toward the altar, on whose face one can see the image and superscription of the almighty dollar stamped as legibly as though it had been done at the Philadelphia mint.

The clergyman who ministers to a congregation of these "solid men" is pretty liable, as a modern writer has intimated, to know no sin but "original sin," and no sinners but Adam and the Devil. In the theology of a man thus situated, all violence and iniquity are, like the scrofula and consumption, *constitutional;* and all righteousness is, like Abraham's, "imputed." We have more than once heard such an one attempt, in euphuistic phrase, to "remember" his brethren "in bonds"; but when it flashed upon him that one of his parishioners — the one, too, who paid the heaviest tax — was engaged in the Southern trade, "vox faucibus hæsit,"— the half-uttered prayer for the slave stuck in his throat, like Amen in the throat of Macbeth. "It is hard," as an old English divine says, "to maintain truth; but still harder to be maintained by it." Duty and pecuniary profit, it is certain, do not always go hand in hand in the "primrose path of dalliance"; they do not stand toward each other in the relation of cause and effect. A virtuous act is not always, in the language of the brokers, a good investment. The dividends on it are small, and, when declared, they are not usually in the current coin. It is no easy thing for a poor minister, especially if in his hunger he have lost faith in the continued existence of that species of raven which fed Elijah, to proclaim unwelcome doctrines to an audience who hold in their hands the keys to his pantry and wardrobe. He soon learns to talk to them in the gilt-edged phrase of the shop and the exchange, and his words fall musically on their ears, like dimes on a counter. But while we thus speak, it is no more than just to our clerical friends to say that, among the faithless, many an Abdiel is found faithful; that, in proportion to their numbers, they furnish, perhaps, more men than any other class who, in spite of all adverse influences, are foremost in every good word and work. There are among them men whom no tyrannical public sentiment can intimidate, no gilded bribes seduce, — men who think more of "the pure river of the water of life" than they do of a Lydian Pactolus, even though every modern Midas should bathe in it, and its waters should glisten with golden sands, as of old.

The power of wealth, again, may be seen in our courts of justice. We do not refer to any peculiar corruptibility in our bench or panel; we do not know that judges stain their ermine or jurymen violate their oaths oftener in this country than in any other. But we refer to the well-known fact that crimes of every hue and dye, from petty larceny up to gaunt murder, have their pecuniary equivalent, — that their prices are marked against them in the statute-book by our legislators, just as merchants mark their goods. It has always been true, that,

> "In the corrupted currents of this world,
> Offence's gilded hand may shove by justice."

The rich man who forges or steals, or commits any offence which lies without or within the shadow of the gibbet, may, at the pleasure of the Supreme Court, pay the bill, take a receipt in full of all demands, and leave for parts unknown; while the poor wretch who never inherited a fortune, and is therefore unable to secure from loss those who might possibly be tempted to become his bail, must do the state some service in the penitentiary. This may be a necessary evil in the workings of the law; but still, when those who are not initiated into the mysteries of jurisprudence see one man who has committed midnight arson hammering stone within high walls at Charlestown or Sing-Sing, and another who has been proved guilty of the same offence driving fast horses or speculating in fancy stocks, they are led to exclaim, with Dean Swift,

> "Strange such difference there should be
> 'Twixt tweedle-dum and tweedle-dee."

It need not be said that a distinction, which exists not in the enormity of the crime, but in the comparative wealth of the criminals, is not likely to be appreciated by the unreasoning multitude, nor is it fitted in its practical application to enhance a poverty-stricken villain's reverence for the majesty and impartiality of law. It only tends to quicken in the community the already riotous sense of the desirableness and omnipotence of gold.

In speaking of the various relations which wealth sustains to human conduct in this country, we cannot, of course, shut our eyes to the fact, that money is an element of no little force in our political action. It is well known that, in some of the States, property is made in their fundamental law a test of a man's fitness to vote or be voted for. He must have a freehold in order to be deemed a safe repository for a civil right so sacred as the elective franchise. His patriotism is virtually measured by the acre, and in some States his qualifications as a freeman are counted up on his fingers by the number of slaves he owns. The Constitution of South Carolina declares, among other things, in its first article, "that no person shall be eligible to a seat in the House of Representatives unless he be legally seized and possessed, in his own right, of a settled freehold estate of five hundred acres of land and *ten negroes*." But it is not of the constitutional disfranchisement of men because of their poverty that we would speak. We refer rather to the influence of money in the elections in those

States where, theoretically, all, rich and poor, high and low, are on a horizontal level. It costs an aspiring individual something now-a-days to get elected to any high political office. To secure the suffrages of an influential voter, he must render a *quid pro quo*, either in ready cash or in magnificent promises of post-offices or clerkships. One of the "general gender" may be enlightened as to his duty, perhaps, with free lunches, free drinks, and an affectionate shaking of hands. It is notorious that the ballot, in some Congressional districts, is coming to have a mercantile value, and the caucus has already become a collection of stock-jobbers. Those grand test questions of Jefferson, — "Is he honest? Is he capable? Is he faithful to the Constitution?" — are gone into disuse, and now the only inquiries interesting to Empire Clubs or bar-room juntos are, whether the candidate for office will stick to the platform, and part with himself; keep his mouth shut on agitating subjects, and his purse open at the call of his party. If he have the proper amount of dough, — dough that will not "*rise*," — nothing more is requisite; his statesmanship is complete. He may know the difference between the Constitution and a kangaroo, or he may not. If he is elected, the Union will be safe; the stars on our national banner will twinkle with an unwonted brilliancy, and the stripes will all run together — *e pluribus unum* — into one broad expanse of glory. "The world," as Samson Brass hath it, "will turn on its own axis, and have lunar influences, and revolutions round heavenly bodies, and various games of that sort." But should he be defeated, then,

> "Hung be the heavens with black, yield day to night!"

But the influence of money does not stop with election-day; the accumulation of wealth is the "be all" and the "end all" both of our national and State legislation. Man is postponed. Cotton in politics, as in fashion, is prominent and foremost, while humanity sweats and pants behind it. We think more of the tunic than of the *toga virilis;* more of the shirt than we do of its wearer. It was in view of the perverse influence which an all-absorbing passion for money exerts, that Plato, in his Republic,* affirms that "virtue is so at variance with wealth, that, supposing each to be placed at opposite ends of a balance, they would always weigh the one against the other." This of course cannot be accepted as a universal proposition; but it is too true, that, to no small extent, the tables of the money-changers do now, as of old, defile the temple of the human soul. It is this greed for gain which flouts at conscience, and would coin the public heart, and "drop its blood for drachmas."

But this *auri sacra fames* — this accursed hungering for gold — is felt as keenly in literature as in politics. Authors catch the spirit of the times in which they live, and their utterance is modulated by the circumstances which surround them. The writer who has learned that books of real merit can find no sale but with the trunk-maker or grocer, and no higher mission than to line a box or enwrap a parcel of damp sugar, is impelled to knock down his talents to the highest bidder, and to write, rather than starve, what he had better starve than write, — sentimental tales for seven-by-nine magazines, puffs of pills and panaceas for penny papers, yellow-covered pamphlets reeking with obscenity and atheism for precocious boys, rose-water novelettes for young ladies in pantalets and pinafores, political tirades for ambitious demagogues or malignant partisans. The mercantile element is a constituent element in book-making. He must use the same discrimination in the productions of his brain that the manufacturer employs in the productions of his mill. It is of vital importance to know "what *prints* will sell."

* Book VIII. chap. 6.

Milton neglected this worldly wisdom, and therefore, through much tribulation, got five pounds for his Paradise Lost; Byron regarded it, and the bookseller was glad to pay him fifteen thousand dollars for the first five cantos of Don Juan. Professor Anthon is shrewd enough to see that text-books in Greek and Latin sell better to students when all the hard places are translated, and so Homer and Horace, Cicero and Virgil, no longer speak to us in their vernacular language, but we hear them, as in Pentecostal days, "every man in our own tongue wherein we were born." Roman sesterces, in the estimation of the learned Professor, are of more consequence by far than American scholarship.

It is a melancholy fact in the history of literature, as well as in the present world of letters, that authors, even the most gifted, are nothing but men,—"forked, straddling animals with bandy legs." However brilliant their talents or ethereal their genius, yet, as Carlyle has said of the French peasants, "every unit of them stands covered with his own skin, and if you prick him he will bleed." They may attempt to "soar in the high reason of their fancy, with their garlands and singing-robes about them," but they always find themselves, even as other men, beating their wings helplessly against the walls of their earthly prison-house. If they would live in the bright creations of thought and imagination, yet they have five craving senses, and their stomachs, like the daughters of the horse-leech, continually cry, "Give, give." The gnawings of the gastric juice, as well as the presence of a money-getting public sentiment, produce in authors, as in other people, a utilitarian materialism. They learn to detect in the running brook so many mill-privileges; in the spreading tree, so many cords of wood; and in the sporting lamb, so many pounds of meat. "See those lambs," said Sir Walter Scott to his wife,—"how beautiful!" "Yes, my dear," replies the appreciating Lady Scott, "beautiful — *boiled!*" The "better-half" of the great Scotch minstrel expressed the inmost conviction of many a hungry poet in all ages of the world. Poetry and mutton! Happy would it have been for the poor children of the Muses in the days of Pope, if they could have effected a reconciliation between good writing and good eating, between rhyming ballads and boiled lamb. Chatterton then would not have poisoned himself to prevent starvation; Otway would not have choked himself to death with a roll of bread, in his eagerness to atone for an unwilling fast; and "poor Goldsmith" might not have incurred the oppressive debt of four thousand pounds, which prematurely crushed out his life.

To the young person, male or female, ambitious of any other distinction than a possible posthumous fame, the annals of literary men do not furnish much encouragement. The dividends do not come until the certificate-holder is gone. Garrets and genius, poverty and poetry, have generally been boon companions. Dr. Johnson, the "colossus of English literature," wrote his Rasselas in six successive nights, to obtain the money for the defrayal of the funeral expenses of his mother. Indeed, during his whole life, the great lexicographer and editor of the Rambler struggled day and night to keep his soul and body together, and yet was worsted in the end. Authors at all times, with the exception of a few, like Scott and Dickens and Mrs. Stowe, have maintained the same struggle, and oftentimes with even less success. Between the appetite of the poet and the stall of the butcher, as between the ancient Sestos and Abydos, an angry Hellespont has rolled, spanned by no bridge of boats. A *sans-culotte* from necessity, his "looped and windowed raggedness" has degraded him to a companionship with strolling mendicants, and left his reputation to the mercy of succeeding generations. With such prospects before them, it is not strange that the class of literary men as such, in this country, has ever been small. We have but few men who devote themselves exclusively to the higher walks of thought; we have many, far more than any other nation, who can read, write, and cipher, — read the Bible and newspaper, write a note for sixty days, and cipher up the interest on it when it falls due. We are not by any means deficient in intellectual power and resources; there is among the shining faces in our school-grounds many a "mute, inglorious Milton"; but we choose rather to do than to dream, especially when wealth is the consequent of the one, and poverty is the shadow of the other. Hence with us the thought becomes at once an act; our ideas do not, as in Germany, lie idle in our heads, like specimens in a cabinet, but they are organized into institutions, engines, reaping-machines, and chloric ether. Not unfrequently, our profoundest thinkers are engaged in the most active pursuits. Our scholars are superintendents of railroads or agents of factories; our men of genius preside over machine-shops; our poets are editors of political papers; our linguists are learned blacksmiths; our mathematicians are building bridges or navigating ships. Elihu Burritt learned some fifty languages between the forge and the anvil. The *Mécanique Céleste*, which could be read by but one person in England, was translated and improved by Nathaniel Bowditch while at the head of an annuity-office in Massachusetts. Familiar facts like these might be multiplied to an indefinite extent.

As a people we are decidedly utilitarian in our notions and conduct. We cultivate table-sauce rather than flower-borders, ruta-bagas rather than roses, parsnips rather than pansies. We like robins and bobolinks, not so much because they sing, as because, when broiled, they are not bad to take. We sympathize with the practical Hibernian, who was sure entirely that he would not keep pigs, the troublesome creatures, if it were not for the pork. We cannot stop to worship the beautiful in nature or art, — such worship does not pay one per cent a month. We think more of a potato-patch than of a painted landscape ; more of McCormick and Manning than of Titian and of Claude Lorraine. Fat oxen and merino sheep look better to us when chewing their cuds in our barn-yards, than when reposing in bright colors on the imaginary hillsides of the artist. Statuary is regarded as well enough for those who can afford to indulge in such luxuries, but the Apollo Belvedere and Venus de Medici would excite the admiration of not a few to a higher degree if they could be turned to any practical use. There are those, I doubt not, to whom the Greek Slave of Powers is an object of less interest and value than one of a darker hue, who could do a man's work in a cotton-field. We look at all things, animate and inanimate, in the light of loss and gain ; and our children are taught the higher law of trade — " Put money in thy purse " — long before they learn the moral code or the "chief end of man." The ingenious Yankee who engraved the Lord's prayer on one side of a dime and the ten commandments on the other, was a representative man. It matters not that the letters on the coin are too small for the naked eye ; the coin itself is visible, and that is the main thing.

In our anxiety to " make " the most in life, if not of it, we give less time to amusements than any other nation. It is with us "all work and no play." We have nothing corresponding with the great national festivals of the Grecian republic. Instead of the Olympic, Pythian, Nemæan, and Isthmian Games, to which every people of the Hellenic race flocked in their holiday attire, and at which genius and patriotism were kindled to a flame, private feuds forgotten in the hilarity of social enjoyment, and grovelling tastes and pursuits rebuked amidst the masterpieces of statuary, painting, and architecture, we listen gloomily to the left-handed prophecies of some world-destroying Millerite at a second-advent camp-meeting, or encore the wordy harangues of flatulent orators. It has been said of us by a foreigner, that our only two amusements are "theology for the women and politics for the men, — preaching and voting." It is certain that the natural cravings of the young for innocent recreation are not properly attended to; while the old, plodding on in their hard-trodden paths of business, lose long before the time all relish for the few pastimes of their youth, — all power to see any "sunny side" in life. This is unquestionably wrong; for the time will come, do all we can to avert it, when the wild roses will all be gathered from the wayside, the bird fly elsewhere with his song, the storm-wind scatter the red leaves from the maples, and darkness settle down upon our path, — a path which has lost all too soon its flowers, its music, and its verdure. There has been abroad in the community a sentiment, zealously inculcated by well-meaning but undeserving men, entirely opposed to amusements of every class and kind. Because

"Life is real, life is earnest,"

it has been thought by many altogether wicked for one to do anything but work with his hands on week-days and rest from his labors on Sundays. This may be good; but "man cannot live by bread alone." A deeper wisdom would enable overweening censors to see that all those recreations which do in reality re-create man, as an intellectual and moral being, are desirable; that those only are sinful which appeal to our passions and debase us; that labor and diversion, like day and night, should alternate; that a pure morality and a rational amusement are congenial, and may go together. There is quite as much truth as poetry in the oft-quoted line of Horace, —

"Dulce est desipere in loco,"—

which, being interpreted, signifieth that that man mows the most grass in a day who stops once in a while to whet his scythe. A cheerful religion should be to us a "thousand-voiced psalm" of life, and not be made a garb to be put on and taken off like a cloak or an overcoat. There was a whole volume of moral philosophy in the remark of a student of Yale College, now a retired veteran clergyman, who, when asked with surprise, on a certain occasion, by a narrow-minded classmate, if he, a professor of religion, was going out to engage in the sports of the gymnasium, resolutely replied, "Yes, I am going to pitch quoits to the glory of God." The time, however, has nearly gone by when it is thought by anybody a virtue to set our nature at strife with itself; when all pleasure is condemned simply because it is pleasant, and all pain is welcomed simply because it is painful. There have been men — we have seen them — who were never comfortable unless they were miserable, — men who were always unhappy in life unless, in the quaint though energetic language of Dr. South, they felt the "fire and brimstone flaming round them." Far different from this was the philosophy of the old Spaniard, who always put on spectacles when he was about to eat cherries, that they might look bigger and more tempting. In like manner, as it seems to me, does it become us in this working world, and especially in this busy country, to make the most of every innocent enjoyment, of every harmless amusement.

Within the last few years the absorbing passion for money has been quickened and intensified by the acquisition of California, and the consequent discovery of exhaustless gold mines. The enthusiasm which animated the followers of Peter the Hermit and St. Bernard, in their march to the Holy Sepulchre, has been matched in the eagerness of the thousands who have gone in crusades to the "placers" of this new El Dorado. The treasures over which the indolent Mexicans had stumbled blindly for centuries have been suddenly poured into our great cities, and thence, as from the fabled Tmolus, they have flowed in a thousand golden streams all over the land. To the political economist there is a startling interest in some of our recent moneyed statistics. A statement from official sources shows that, during the five years ending December 31, 1853, the total production of gold in California was the enormous sum of $300,000,000. Down to this same date, Australia, though her mines had been worked but two years and a half, had yielded to the English $176,000,000. Now the whole estimated stock of gold in Europe and America both, in 1848, was $2,785,000,000. The produce of California and Australia for the five years succeeding that time, therefore, was more than *seventeen per cent* on the whole amount of gold in the whole civilized world! What addition to this extraordinary percentage has been made during the last eight years, we have not the means of determining. Nor is it easy to foresee what the final result of this unprecedented influx of gold into our channels of trade will be. We do know, however, that Mexican and Peruvian mines did much to overthrow the Spanish power and nationality; that it diverted industrial energy from honest labor into reckless adventure, and contributed more than anything else to change a hardy and enterprising people into a herd of indolent, imbecile, intriguing cut-throats, with scarcely any trait of their former character remaining, except their indomitable pride. That California gold will work similar effects on us, we do not like to believe. Our commercial activity, our internal improvements, the railroads which are checkering our land and uniting our oceans, the manufactories which are mingling the music of spinning-jennies and power-looms with the music of waterfalls, — these all require capital, and all serve to scatter the shining dust of the Sacramento and Sierra Nevada to every village and hamlet in the Union. Still, it cannot escape the notice of the most careless observer, that a revolution is going on in our every-day life. Our social habits are changing; the relation of labor to a physical subsistence is undergoing no slight modification. The increase in the amount of money is followed by a proportionate diminution in its value.* It takes more of it now than it did a few years ago to pay for "food convenient for us." It is manifest that the laboring classes, whose wages per diem or salary per annum were fixed under the old *régime*, must either, like Oliver Twist, "ask for more," and, unlike him, get it, or else they must put their wives and children upon short allowance.

The increased wealth of the nation, it is obvious, therefore, is in some respects operating to the disadvantage of the many whose daily bread is dependent on their daily labor; it is no less obvious that the accumulation of this national wealth in the hands of a class or limited number, as will inevitably be the case, can hardly fail to affect unfavorably these favored few. There is a Nemesis which always rules in human affairs. When weak men have all the means of personal gratification at command, the temptation to wasteful extravagance and dissipation, hurtful to themselves as well as to the community, is ordinarily too strong to be resisted. The truth of this assertion is forcibly illustrated in the fashionable follies running riot in some of our principal cities. The cost of a new suit for an exquisite Broadway dandy of the first water, including finger-rings, watch-chain, snuffbox, and eye-glass, would be amply sufficient to purchase in Minnesota a whole township of government land; it would even go far, if invested in a constitutional way, to entitle him to the privilege of voting in the empire of South Carolina! Carlyle

* Bank capital in 1860, $421,890,095. Report on Eighth Census, p. 193.

must have had his eye on one of these specimens of humanity when he defined man to be a "clothes-wearing animal." Such characters as these clothes-horse dandies are not mythological; we see them on pleasant days in the streets, or catch the perfume of their presence in drawing-rooms, never employed, but always and everywhere serene and "idle as Solomon's lilies"; not real flesh-and-blood men, but padded and elaborate figures of speech. But outward show is not the prerogative of one sex. There is, I doubt not, to-night, in many a fashionable saloon, many a lady whose costume, scanty though it be, at a fair mercantile value, the whole Plymouth Colony, in the time of John Carver, could not have bought.

Luxury in some of its multitudinous forms has always been the result and accompaniment of wealth. It was true in Rome and Corinth; it is true in these United States. Its most common and absurd mode of development, however, has been rather in the extravagance of the table than of the dress. Men have coveted riches for their own sake; not as a means, but as an end; not to relieve human want or to embellish cultivated life, but to minister to the unnatural appetences of their own pampered bodies. In the reign of Augustus, after the conquest of Asia, we read that, notwithstanding the strictness of the sumptuary laws, epicurism had attained such a pitch of sickly refinement that Maltese cranes, peacocks, and nightingales, though hardly eatable, were considered great delicacies, and their tongues and brains still greater. It is a sober historical fact, that a single surmullet, a fish of the perch variety, was sold for a sum equivalent to two hundred and fifty dollars of our money. Æsop, the tragic actor, treated his guests to a dish of birds which had been taught, with infinite pains and expense, either to sing or to speak, and set before them also a flagon of wine whose flavor he had attempted to improve by a solution of pearls. Horace, however, ascribes this fact of hospitality to the son of Æsop:

> "An actor's son dissolved a wealthy pearl—
> The precious ear-ring of his favorite girl—
> In vinegar, and thus luxurious quaffed
> A thousand solid talents at a draught."

In the reign of Domitian, the Senate, the grave and reverend Roman Senate, was convened by imperial proclamation, to consult on the best mode of dressing a turbot of unusual size which had been presented to the Emperor. The despot knew, says the historian, that no council of cooks could furnish him with better advice. Some of the rarest dainties which regaled the senses of the Roman epicure have not yet, so far as we know,

> "Risen, like a stream of rich distilled perfumes,"

from the tables of American gastronomists. Snails, and a species of large borer found in old timber, were, if we may believe Apicius, who tells us how to cook them, fattened with peculiar care, as a delicate morceau for the fastidious human palate; while, according to Pliny, fricasseed nursing puppies were worthy of being served at a supper for the gods. The aristocracy of our great cities have not yet reached this refinement of luxury. Still they are quite as flaunting and showy in their public exhibitions of wealth. Armorial bearings emblazoned on the doors of carriages, footmen in gaudy liveries, and grand parties, in which the host may smile upon the beauty and the chivalry from a halo of gas-light glory, amidst the fragrance of Weller's fricandeau and the hired music of "flutes and soft recorders,"—these are the modes in which the pride of some of our millionnaires finds expression.

But, notwithstanding the thousand absurd follies constantly perpetrated by the worshippers of the golden calf in our great cities, we should do violence to our own convictions of truth and justice should we attempt to convey the impression that they are a fair type of our wealthy men. Many, if not most, of our rich men have been the artificers of their own fortunes; they have risen to opulence by their own skill and exertions. The concentration of mind, the persistency of purpose, the indefatigable industry, which made John Jacob Astor worth his millions, might, if these same faculties had been applied to books, have made him a Sir William Temple or a Dr. Parr. The liberality of the mercantile class is as munificent as it is proverbial. The names of our merchant-princes, whose hands are ever "open as the day," are known and honored throughout the land, in connection with our highest and most cherished institutions of learning and charity and religion. While there can be no doubt that, by a large majority of the American people, an undue importance is attached to wealth as the chief, if not the only good, yet we would by no means depreciate its desirableness to an individual, or its necessity to an enlightened community. The elevation of man in civilized life above the fisher and hunter is owing to the increased amount and secure possession of property. Without this we should relapse into barbarism. The hum of industry would cease; the pant of the engine would be hushed; briers and thistles would overspread the garden and fruitful field; its acorns and honey would again render the oak sacred to Jupiter in the eyes of the hungry multitude; the sails of commerce would flap idly over rotting hulks; the warehouse and granary would be empty; learning would forsake the halls of the university, and invention sit listless among broken crucibles and half-finished implements of skill; the monuments rising from the red fields of our fathers' valor would pause in their ascent; the hospital would no longer open its doors to the sick and mutilated and insane; the owl and the raven would congregate in the temple, and from chancel to porch "the satyr would cry to his fellow." It is in the contempt which our Indians feel for labor and its material products that the missionary finds the most serious obstacles to his efforts for their improvement. The Bedouin Arabs have no conception of the sacredness of our household gods. The root which they plant in the soil is plucked up without blood, and they need no ghost of Polydorus to induce them to seek Lavinian shores. It is only where there is an accumulation of property and a "local habitation" that all the sweet charities of society, friendship, and home gather. The nomadic herdsman, following the caprice of his grazing cattle, must, in the nature of things, be solitary and selfish. The famous line of Terence — "I am a man, and deem nothing human unrelated to me" — could have no meaning to him. With him it is all of life to live. There is no care for others in the present, none for himself in the future. The law of appetite is the highest law he knows.

Few people are aware how great an accumulation of values, how vast an amount of capital, is required, not only to promote, but even to maintain our civilization. The school systems of different countries are not bad illustrations of this fact, while at the same time they are indices to the degree of a nation's progress and culture. The young of the Free States in this Union do not comprehend the magnitude of the sacrifice which is made every year to secure to them the opportunities of a good education. The most important item in determining the liberality of a State in this particular — an item generally overlooked — is not the money raised for common schools, but the time which the young are permitted to appropriate to their books. It makes a wonderful difference with a family, whether its members are producers or consumers only. The state is but a family of larger growth. The actual value of the twenty weeks' time spent last year by the ninety thousand children of New Hampshire in the public schools, was, at the lowest estimate, half a million dollars, or an average of not less than six dollars to each tax-payer of the State. In Massachusetts the proportional amount is much greater than this. Now, such an expenditure can only be made by a wealthy people. It could not be done in China, or even in a large part of Great Britain; for there, as soon as a child can earn a penny a day, he must earn it or starve.

But the amount expended in time and money on our free schools, though fraught with the most momentous consequences to the country, is but a trifle compared with the vast sums required to sustain the other great interests which distinguish us from the savage and barbarous nations of the earth. The characteristics of an enlightened civilization are these six: a common-school education, to which we have referred, the Christian religion, a skilful culture of the soil, manufactures by steam and water-power, rapidity of intercommunication, and commerce. These all cost money, — how much not many of us, perhaps, ever stop to inquire. According to the report of the Superintendent of the Census, the value of our church property in 1850 was $ 86,416,639. It appears also, from the same document, that $ 151,000,000 were invested in agricultural implements and machines.* The capital employed in our various manufactures, on the 1st of June, 1850, not including any establishments whose gross income was less than $ 500 per annum, was $ 530,000,000.† On the first day of January, 1852, ten thousand eight hundred and forty-three miles of railroad had been built in the United States, at a cost of $ 592,770,000. How many miles have been finished since that date, and how many are now in process of completion, we have not the data to determine.‡ Of

* Value of agricultural implements and machinery in 1860, $ 247,027,496. Report on Eighth Census, p. 197.

† The total value of domestic manufactures produced in the year ending June 1, 1860, was $ 1,900,000,000. The amount employed in this production was $ 1,050,000,000. *Ibid.*, pp. 59, 190.

‡ At the close of the decade in 1860, 30,599 miles of railroad in the United States had been completed, at a cost of $ 1,134,452,909. *Ibid.*, p. 103.

the amount of money invested in commerce I have no definite knowledge; but the enormous sums already enumerated are sufficient to show that there is an intimate connection between capital and civilization.

We have thus spoken of wealth in some of its relations to a democratic government. We have seen that out of the freedom of our political institutions there has sprung up an unexampled physical and mental activity; that this activity is especially manifested in the intensity of our haste to be rich; that money exerts a controlling influence in all the departments of our energetic life,—entering the school-room, ascending the pulpit stairs, paying the penalty for crime, withholding or bestowing as by a divine right the elective franchise, making merchandise of our political principles, tempting the man of letters from the shades of the academy into the marts of trade, destroying our relish for rational amusements, and shutting our eyes and petrifying our hearts to the beautiful in nature and in art. We have seen, too, that, notwithstanding these multiform abuses of wealth, it is indispensable to the success, and even existence, of those magnificent interests which characterize an enlightened nation. We have endeavored to show that, though some rich snobs in Fifth Avenue are guilty of all sorts of grotesque and absurd extravagances, still the beneficent influence of wealth upon our social, industrial, educational, and religious relations is such as to render it an object worthy of individual exertion and of national concern.

Two very brief remarks shall finish what we have to say.

In the first place, "a man," as Theodore Parker, in his quaint way, expresses it, "was meant to be something more than the tassel to an estate." Thought and labor, at least in the Free States, may go hand in hand in a path, not unstrewn with flowers, to competency and fortune.

> "The fool, who holds it heresy to think,
> And knows no music but the dollar's chink,"

is not a fool of the highest style. When Shylock asked,

> "Hath a *dog* money? is it possible
> A cur can lend three thousand ducats?"

he thought, undoubtedly, that he had made the grand distinction between the *genus canis* and the *genus homo*. But it is coming to be generally conceded, that to be a man, a full-grown, well-developed man, somewhat more is necessary than skill in shaving notes without drawing blood. There is a significance in the exclamation of Solomon: "How much better is it to get wisdom than gold, and to get understanding, rather to be chosen than silver!" But let the gold and silver, and the high thought and warm heart and open hand, go together, as they may, and then you shall follow the path of the rich man through life by the fruits of his culture and the splendid monuments of his generosity.

The last remark which I have to make is this: material wealth and physical power will not alone insure permanency to a free government. Sir William Jones has well answered the question of his own asking:—

> "What constitutes a state?
> Not high-raised battlement or labored mound,
> Thick wall or moated gate;
> Not cities proud, with spires and turrets crowned;
> Not bays and broad-armed ports,
> Where, laughing at the storm, rich navies ride;
> But *men*, high-minded *men*."

The soil of Attica is as fertile, its valleys as beautiful with vines, and its hills as redolent of olive-blossoms, as when Miltiades conquered at Marathon, or Demosthenes hurled his terrible Philippics at the king of Macedon. The sky of Italy is as serene and blue, and the Adriatic is as exultant with white-winged commerce, as when Cato, with vindictive pertinacity, repeated in the ear of the Roman Senate his famous *Delenda est Carthago;* and the Seven Hills are as firm as when they echoed to the tramp of Cæsar's victorious legions. But the Genius of their liberty was like the image which the Chaldæan king saw in his vision. "Its head was of fine gold," but in its iron feet there was a mixture of "miry clay." Athens — splendid, ivy-crowned, poet-sung, world-renowned Athens *— talked eloquently of human rights with her sandalled foot upon the neck of four hundred thousand slaves, and worshipped devoutly in glorious temples dedicated to "the unknown God"; and Rome, in her lust of dominion, in the realization of her "manifest destiny," became the bloated oppressor of the world; — and so they fell. On the banks of the Ilissus and the Tiber their shadowy forms still rest, beautiful in desolation, mementos of the past and prophecies of the future,

> "So coldly sweet, so deadly fair,
> We start, for soul is wanting there."

From amidst the broken arches of their civilization, and the mouldering monuments of their military triumphs, there comes to us, in one of the inspired utterances of Cicero, a voice hollow as the sepulchre, and awful in its admonition as the voice of doom: "No Republic can stand unless its pillars rest upon the foundation-stones of Eternal Justice!" †

* *Ἅι τε λιπαραὶ καὶ ἰοστέφανοι καὶ ἀοίδιμοι, κλειναὶ Ἀθᾶναι.*

† "Sine summa Justitia Rempublicam geri nullo modo posse." — Cicero de Rep. Lib. II. c. 44.

THE PHILLIPS FAMILY AND PHILLIPS EXETER ACADEMY.*

[North American Review, July, 1858.]

THE failure of a contributor to fulfil his engagement has prevented, until this late day, any notice in our pages of Mr. Taylor's Memoir of Judge Phillips. The intrinsic merits of the work, as well as the elevated character of its subject, deserve a larger space than we can even now bestow. We can do little more than to express our high sense of the research and fidelity of the writer, and our admiration of the "Christian statesman, scholar, and philanthropist" to whose intimacy he has introduced us. The ancestry and personal history of a man remarkable in all the relations of life, sketched in an appreciative spirit and with a skilful hand, are never without interest. Especially in these days, when politicians are publicly bought and sold at the Washington brokers' board, and quoted daily in the money articles of the commercial press like fancy railroad stock or copper-mine shares, it is pleasant, for the novelty of the thing, to contemplate the character of a patriot of the olden time. It is a consolation, too, to know that the wealth which now flaunts in the grotesque extravagance of our modern pill and panacea aristocracy, once was employed in founding institutions of

* 1. *A Memoir of His Honor Samuel Phillips, LL. D.* By Rev. John L Taylor. Boston: Congregational Board of Publication. 1856.

2. *Catalogue of the Officers and Students of the Phillips Exeter Academy for the Academic Year* 1857 - 8.

learning, and consecrated with many prayers "Christo et Ecclesiæ."

Among the distinguished passengers on board the ship Arbella, which entered the harbor of Salem on the twelfth day of June, 1630, was the Rev. George Phillips, "a godly man, specially gifted," who used to talk to the sturdy old Puritans at Watertown "at such a rate as marvellously ministered grace unto the hearers." He was the intimate friend, as well as fellow-voyager, of Governor John Winthrop and Sir Richard Saltonstall, and seems to have been a leading spirit in moulding the civil and ecclesiastical institutions of the early New England Colonies. Cotton Mather's quaint epitaph upon him introduces us to his son Samuel: —

> "Hic jacet Georgius Phillippi,
> Vir incomparabilis, *nisi Samuelem genuisset.*"

This same son, whose lustre had dimmed the father's fame, was an eminent preacher of the Word at old Rowley for forty-five years, from 1651 to 1696. Among the fruits of his ministry we find, in the line of regular succession, a son who inherited the paternal prænomen, though the prophetic mantle fell upon a younger brother. We know of this patronymic descendant, only that he was a successful goldsmith in Salem, and that he transmitted the favorite family name to the Rev. Samuel Phillips, a man of striking individuality and energy of character, whose pastoral relation to the old South Church at Andover commenced with its origin, in 1711, and continued without interruption for a period of sixty years. His charge of ordination, on the eighteenth day of November, 1730, to the Rev. Timothy Walker, the first minister settled in that "remote part of the wilderness" then called Penacook, but now known as Concord, New Hampshire, is still extant. Besides this, he left behind him numerous sermons of marked ability, and three sons, Samuel, John, and William, the founders of the

Phillips Academies at Andover and Exeter. Of these, the first was the father of his Honor Samuel Phillips, Jr., or, as he is more commonly called, Judge Phillips, the subject of Mr. Taylor's Memoir. The former of these titles, the office of Lieutenant-Governor of Massachusetts, held during the last year of his life, gave to him; the latter he earned by sixteen years' laborious service on the bench of the Court of Common Pleas for Essex County.

The son of religious parents, without brothers or sisters, young Phillips grew up, in the companionship of his elders, a grave and manly boy. The defeat of Braddock, the capture of Nova Scotia by Massachusetts troops, the repulse of Baron Dieskau by General Johnson near Lake George, and the thousand thrilling tales of the French and Indian wars, stirred the blood of his early childhood, and gave a military glow to his future life. In his quiet retreat at Byfield Academy, in 1765, he could hear the forensic thunders which foreboded the storm of revolution. The two Adamses were denouncing the Stamp Act, and proclaiming the doctrines of republican liberty; the breath of James Otis, like a flame of fire, was consuming writs of assistance, and kindling the patriotism of his countrymen; the clarion voice of "the Boston Cicero," Josiah Quincy, the honored sire of a no less honored son, was waking the echoes in old Faneuil Hall. Having completed his preparatory studies at Byfield, he entered Harvard in 1767. But the silence of its classic grounds was soon disturbed by the din of martial preparation. The legislature, in 1768 and in 1770, indignantly refused to sit in Boston, occupied as it was by British troops, and held their sessions in Cambridge. The students caught the spirit of their deliberations; and some of Phillips's college themes, still preserved, sound more like the Philippics of the Athenian orator than like the literary essays of a smooth-faced boy of eighteen summers. He was graduated in 1771, with the Salutatory Oration. He seems to have been in college, as he was in his whole subsequent life, a model, not only of scholarly industry and refined manners, but of pure morals and rational piety. In 1773, at the age of twenty-one, he married Miss Phœbe Foxcroft, a highly cultivated and accomplished lady, his senior by nearly nine years, yet his junior in temperament and constitutional vivacity. The marriage was eminently happy. The wife was a beautiful counterpart of the husband. The self-possessed dignity and solid virtues of her character admirably fitted her to preside over his household, and to manage his affairs during the long periods of his absence; while her exuberant hopefulness irradiated the clouds which sometimes lay dark in the western horizon of his life. Whether she was keeping for him the records of the town, or dispensing a generous hospitality, or the "cynosure of neighboring eyes" in the social circle, she was always and everywhere to him, as he used to express it in his stately, though affectionate letters, "his invaluable partner," "his best friend." She survived him nearly eleven years, and died in 1812, having almost reached the allotted threescore and ten. Some five years before her death, she, in connection with her son, contributed $20,000 toward the establishment of the Theological Seminary at Andover, and thus carried into execution the partially formed plans of her husband. This institution was still further endowed by other members of the Phillips family. His Honor William Phillips, cousin of the Judge, bestowed upon it during his life $4,000, and at his death left it a legacy of $10,000. Samuel Abbot, grandson of the Samuel Phillips of Salem, and the wife of Moses Brown, great-granddaughter of the same, founded the Abbot and the Brown Professorships, — the former giving for this purpose $20,000, and the latter, together with her granddaughter, Mrs. Sarah W. Hale, $24,000. It is a noteworthy fact, too, that the

Abbot Female Seminary had its origin in the munificence of a descendant of the same Salem goldsmith.

In contemplating the career of Judge Phillips, we are amazed at the amount and variety of labor which he performed. There was hardly any sphere of action, public or private, into which he did not enter, and in which he did not succeed. His body was literally a "living sacrifice" to God and duty. Though "he completed his self-immolation at mid-life," yet, philosophically speaking, his death at fifty was not premature. He died old and full of years, because his life had been crowded with action and with thought.

> "We live in deeds, not years, — in thoughts, not breaths, —
> In feelings, not in figures on a dial;
> We should count time by heart-throbs. He most lives
> Who thinks most, feels the noblest, acts the best."

At the age of twenty-three years, he was chosen a representative to the Provincial Congress, which met at Watertown, July 19, 1775. The records show that he was especially efficient and influential in all the deliberations of its four successive sessions. When the tide of war turned towards the South and West, and the people began to think of inaugurating a new government upon the basis of republican principles, he was elected a delegate from Andover to the Constitutional Convention, which met at Cambridge, September 1, 1779, and was a conspicuous member of the committee of thirty-one, chosen by ballot to prepare "a frame of government and declaration of rights." His associates were such men as John Adams, Samuel Adams, John Hancock, James Bowdoin, Levi Lincoln, John Lowell, Theophilus Parsons, John Pickering, and Caleb Strong. There were giants in those days. After the formation and adoption of the Constitution, he was chosen under it to the Senate, in 1780, and continued to be reelected for twenty years, for fifteen of which he was President of that body. He occupied this high position, too, it should be remembered, when statesmen, as Josiah Quincy quaintly remarks, "were not made out of every sort of wood." It was during this period, in the summer of 1786, that Shays's rebellion assumed an alarming aspect. The conspirators had gathered in large numbers, with arms in their hands, at Northampton and various other places in Western Massachusetts. The same riotous spirit had begun to exhibit itself in New York and Vermont; and in New Hampshire it had menaced the legislature, then in session at Exeter. John Sullivan, the President of New Hampshire, (as the governor was called under the constitution of 1784,) attempted to convince the insurgents of the unlawful and revolutionary character of their proceedings; but "inter arma leges silent." At the point of the bayonet, they demanded, among other things, an emission of paper money, a release from debts, and an equal distribution of property. The citizens of Exeter, incensed at their audacity, flocked together at once, in such numbers, and with such manifest hostility, that the rebels retired to a hill a mile distant, where, on the next morning, General Cilley charging upon them with a troop of horse, "they were instantly broken, and fled without firing a gun." The dispersion of the rebels in New Hampshire had disheartened their confederates in Massachusetts. Governor Bowdoin, February 19, 1787, issued his proclamation, "setting a price of £150 upon the head of Shays, and £100 upon each of the other three leaders, Wheeler, Parsons, and Day." These men soon found it discreet, if not valiant, to leave the State, and it became evident that large numbers of their followers were anxious to return to their allegiance to the government. A special commission, therefore, was created by the legislature, to treat with the disaffected, and receive their submission. Judge Phillips, General Lincoln, and Samuel Allyne Otis were appointed commissioners. The delicate and responsible trust confided to them was discharged with most gratifying success, and the clouds which overhung the infant commonwealth passed away. The next year Judge Phillips returned to his position in the Senate, which he continued to occupy until he was elected, the year before his death, Lieutenant-Governor. In addition to the arduous duties connected with these public stations, he served, with eminent ability, as one of the judges of the Essex Court of Common Pleas from 1781 until 1798, — having been absent in all that time in but two cases, when some other public duty rendered his presence impossible. His associates on the bench were Benjamin Greenleaf, Samuel Holton, and John Pickering.

It would seem that these manifold civil labors were enough to absorb the interest and exhaust the energies of any common man. But yet, in the midst of them all, he gave, as Knapp expresses it, "incredible attentions to business." He was an extensive and successful farmer. His saw-mill, grist-mill, and paper-mill, under his watchful supervision, were constant sources of revenue. The powder-mill which he had erected in the winter of 1775-6, when Washington was compelled to lie inactive at Cambridge for want of ammunition, and General Putnam was roughly praying, "Powder, powder, powder! ye gods, give us powder!" after playing a most important part in the Revolutionary drama, was blown up in 1796. His stores at Andover and Methuen felt the influence of his ubiquitous presence, and became places of extensive traffic and corresponding income. His thrift is sufficiently indicated in the fact, that his property, exclusive of the estate of Madam Phillips, was appraised after his decease at nearly $150,000. But neither the pursuits of wealth nor the discharge of civic trusts could divert his interest from the subject of education. "The times had made him a man of business; had associated him with powder and politics; had agitated him with public cares, and consumed him with public toils; but in all this he had shown how completely a far-seeing patriot scholar can sacrifice his predilections in great public exigencies." His native temperament, his intellectual qualities, his moral affinities, are all exhibited in his enthusiastic exertions in behalf of sound learning and the Christian faith. He gave $ 5,000 as a perpetual fund, for the purpose of lengthening the common schools of his native town, and scattering religious books among the people. As Senator, he was *ex officio* an Overseer of Harvard University for twenty years, and his paternal counsels to the students were not the least attractive feature of the Senior examinations. He was one of the original members of the American Academy of Arts and Sciences, incorporated May 4, 1780. His address from the bench to the grand-jury, upon the importance of educating the youth of the community and the pitiable parsimony of employing cheap instructors, is replete with profound thought and wise suggestions, not inappropriate to these times and this meridian. But he is more widely and favorably known as the projector of the Phillips Andover Academy. In the establishment and well-being of this institution he exerted a controlling influence, and its honorable fame is a monument to him more lasting than brass. Though he did not himself bestow upon it any very considerable sums of money, yet he "subsidized a family of kindred spirits, and unlocked their hoards and hearts." His father gave to it $ 6,000, his uncles John and William $ 31,000 and $ 6,000 respectively, and his cousin William $ 28,000. The various benefactions of this extraordinary family, amounting to more than $ 100,000, have made Andover a place sacred forevermore to letters and religion.

But, commending Mr. Taylor's book to the general reader, as a beautiful tribute to the fragrant memory of "the accurate scholar, the enlightened statesman, the accomplished gentleman, and the exemplary Christian," we propose now to turn aside, and spend an hour among the trees and in the halls of an institution, planted by one of the uncles just alluded to, in the pleasant town of Exeter.

PHILLIPS EXETER ACADEMY was incorporated April 3, 1781, just six months, lacking one day, subsequent to the incorporation of the Phillips Andover Academy. It is the oldest institution of learning in New Hampshire established by the legislature, Dartmouth College having been chartered by royal grant in 1769. The provisional government, which, commencing with the Declaration of Independence, was supplanted at the close of the Revolutionary war by the constitution of 1784, was then in force. The act of incorporation, signed by John Langdon, Speaker of the House of Representatives, and Meshech Weare, President of the Council, is a liberal and enlightened document, worthy of a people who knew that the freedom for which they were battling could rest secure only on the basis of intelligence and virtue. After setting forth in its preamble the great advantages accruing to society from the education of the young, the act proceeds: "Be it therefore enacted, by the Council and House of Representatives in General Assembly convened, and by the authority of the same, that there be and hereby is established, in the town of Exeter and County of Rockingham, an Academy, for the purpose of promoting Piety and Virtue; and for the Education of Youth in the English, Latin, and Greek languages; in Writing, Arithmetic, Music, the Art of Speaking, Practical Geometry, Logic, and Geography, and such other of the liberal Arts and Sciences or Languages as opportunity may hereafter permit, or as the Trustees hereinafter provided shall direct." The entire management of the institution is vested in a Board of Trustees, not to exceed seven in number nor to be less than four, a majority of whom must be "laymen and respectable freeholders," and a majority, too, non-residents of Exeter. These Trustees constitute a close corporation; and whenever any vacancies occur in their number, the survivors are authorized to fill them by ballot "in perpetual succession forever." The last clause of the act declares, that "all the lands, tenements, and personal estate, that shall be given to said Trustees of said Academy, shall be and hereby are forever exempted from all taxes whatsoever." The Academy was named after the person who was the prime mover and efficient agent in its organization, and to whose princely munificence it is indebted for its capabilities of usefulness. Of the character of "the founder," the scanty materials at our command enable us to give only a meagre sketch.

The Hon. John Phillips, LL. D. was born December 27, 1719. Of his early youth we know but little. He was graduated with distinction at Harvard College in 1735, the same year in which Rev. Eleazer Wheelock opened, in Lebanon, Connecticut, the school, which, thirty-five years afterwards, was removed to Hanover, New Hampshire, and transformed into Dartmouth College. After his graduation, he pursued the business of teaching for several years, during which time he studied theology with such helps as he could command. The religious element was the controlling one in his character. "An angel had troubled" the fountains of his being; and in the outflow of his life there were cleansing and health. While in charge of a private classical school at Exeter, he was unanimously invited to the pastorate of the First Church; but not being able to overcome his natural diffidence, he declined, and the vacancy was filled by the Rev. Woodbridge Odlin. The wonderful eloquence of Whitefield, whose preaching at that time in the region round about had caused the "Great Awakening," seems to have elevated the standard of pulpit oratory in the esteem of young Phillips to such an unattainable height, that he abandoned at once his ministerial plans, and devoted himself to business. The energy and sagacity of a mind vigorous by nature and quickened by careful culture, could hardly fail of success in any sphere of effort. The unpretending house in which he both lived and "kept store," is still standing, on Water Street, in Exeter. After the decease of his widow, who did not survive him a long time, it was the residence of Dr. Abbot, the Principal of the Academy; but during the last half-century it has experienced various vicissitudes of fortune, until now it is said to be devoted by its colored occupants to *billiards and bad liquor!* The dog-kennels of Louis XIV. and his kingly successors have become a famous normal school at Versailles; the very buildings and grounds, once dedicated to pointers and fox-hounds, are now the beautiful home of young men and women preparing themselves to be the teachers of France. The transformation of the Phillips mansion is quite as absolute as that of the royal doggeries, though in the opposite direction.

Dr. Phillips was a vigorous old Puritan, a little sombre in his exterior, but genial and warm-hearted with his friends. He was punctilious in his exactions of outward respect. While expending his fortune for the welfare of the young, he would not give a boy a cherry from his trees, unless the favor were asked with a low bow and in the most reverent tone. The failure of a little girl to make her accustomed courtesy on meeting him in the street would overshadow his face with a frown, which hours of sunlight could not dissipate. He was conscious of his position in society, and was not unwilling to receive the homage of youth or age. And yet he did not walk in a vain show, nor were his thoughts all concentred on himself. He was simple in his habits, and far-seeing in all his plans. As a natural consequence, his accumulations of property were rapid, — outstripped only by his benefactions. The wealth which he acquired was not wasted in personal extravagance, nor hoarded with miserly greed; but it was used in large measure during his life for noble ends, and the residue was consecrated at his death to the promotion of knowledge and virtue. His charities did not flow in a single stream, but distilled like the dew. He endowed a professorship of theology in Dartmouth College, and served for twenty years as one of the Trustees of that institution. To Princeton College also he dispensed his bounties with a liberal hand. Every enterprise which his judgment approved, as tending to elevate and enlighten the young, was sure to command his sympathy and unwavering support. The honor of originating the *idea* of the institution at Andover, it is affirmed, belongs to neither of the three brothers referred to above, Samuel, John, and William; but rather, as we have seen, to the only son of the eldest, Samuel Phillips, Jr. But it is agreed on all hands, that the *execution* of the various plans for a model school depended to a great extent, if not chiefly, upon the intelligent counsel and material aid of Dr. Phillips. The benevolent purpose of the nephew would never have taken form and fulness, had it not been for the practical wisdom and enlightened efforts of the uncle. He was one of the two original signers of the constitution of Phillips Academy at Andover. From its organization to his death, he was one of its most efficient Trustees, and, during the last five years of his life, President of the Board. For its endowment he did more than any other man. He gave to it at the outset, in equal shares with Samuel Phillips, senior, three hundred and forty-one acres of land and the sum of £1,614 sterling. His interest in it continued through life, and his contributions to it, as has been stated before, were not less than $31,000.

But, besides these liberal benefactions to Andover, Dr. Phillips was the originator and sole founder of the Academy at Exeter. "Without natural issue, he made posterity his heir." How much he gave at various times to the Phillips Exeter Academy, it is not easy to determine with mathematical accuracy. But it is indebted solely to him for all its funds, with the exception of a bequest by Nicholas Gilman of $ 1,000, the income of which is expended for instruction in music, and a donation of $ 100 by the late Hon. Leverett Saltonstall, for the library. The present property of the Academy may be stated approximately as follows: —

Real estate, including six or seven acres of land in the village, the Academy building, Abbot Hall, and the house of the Principal, .	$ 35,000
Productive funds in notes and stocks, . .	$ 100,000

It is safe to say, that it is altogether the best-endowed institution of its class in the State of New Hampshire, if not in the country. The founder, however, did not merely bestow his wealth and then leave it to the control of others, but he watched over its use with a sleepless interest. The same breadth of vision in general plans, and the same economy in minute details, which characterized the man of business in his accumulations, were characteristic of the Trustee in the application of funds which he considered sacred to God and humanity. He was constant in his attendance upon the meetings of the Board, as its President, and fruitful in his expedients to promote the prosperity of his favorite institution. When the burden of increasing years grew heavy upon him, he appointed as his successor his Excellency John Taylor Gilman; but still he labored on in the vineyard of his planting, and death found him watching. He died, April 21, 1795, at the age of seventy-five years and four months. The Rev. Benjamin Thurston was invited by the Trustees to deliver a eulogy upon the deceased, at their next annual meeting. This tribute of friendship was paid, October 14, 1795, in the meeting-house; but no copy of the eulogy has come down to us. The portrait of the founder was taken by Stewart, and placed in the library. A marble monument in the old cemetery covers his remains, and the inscription, from the classic pen of Nathaniel A. Haven, Jr., tells us of his manifold virtues.

The animating purpose of the founder, as expressed near the commencement of the Constitution, which he drafted himself, was "the instruction of youth, not only in the English and Latin grammar, writing, arithmetic, and those sciences wherein they are commonly taught, but more especially to teach them the *great end and real business of living.*" Further on, he expresses himself on the same point, in a style worthy of the elevated sentiment which he is enforcing. "Above all, it is expected that the attention of instructors to the disposition of the minds and morals of the youth under their charge will exceed every other care; well considering that, *though goodness without knowledge is weak and feeble, yet knowledge without goodness is dangerous, and that both united form the noblest character* and lay the surest foundation of usefulness to mankind." If he had been writing a text-book on ethical philosophy, he could not have enunciated with more conciseness, and at the same time fulness of truth, the great proposition which must underlie every system of Christian education. Near the close of the Constitution, he says: "And in order to prevent a perversion of the true intent of this foundation, it is again declared, that the first and principal design of this institution is the promoting of virtue and true piety, — useful knowledge being subservient thereto." To put this purpose more effectually into execution, as well as to give special instruction to those who had the ministerial profession in view, it was voted at a meeting of the Trustees, October 15, 1791, "to proceed to the choice of a Professor of Divinity in the Phillips Exeter Academy, and joint instructor with the Preceptor thereof." The Rev. Joseph Buckminster was chosen, and his salary fixed at "one hundred and thirty-three pounds six shillings and eight pence, lawful money, per annum." But it does not appear that he accepted the responsibilities of the position. No further movement was made in that direction during the life of the founder, nor indeed until 1817, when the Rev. Isaac Hurd, pastor of the Second Church in Exeter, was elected "Theological Instructor." The duties attached to this office were stated lectures on the principal topics of theology, together with more frequent moral and religious instruction of a familiar character. At a meeting of the Trustees, August 22, 1838, — present, Jeremiah Smith, Samuel Hale, Daniel Webster, and Charles Burroughs, — it was "Voted, that the office of Theological Instructor be discontinued from and after the eleventh day of March next." The propriety of this action of the Board was sustained in an elaborate report by Dr. Dana. Since that time, the moral training of the students has been committed to no particular individual as his specialty; but the culture of the heart, as well as of the intellect, has devolved upon the regular instructors. So far as they may be faithful to their trust, the Academy will be what its founder intended it should be, — "not," in the words of another, "a sectarian school, and not a mere scientific school; but a classical and Christian gymnasium, in close alliance with the university and the learned professions." It is proper to add, that, though Dr. Phillips was a thorough Calvinist, yet he did not establish the Academy for any one sect. This is manifest from the fact that, of the seven original Trustees appointed by himself, two, John Pickering, LL. D., and Rev. Benjamin Thurston, were Arminians; and three others, Hon. Paine Wingate, Hon. Oliver Peabody, and Hon. John Taylor Gilman, together with the second Preceptor, Benjamin Abbot, LL. D., men of his own selection at different times prior to his death, all entertained theological views at variance with his own. The truth is, the school is not, never was, never was meant to be, and we devoutly hope never will be, in any sense sectarian.

Having thus spoken of the establishment of the Academy in connection with the elevated character and aims of Dr. Phillips, it is proper to refer to the early teachers, whose scholarship and ability are attested, not only by the reputation of the institution, into whose inanimate organism they breathed the breath of life, but also by the world-wide fame of a multitude of their pupils.

The first meeting of the Trustees was held, December 18, 1781, eight and a half months after President Weare put his name to the act of incorporation. The school does not seem to have been opened in due form until February 20, 1783, on which occasion a discourse was delivered by the Rev. David McClure. It is probable that on that day the Rev. Benjamin Thurston, as temporary instructor, gave the first lessons ever given to the students of Phillips Exeter Academy. The old records, however, are somewhat misty on this point. William Woodbridge, A. B., who had been appointed Preceptor by the founder, was not inducted into office until the first day of May following, at "two o'clock, P. M." The Academy building, which was of moderate size, was situated a few rods west of Tan Lane, on a swell of land now owned by Mr. Jeremiah Robinson. It was removed, after the erection of the present structure in 1794, nearly a mile, and transformed into the dwelling-house occupied at the present time by John T. Gordon, Esq. The salary of the Preceptor, it was voted, should be one hundred pounds sterling per annum. The failure of his health, and his consequent inability to discharge the duties of instruction and government, constrained him to resign his position. In accepting his resignation, on the second Wednesday of October, 1788, the Trustees tender to him their thanks for his "faithful services and unwearied exertions," and express the hope, that, "in whatever sphere he may hereafter move, his efforts may be crowned with distinguished usefulness." He afterwards, in connection with his sister, opened a school for young ladies in Medford, Massachusetts, and exercised his gifts as a preacher at Jamaica Plain and in other places. Of his personal characteristics and history, we have no very definite knowledge; but we infer, from some floating traditions, that, though the Trustees wished him well at his departure from Exeter, as Christian men should, yet they economized their tears on the occasion, and proceeded in a business-like way to elect his successor.

Benjamin Abbot, LL. D., a native of Andover, Massachusetts, was born September 17, 1762. He labored on his father's farm until he was nearly twenty-one years of age, and then, with his face towards college, he commenced his Latin grammar, under the instruction of Professor Eliphalet Pearson. He evidently studied to some purpose; for he delivered the Salutatory Oration in the class which was graduated at Harvard in 1788. In the autumn of the same year, he was employed as an instructor at Exeter, where he labored successfully for two years, when, on *Friday*, October 15, 1790, he was regularly chosen Preceptor, with a fixed salary of one hundred and thirty-three pounds six shillings and eight pence, lawful money, per annum. Friday did not in this case prove to be one of the old Roman *dies nefasti.* The school, when he took charge of it, was small in point of numbers, and backward in scholarship. There were but *two* pupils who had looked beyond common reading and spelling into the mysteries of Latin. The aspect of things was soon changed. Students were multiplied, a new building was erected for their accommodation, the course of study was enlarged, and a spirit of order and system "moved upon the face of the waters." It became necessary, in a short time, to procure for the Principal some assistance. Inexperienced youth just from college proved inadequate to the task; and it was therefore voted, in a meeting of the Trustees, August 23, 1803, "that there be established in the Academy a permanent instructor, to be denominated the Mathematical Instructor." His title was afterwards changed, by formal vote, to "Professor of Mathematics and Natural Philosophy," and Ebenezer Adams, who had been Principal of the Academy at Leicester, Massachusetts, was in 1808 elected to the Professorship. But in the course of the next year, he accepted an invitation to a similar Professorship in Dartmouth College. The place thus made vacant was filled in 1811 by Rev. Hosea Hildreth, a man of eminent ability and fine scholarship, full of quaint wit and irony, with an exceedingly expressive face, which Robert Treat Paine affirmed might be cut up into a thousand epigrams. His connection with the Academy continued until 1825, when he left it, and devoted himself exclusively to the ministry, — a sphere of labor in which his power as a writer found scope and verge. The distinguished American historian is his oldest son. Mr. Hildreth's successors were John P. Cleaveland, D. D., Charles C. P. Gale, Joseph Hale Abbot, Professor Francis Bowen, and William H. Shackford. In 1841 the Trustees elected to the office Joseph G. Hoyt, the present incumbent. In the classical department, too, Dr. Abbot was always assisted by some young man who had sustained a high rank in college, and who wished to furbish here his armor in preparation for the conflicts of life. Among these assistants we find no small array of brilliant names, — Daniel Dana, D. D., Abiel Abbot, D. D., Peter O. Thacher, Judge of the Municipal Court in Boston, Nicholas Emery, Judge of the Supreme Court of Maine, Joseph S. Buckminster, one of the most accomplished Biblical scholars in the country, when

> "Snatched all too early from that august Fame
> That on the serene heights of age
> Waited with laurelled hands,"

Ashur Ware, Judge of the United States District Court of Maine, Nathan Hale, senior editor of the Daily Advertiser, Alexander H. Everett, the writer, diplomatist, and statesman, Nathaniel A. Haven, Jr., the profound lawyer and man of letters, the saintly Henry Ware, Jr., D. D., Nathan Lord, President of Dartmouth College, and James Walker, President of Harvard University.

Dr. Abbot combined in himself, in a wonderful degree, the various elements of a model teacher. He was a gentleman. We do not mean that he was a Chesterfield or a Count d'Orsay. He was something more and higher. Though scrupulously exact in all the externals of life, yet he was not dependent on them for his position either in society or in the school-room. The finest broadcloth did not so much dress him as he the broadcloth. The lofty bearing of a nobleman sat easy on him, simply because he was a nobleman. His were not the titular dignities of a partisan parliament, that

> "Hung loose about him, like a giant's robe
> Upon a dwarfish thief";

but they were the choicer gifts of imperial nature. He knew how to be dignified without being ungenial. There was in him the rare quality which Cato attributes to his friend, *comitate condita gravitas.* His greatness did not repel the trembling school-boy, but rather attracted him; and the attraction was the stronger, as in the planetary system, the nearer he was approached. His pupils feared him, but not half so much as they loved him. They never doubted his honor or his truth. They knew that he was their friend, great-hearted and strong. There was, it is true, an indefinable distance between him and them which was never passed, — a sort of ἀορίστη γῆ, a sacred belt of land, which no Megarean stripling, however venturesome, ever dared to invade. When his face was lighted with a smile, it shone all the sunnier because its sedate seriousness was not often disturbed. The earnestness of his labors left him little time for simpering small-talk or idle ceremony. Manners and morals meant the same thing to him in his life, as well as in his Latin lexicon. He was never surprised into an uncourteous word or an unchristian act. Never for a moment, either in the sovereignty of his own immediate realm, or in the intercourse of the social circle, did he forget or undervalue the beautiful amenities of life.

He was a scholar. The standard of scholarship is variable, — different in different times and places. It is undoubtedly much higher in this country to-day than it was seventy years ago. But Dr. Abbot, in his time, was foremost among scholars, as he was a primate among teachers. His high position in college was but the foundation on which he was rearing a superstructure, story after story, all his life. He knew that, among regal minds, progress is the supreme law; and he was not content to sit by the roadside, a wondering spectator, while the grand procession moved on. He did not, like some men, merely mark time, but he fell into line and marched. New books and new educational systems did not come and go without his knowledge. By his request, his brother-in-law, James Perkins, Esq., who visited Europe in 1802, examined the methods of instruction in Eton and other prominent schools in England, and transmitted the fruits of his observations to him. He made the Academy the centre of his efforts and his thoughts. Everything else he compelled to pay tribute to this. Invitations to the Boston Latin School and to other positions, though offering larger rewards for less labor, he resolutely declined. Prevented by his continuous duties from seeing much of the great world, he was nevertheless emphatically a *live* man. His mind was a fountain, not a reservoir. His knowledge came gushing up from the overflowing depths of his own being; it was not drawn up with rope and bucket from the moss-grown wells of antiquity alone. He breathed his own spirit into the worn text-books of the recitation-room, and the mystic page glowed with his inspiration. The Latin of Cicero and Horace, his favorite authors, when pronounced by him, seemed instinct with new life and meaning. The denunciations against Catiline sounded to his electrified pupils as terrific as when they were first uttered in the old Roman senate-chamber; while the rhythm of the Carmen Sæculare was as musical as when, two thousand years ago, it won the "friendly ear" of Diana. He was a scholar of breadth as well as depth, knowing something more than the mere routine of daily study. Modern literature, politics, and theology, as well as the ancient classics, found a place in the circle of his reading. Few men were so deeply versed as he in that most abstruse of all studies, *the human nature of boys*. He had striven to obey the precept emblazoned on the Delphic temple; and, as a natural consequence of his self-knowledge, he had an intuitive perception of the modes of thought and springs of action in others. He had the faculty of making his classes believe that the particular subject on which they were engaged was the most important and attractive branch of study in the world. They caught fire from him, and teacher and pupils alike glowed with the same enthusiasm. He knew how to put himself in communication with youthful minds. Age did not make him morose; but he was always fresh in his feelings and sympathies, and his heart was young to the last in all its pulsations. It is fitting to add, that the light of a Christian faith irradiated all his intellectual attainments, giving them a brighter lustre, just as a lamp in an alabáster vase brings out into bolder relief and clearer expression the beautiful figures sculptured upon it.

He knew how to govern. It is not every man whose name is tasselled with an A. B. that is able to manage boys. Many a college graduate would feel as helpless and unhappy in a populous school-room as a frog in a beehive. He may find no difficulty in unravelling the knottiest problem, or in resolving the longest Greek verb into its elements, and yet may fail entirely in his attempts to command the smallest company of light-infantry. Reducing equations and reducing rebellions are very different things. If of the various attributes of a teacher Dr. Abbot had any one in pre-eminence, it was the attribute of imperial authority,— the *auctoritas* of Cicero. His pupils came from every State in the Union, and from foreign countries. There was among them every variety of character and disposition,—the spoiled child of fortune, the untrimmed sapling from the backwoods, the haughty son of the old Castilian; but to all of them alike, the *ominous shake of that long forefinger* was as decisive as the nod of Jove. There was no appeal from him,—no escape from the penalty of violated law. But in his bearing there was nothing harsh or severe, and in his quiet tones no "sound and fury signifying nothing." Though he had a voice like the voice of many waters, yet he seldom spoke so loud as to be heard across the recitation-room. The scarcely audible tap of his penknife on his desk hushed his room to silence in a moment. However indignant he might be at any act of wickedness or folly, his speech was always gentle. Of a temper naturally quick and passionate, it often cost him a struggle to rule his own spirit. But if the volcano sometimes heaved and surged, yet the hot lava was never allowed to blast the verdure which clothed the outer slopes with beauty to the crater's very rim. The moral suasion of his manner was the principal element in his governing power. Still occasionally, at rare intervals, there would be an individual whose incorrigible depravity required extraordinary treatment. But the day when the culprit, especially if he had been guilty of a *lie*, was sent up into the library, and, after listening for a time in anxious suspense for the slow step and creaking shoes on the stairs, was visited at length by the Doctor with his *rattan*, was a day in his history to date from and be remembered. He never wished to consult the library a second time.

Dr. Abbot had many characteristics, both as a man and a teacher, which belonged also to Dr. Arnold; and it is not strange, therefore, that an "old boy" of the latter should be struck, as one recently was, with the strong points of resemblance between the school at Exeter and that of Rugby. The enthusiastic regard which the pupils of each entertained for their teacher is the highest encomium which could be paid to their excellence.

When Dr. Abbot had passed beyond his seventieth year of life, he wished to resign his position; but was persuaded to retain it until he had completed a term of *fifty years' service.* The reluctant acceptance of his resignation, August 23, 1838, was the signal for such a gathering at Exeter as is seldom seen. During the half-century, there had gone forth from the institution more than two thousand who had sat at his feet, and now they came thronging back to do their old instructor reverence. They came from the senate-chamber, the cabinet, the court-room, the gubernatorial chair, the hall of the university, the pulpit, the fields of literature, and the laboratory of science; and they held a high festival of the heart. The arches of the crowded church reverberated with their glad song: —

"From the highways and byways of manhood we 've come,
And gather like children about an old home;
We return from life's weariness, tumult, and pain,
Rejoiced in our hearts to be school-boys again.

. . . . .

"O, glad to our eyes are these dear scenes displayed,
The halls where we studied, the fields where we strayed;
There is change, there is change; but we will not deplore;
Enough that we feel ourselves school-boys once more.

"Enough that once more our old master we meet,
The same as of yore when we sat at his feet;
Let us place on his brow every laurel we 've won,
And show that each pupil is also a son.

"And when to the harsh scenes of life we return,
Our hearts with the glow of this meeting shall burn;
Its calm light shall cheer till earth's school-time is o'er,
And prepare us in heaven for one meeting more."

Daniel Webster presided on the occasion, assisted by Edward Everett, — the Demosthenes and Cicero of the American forum. Eloquent speeches were made by them, and by Judge Thacher, Judge Emery, Judge Merrill, Dr. Palfrey, Dr. Henry Ware, Jr., Leverett Saltonstall, Jonathan Chapman, A. H. Everett, John P. Hale, and many others, whose names will illuminate the page of history. Some of the most distinguished alumni were prevented from being present, among whom was Lewis Cass, — a pupil for seven or eight years, and the commander of the first military company formed in the Academy, in 1799, — from whom Dr. Abbot, to the close of his life, continued to receive delicate and gratifying evidences of affectionate regard. After the dinner was over, Mr. Webster, in behalf of the old pupils present, and of many who were absent, presented to their venerable teacher a massive and elegant silver vase, as a token of their profound respect and abiding reverence. His portrait, taken by Chester Harding, had been secured for the occasion, and it now hangs side by side with that of his early patron and constant friend, the founder. Besides this, some two thousand dollars were subscribed for the establishment of the "Abbot Scholarship" at Cambridge, the annual income of which is now appropriated to the college education of some meritorious student from the Academy at Exeter.

Dr. Abbot lived more than ten years after the semi-centennial celebration, in the full possession of his faculties, honored and revered, in the enjoyment of a true fame, and surrounded by troops of friends. His pupils did not forget him; but, in the beautiful language of one who was worthy to be his companion while he lived, and who still dwells among us, a cherished remembrancer of the past, "their kindly visits made many a green spot in the winter scenery of his life." October 25, 1849, at the age of eighty-seven, he was permitted to rest from his labors; "for so HE giveth his beloved sleep."

His successor in office was GIDEON L. SOULE, LL. D., the present Principal. The prosperity of the Academy continues unchecked; its students are steadily increasing in numbers, drawn thither in part by its ancient renown, and in part by its present reputation and charities.

It may be safely affirmed, that no academic institution in the country is doing more, pecuniarily, for young men, than Phillips Exeter Academy. First, tuition is uniformly remitted to all whose circumstances require a careful husbandry of their resources. More than half of the students pay nothing for instruction. Secondly, Abbot Hall, an exceedingly well-built and well-arranged brick edifice, with accommodations sufficient for fifty students, was built, at a cost of more than $17,000, expressly for young men of limited means. It contains, in its four upper stories, twenty-six studies, with bed-alcoves attached, all neatly and substantially furnished. Not only is no charge made for rent, but the trustees pay one fourth of the sixty cents per week which the matron receives from each occupant for her services in cooking the food provided by the steward of the club, and in keeping the rooms in order. Thirdly, in addition to this, about $21,000 of the funds have been appropriated to the establishment of twenty scholarships. At the close of the first academic term of each year, the Trustees elect to these scholarships, from a large number of applicants, twenty students in indigent circumstances, but of good character and "excelling genius." The successful candidates receive the average sum of $63 each per annum, for three years, less as a charity than as a reward of merit. It is easy to see, that an enterprising young man in the receipt of this stipend, and at the same time exempted from all tuition-fees, and allowed to board in Abbot Hall at a cost, in ordinary times, of only about $1.50 per week, may fit himself for college without distressing his friends, or involving himself very deeply in debt. Among the beneficiaries of the institution, we find the names of some of its most celebrated alumni. The money bestowed upon such men as Jared Sparks, and John G. Palfrey, and George Bancroft, was certainly not a bad investment. In the Doric dialect of trade, "It pays."

The internal economy of the school is not unlike that of a well-ordered college. The teachers constitute a faculty, in which are vested the government and instruction. Their support comes exclusively from the funds. They do not, therefore, "hang on princes' favors," or on the still more fickle favor of the populace. As a natural consequence, they are not obliged, by any considerations of interest, to listen to the capricious whims of boys, or to pander to the taste of a superficial, hurrying people. The precocious youth who disliked to join either of the regular classes, but wished to devote himself solely to Greek and astronomy, because he expected to be a public speaker, could not be accommodated. The amount of his tuition was, as Mr. Toots would express it, "of no consequence." The Faculty can be systematic and thorough, without becoming a topic for debate and denunciation in town-meeting. The

Trustees can build a club-house or a gymnasium without increasing anybody's taxes. A rigid classification, without which no institution can attain to its highest efficiency, has been adopted, and is enforced. There are in the Academy four classes only, — the Junior, Middle, Senior, and Advanced, — the first three preparatory, and the last covering the ground of the Freshman year in college. Latin, Greek, and mathematics go together, *pari passu.* Of the students who leave the Academy each year, a majority are fitted for Sophomore standing. The course of study is arranged with special reference to young men of ability and industry. It is not thought worth while to attempt to thrust a liberal education upon drones, and there are eleemosynary asylums provided expressly for persons of "weak understanding." The Academy makes no show or parade to catch the favor of the public. It has no exhibitions, and seldom publishes even the calendar of its terms in the newspapers. It seems to act in accordance with the sentiment of Cowper: —

> "Stillest streams
> Oft water greenest meadows; and the bird
> That flutters least is longest on the wing."

For its advertising, it depends to a large extent upon the friendly interest of its graduates; and, in not a few instances, there appear in its general Catalogue three successive generations of the same name and blood, — the living stream growing wider as it flows on. The area of its usefulness might of course be enlarged, if still more ample means were put at its disposal. There are new fields in literature and science to be explored; new departments of instruction to be filled; new books to be placed upon the library shelves. And then, too, there is many a soil-stained child of genius in the valleys and mountain shadows of life, uttering in the dawn of his awakening intellect Goethe's dying cry, "More light!"

It is a pleasant thing to be vitally connected with outward nature, — to be mirrored in Avon and Windermere, to be a felt presence at Marshfield and Mount Vernon. But Dr. Phillips, in establishing the institution which bears his name, has secured to himself an immortality more beautiful and grand than that of poet or statesman. He lives not merely in the sacred, though fading, associations of a single spot, but the light of his spirit shall shine in every one of the thousands of radiant minds, which, age after age, his munificence shall call from obscurity and quicken into newness of life.

ORCHARD CULTURE,

IN CONNECTION WITH THE LAWS OF VEGETABLE GROWTH.*

" Nec longum tempus, et ingens
Exiit ad cœlum ramis felicibus arbos."

THE saying of rare Ben Jonson — " A certain amount of *soul* is necessary to save the expense of *salt* " — is as true of every profession as it is of every individual. But in no profession is earnest, thinking, cultivated mind more in demand than in that of the farmer. It is true that any clown who knows enough to manipulate a shovel or trundle a wheelbarrow by day's work, and find his way home at sunset, may get a living, so called, from the land. But to develop the latent resources of the soil, and to make the most of his profession and from his profession, requires of the agriculturist, in our judgment, a wider range of studies and a closer power of thought and analysis, than are required in any one of the *learned* walks of life. It is related of Cuvier, we think it was, that, sitting one day in the shade of a tree, with his hand upon the ground, he exclaimed, with no little emphasis: " I could, with the highest pleasure as well as profit, spend my life in studying upon the nature and properties and laws of the little spot of earth which is covered by my single hand." There was nothing extravagant in this declaration of the great naturalist. It would puzzle the wisest of us to give an

* New Hampshire Agricultural Transactions. 1850 - 52.

intelligible and intelligent exposition of the laws which control the growth of the smallest blade of grass, or which regulate the mingling and shading of colors in the simplest flower of spring.

There is no department of agriculture which can afford to dispense with the "aid and comfort" of science. Mechanical philosophy assists the farmer in selecting the best implements of husbandry, and in applying his horse-power or ox-power or water-power, as the case may be, in the most efficient manner, and with the least possible waste. Physiology teaches him what breeds to cross and what fodder to provide in order to improve his stock. Ornithology enables him, not only to make the most of his Shanghais and Cochin Chinas and Bolton Grays, but also to appreciate the worth and secure the friendship of the forest birds. Entomology shows him the way to distinguish his foes from his friends among the insect tribes, curculios from lady-bugs, codling-moths from ichneumon-flies, and tells him how to crush the one and protect the other. Chemistry enables him to look, with Lynceus, into the earth, and to gather from the wonderful experiments which Nature is ever performing in her dark laboratory, some hints about the relation which subsists between the growth of plants and the constituent elements of soils and manures.

But in no branch of agricultural labor is scientific information, or at least enlightened common sense, more important, than in the raising of fruit. Now, though we disclaim all pretensions to profound knowledge in agricultural science, yet we will venture to submit a few suggestions in relation to the mode of planting and cultivating an apple orchard.

If we had an acre of land which we wished to plant with apple-trees, embracing those varieties which we know from our own experience and observation are of the highest quality in their respective seasons, we would plant it with some fifty trees of about a dozen different kinds. Fifty trees, set at equal distances on a square acre, would stand thirty feet apart, and leave a margin of fourteen feet on all sides of the field. A weak, poor soil permits a greater number of trees; but if the soil is strong and rich, fewer should be set, for the simple reason that the better the soil, the larger will be the growth of the trees, and, of course, the greater the space required by each one in the orchard.

In respect to the varieties, we would plant, for early summer eating, the Williams Favorite, and especially the Early Sweet Bough; for September and October, the Orange Sweeting, Ramsdell's Sweeting, the Porter, and the Gravenstein; for November and December, the Hubbardston Nonesuch, and by all means Jewett's Red, or, as it is more generally known, the Nodhead; for January and February, the Rhode Island Greening, Red Russet, and Baldwin; for March, April, and May, the Sweet Greening, Roxbury Russet, and Northern Spy. We do not say that these are the best apples in New England, but we do say that of the one or two hundred varieties with which we happen to be familiar, they are the best selection which we could make.

In choosing these trees from the nursery, the largest and stockiest should be taken, rather than the tall, slender, citified-looking saplings. Two years old from the bud is generally the best age for transplanting. The holes for their reception should be dug five or six feet square, and not less than two and a half feet deep, and then filled up again to the requisite height with turfs, rich loam, soft-burnt brickbats, rotten wood, leaves, or anything else which is good, not excepting a little well-rotted, thoroughly fermented manure. The trees should ordinarily be set just as high as they stood in the nursery; on very wet land, a little higher. The roots should be spread out carefully with the fingers, and, if dry, should be sprinkled with water, so that the fine loam may the more readily adhere to them. Great pains should be taken in saving the fibres, for at the end of each rootlet there is a little sponge, or spongiole, as it is called, which is the principal instrument in supplying the tree with its nutriment. When the roots are covered, and the holes filled up within an inch or two of the surface, a fork full of salt hay, or, in default of this, an equivalent amount of straw or sawdust, should be put around each tree, and slightly covered with good soil. After this mulching, not before, the earth may be trodden down, and the tree considered planted.

The land among our trees we should keep under high cultivation, ploughing as deep as possible without interfering too much with the roots. The crop taken off should be potatoes, carrots, or some similar vegetable, and never grain, corn, or anything else which exhausts the soil by maturing the seed, or wastes its ammonia by exhalations from the flower. As for pruning, the main object should be to give beauty and symmetry to the head of the tree, and to let in as much sunlight as possible to the fruit. To accomplish this, we should begin with the youth of our trees, and never use a larger tool than a small penknife. We should be slow to shock their nervous system by carrying into our orchard an axe or a handsaw. To make the bark healthy and vigorous, and at the same time to destroy insects and their eggs, the trees should be washed thoroughly in April or May, with soapsuds, — about half soft soap and the rest warm water. This we should "lay on" in true Macbeth style, — not gently or genteelly, with a long-handled paint-brush, but with a crash towel, as a faithful, hard-handed nurse would scour down a "slovenly Peter" once a year. As a further protection against the borers, in particular, a few quarts of ashes, more or less, according to circumstances, should be put around each tree-trunk early in the spring. Above all things else, the ground about the trees should be kept mellow and entirely free from weeds and grass of every name and kind.

We have thus mentioned the more obvious physical facts connected with the planting and culture of an orchard. Let us now look for a few moments at the philosophy of these facts, — at some of the laws and conditions of vegetable growth.

The first and most important proposition in agricultural science is nothing more nor less than this: *all plants live and grow by eating.* From the hyssop on the wall up to the tallest cedar of Lebanon, every green thing in the vegetable world must eat to live. Each particular plant, too, whether it be a cabbage or a crab-apple, requires, by its constitution, a particular kind of food. Clover is fond of lime, and hence the reason why the intelligent farmer besprinkles his premium clover-field with gypsum or sulphate of lime. Beans have an appetite for sulphur; while turnips, potatoes, and grape-vines possess an "unbounded stomach" for potash, and are therefore called potassa plants. The same law, in a word, obtains in the vegetable as in the animal kingdom. It is well known that there is a certain plant, commonly called lamb-kill, which is death to sheep, but upon which horses, like Jeshurun of old, will "wax fat and kick." So, too, black-cherry leaves and peach leaves will kill calves, because of the prussic acid which they contain; but this same prussic acid, a single drop of which would kill a cat as soon as a rifle-ball through her heart, may be fed out to birds of prey, or at least to eagles, "with perfect impunity and great boldness."

Now an apple-tree is by no means an omnivorous vegetable. It does not eat everything, but is as particular as an epicure about its diet. It becomes a question, then, of some interest, What does an apple-tree eat? One thing is certain: aside from a few gaseous compounds which it absorbs, it lives exclusively on "spoon victuals," or, to be more explicit, it receives nothing into its stomach but liquids, — it takes no bread in its milk, no crackers or cod-fish or old cheese with its toddy. A definite and full answer to the question, "What does an apple-tree eat?" would involve the necessity of subjecting the tree, or some portions of it, to the crucible of the chemist. We must know what it is made of, — what ingredients have gone into its construction, and in what proportions. It has been ascertained, by actual chemical analysis of the ashes of the apple-tree and of the apple itself, just what the constituent elements of this tree and of its fruit are. It should be premised, however, that combustion of wood, or of anything else, is not its annihilation, but only a change in the form of the thing consumed, or, as scientific men would tell us, a chemical union of the fuel with the oxygen of the air. The rusting of a ploughshare, left by a careless farmer in his field, is just as truly a case of combustion as the burning of pine-shavings in a cooking-stove. Now equal portions of the heart-wood, sap-wood, and bark of the apple-tree have been burnt, and an analysis of the ashes remaining shows that of this tree a little more than one third is carbonic acid, about the same amount is lime, a little more than one twelfth is potash, a little less than one twelfth is phosphate of lime, a little less than one twentieth is magnesia, and nearly the same quantity is soda. In addition to these, various other ingredients are found in smaller proportions.

J. H. Salisbury, M. D., analyzed several kinds of apples a few years ago, and communicated the results to the Secretary of the New York State Agricultural Society. While the constituents were the same in each case, the proportions varied somewhat with the different varieties. Of one hundred pounds of the ashes, according to his analysis, the average amount of lime was about four and a half pounds; of potash, about thirty-six and a half pounds; of phosphoric acid, about thirteen pounds; of magnesia, chlorine, and silica, about two pounds each; of soda, about twenty-four pounds; of sulphuric acid, about seven and a half pounds; of phosphate of iron, a little more than one pound; and of malic acid, albumen, sugar, and other organic materials, a little more than six pounds. The carbonic acid formed in the process of combustion was about sixteen pounds.

In answer, therefore, to the question, "What does the bearing apple-tree eat?" we say that, besides the hydrogen and oxygen which it drinks in with water, it lives principally upon carbonic acid, lime, potash, phosphoric acid, magnesia, soda, sulphuric acid, and iron.

How shall the hungry tree obtain this food? The carbonic acid it gets in part from the air in an aeriform state, by absorption through its leaves, but chiefly from the soil, the spongioles of the roots sucking it up in a liquid state. But how shall it be furnished to the soil? We know that it is always the product of decay, — of decaying vegetables as well as animals of every kind. It is supplied to the soil, therefore, in great abundance, by ploughing in green crops, — green clover and buckwheat, — and by the fermentation of barn-yard and stable manures. Charcoal-dust, spread upon the ground and mixed in with the soil, is good, not because it produces carbonic acid, as Cole says in his Fruit-Book, (for it does not produce a particle,) but because it is capable, in consequence of its extreme porosity, of absorbing some eighty or ninety times its own bulk of carbonic acid, and thus holds it in custody for the groping rootlets of the tree. Clay produces the same effect, only in an inferior degree.

The lime necessary to the growth and life of the apple-tree may be furnished to the soil, in which it is deficient, by spreading on air-slaked lime or plaster of Paris, or the plastering from old walls.

The potash, when wanting, is easily supplied by besprinkling the ground in the orchard with dry wood-ashes. The process of leaching changes essentially the character of ashes, as we shall see, if we consider for a moment their constitution. All vegetable ashes contain the alkaline salts of potassa and soda, which are soluble in water, the earthy salts of lime, magnesia, and the sesquioxide of iron, which are soluble in muriatic acid, and the silicates, which are soluble neither in water nor in acids. The soap-maker, in drenching his ashes with water, dissolves the potash and soda, and draws them off in the lye; but he produces no sensible effect upon the other constituent elements. If, therefore, the orchardist wishes to feed his trees with potash, he must obtain it from dry ashes or from soapsuds, and not expect to find it in the leach-tub. If, on the other hand, his soil is rich in potash and soda, but deficient in lime, magnesia, and sesquioxide of iron, leached ashes are as good for him as dry. We see, in the light of these facts, why a thorough, liberal washing with soapsuds always promotes the growth of our trees. It not only destroys noxious insects, but it supplies them, in the most convenient form, with the most important ingredient which enters into their constitution.

The phosphoric acid, which constitutes more than one seventh of the ashes of a Roxbury Russet apple, constitutes also one fourth part of the bones of mammalia and of birds. To enable the tree, therefore, to gratify this want of its nature, we have only to dress our land with bones unmashed, bone-dust, or, better still, with superphosphate of lime.

The magnesia and soda and chlorine which the apple requires are all found, as we have seen, in dry or recent ashes. They also exist in common salt. Indeed, common salt is but another name for muriate of soda or chloride of sodium, and the peculiarly bitter taste of the salt water of the sea is owing to the presence of sulphate of magnesia.

The sulphuric acid, of which there are more than eight

pounds in every one hundred pounds of the ashes of the Rhode Island Greening, may be supplied to the tree by bestowing upon the soil liberal doses of sulphate of lime. The same result may be effected by irrigating the land among our trees with sulphuric acid, diluted with one thousand times its own weight of water. The acid decomposes various kinds of earth, and forms from them soluble sulphates, which are absorbed by the rootlets of the tree, and thus accelerate its growth.

The iron, which is a never-failing constituent of plants as well as animals, may be obtained for our trees by mixing with our soil the sweepings of the blacksmith's shop, or by sweetening our manures with copperas, — an inappropriate name for sulphate of iron.

The great staple articles of food, therefore, for the apple-tree, are animal manures, lime, ashes, bones, common salt, gypsum, and copperas. If these particular ingredients are not present, in some form, in the soil where we plant our orchard, however rich the soil may be in other things, we have no more right to expect our trees will grow in it, than we have to expect that our horse will thrive on clam-chowder or our dog on white beans. Nor will it answer the purpose of vegetation to substitute for one of these ingredients a double portion of another totally unlike it. They are all at the same and at all times and equally indispensable, not only to vegetable growth, but to vegetable life. A certain amount of iron is as absolutely essential to the formation of a Baldwin apple, as is a certain amount of albumen to the formation of a baby's brain.

It must be remembered, however, in dressing our land, that Nature herself is a chemist, and that the surface-soil is in a special manner her laboratory. Should it, therefore, be inconvenient for us to furnish a given plant the very thing which it may need, yet we may be able to furnish something which will combine with some ingredient already in the soil, and so produce the very thing it needs. It is to be remembered, too, in case we are troubled either in determining the wants of our soil, or in providing any particular article of food for our orchard, that the manures of animals, herbivorous and carnivorous, contain all the materials, in a greater or less degree, which enter into the growth of the apple-tree. The fæces from the barn-yard are rich in undissolved vegetable tissue and insoluble salts, while the urine, like the guano of commerce, abounds in the soluble salts of potassa, soda, lime, magnesia, and ammonia. We need not, then, despair of being able to satisfy the appetites of our trees, so long as we allow them access to our manure-heap. If we are obliged to buy, we should not forget that, other things being equal, that manure is best which comes from full-grown, well-fed animals. Young cattle appropriate all the best of their food to the formation of flesh, and therefore what they leave behind them is of little value.

We have thus seen that a liberal supply of food, and food too of a particular kind, is one of the essential conditions of vegetable growth.

We may mention, as the next condition of vegetable growth, the presence of a certain amount of light. That light is indispensable to the production alike of tree and fruit is obvious. Every plant is a *heliotrope.* The apple-blossoms and the flowers in the border all turn their faces toward the rising sun with a more than Persian devotion. One of the most important functions in the vegetable economy — the absorption of carbonic acid and the exhalation of oxygen by means of the leaves — is performed only in the daylight. The necessity of light to the perfection of fruit is a simple fact indeed, but it has a very intimate relation to apple-raising in New England. We cannot, of course, control the weather, but we can avail ourselves of the fact that we have more sunshine, and sunshine of a higher style, than any other portion of the apple-growing world. It is generally understood, we believe, that flowers never have a strong fragrance, nor fruits a high flavor, in countries where the weather is generally rainy, or even cloudy. This law of nature has been recognized by observing men in all ages. Pliny the elder, who wrote more than eighteen hundred years ago, says in reference to this subject, "In Egypto minime odorati flores, quia nebulosus et roscidus aer est a Nilo flumine"; or, in plain English, "Flowers in Egypt have very little fragrance, because the air is cloudy and humid in consequence of exhalations from the river Nile." It is on the same principle, too, we suppose, that the onion, a somewhat pungent vegetable with us, is in Egypt a mild-flavored, commonplace article of every-day diet. Indeed, Herodotus assures us that sixteen hundred talents of silver — a sum equal to nearly two millions of dollars of our money — were expended in the purchase of onions, garlic, and radishes for the workmen, during the twenty years they were employed in building the great Pyramid of Cheops.

It is easy to see why our apples are the best apples in the world. They are ripened beneath a blazing sun. It is not strange, therefore, that they have been for years supplanting the insipid things grown amid the fogs and rain of the British Islands, until at length the English nobility have the good taste to consider our Baldwins and Newton Pippins indispensable to every well-furnished table, and the Queen herself, unless she has one of our big apples under her bodice, feels within, as the hymn hath it,

> "An aching void
> The world can never fill."

The next condition of vegetable growth may be said to be a certain degree of heat. In our climate it is important to make the season of vegetation as long as possible. In looking about for a suitable piece of land for an orchard, we should, in a latitude as high as ours, select the warmest and quickest soil, — a light, sandy loam. Some of our crops, particularly corn, are very often cut off for the want of a week or two more of warm weather. This amount of time, and more too, is lost every spring on many farms, in consequence of the accumulation of surface water, — an evil which might be easily avoided by under-draining, or oftentimes by deep and thorough tillage. Surface water operates badly in two ways at least. It packs the soil, stops its pores, and thus renders it impervious both to the warm air and to the warm rain of the spring weather. But it exerts a more positive injury ; its evaporation cools both the soil and the air above it down below the possibility of vegetation. Few persons are aware of the rapidity with which the temperature of a body is reduced by means of evaporation. We have no doubt that a horse could be frozen to death at noonday, in the hottest blaze of a July sun, by simply sprinkling him for an hour or two with ether. There is nothing poisonous or hurtful in the ether itself. It is the chilling power of the evaporation which kills him. Every particle of the ether, as it flies off from him, carries with it a portion of the animal heat, until at length his temperature is reduced below the level of life; he is a dead horse. We "catch colds" on the same principle. The act of getting wet does not hurt us; it is the act of getting dry that does the mischief. Not unlike this is the effect of the evaporation on the soil, — it is chilled; "the sensible warm motion becomes a kneaded clod." The seed cannot germinate in it; the root-fibres remain torpid, when they should be supplying the tree with its currents of life.

The last condition of vegetable growth which we shall mention is the necessity of a certain amount of moisture. Water is indispensable to vegetation, not only because it supplies the oxygen and hydrogen, which are two of the four proximate elements essential to living plants, but because it dissolves and holds in solution the various salts which, as we have seen, serve as food for everything that grows in the vegetable kingdom. The Egyptian priests, according to Vitruvius, taught that "all things consist of water"; and it was Pindar who sang,

"Of all things, water is the best."

The means and methods of irrigation was, in ancient times, and is now in many places in the Old World, the great problem in farming. The definition of Oriental agriculture was "valuable machinery for raising water"; and even one of the signs of the zodiac is a somewhat significant emblem of the primeval mode of artificial irrigation. But with us there is no need of tanks and lakes, or of hydraulic engines, or that "the rivers of water be turned." The easiest and surest way to secure the necessary moisture to our plants, whether corn or trees, is nothing more nor less than deep and thorough tillage. Besides the mixing of vegetable and mineral elements together, subsoiling benefits trees in two ways at least: In the first place, it enables the tree to send its many-mouthed fibres down into the earth, and thus drink of deeper fountains when those near the surface are dried up. The roots of apple-trees run down much farther than is generally supposed. In taking up a well last summer, a gentleman of Exeter, G. L. Soule, Esq., found the roots of a New York Pippin below the bottom of his well, a depth of thirteen feet. Professor Johnston, in his agricultural chemistry, states that the roots of sainfoin, a sort of grass cut for hay in France, "penetrate through a calcareous, rubbly subsoil ten or twelve feet." It is obvious, therefore, that, if the hard-pan which underlies the surface-soil be thoroughly broken up, the tree will strike deep enough to secure itself ordinarily from the effects of the severest drought. We see the reason, then, why, in planting an orchard, we should make the depth of the holes not less than two or three feet.

But there is another way in which subsoiling and fine tillage is beneficial to trees. If we should dip one end of a dry sponge into a washbowl of water, everybody knows that, in accordance with the laws of capillary attraction, the sponge will suck up water from the bowl until it is itself saturated, or the contents of the bowl exhausted. The sponge will not only do this, but it will also retain the water indefinitely long. Let us see if we can make this simple fact illustrate the law which we wish to present and explain. The earth, we know, grows moister the deeper we dig into it, until we come to unfailing water. The lower strata we will call the "washbowl." The upper stratum, when deeply and thoroughly pulverized, acts the part of the "sponge." It must be deeply pulverized, otherwise the spongy mass will not reach down to the moisture below, and so will not be able to draw it up from the roots. The sponge can suck no moisture from the bowl unless it comes in contact with it. It must be thoroughly pulverized, for the finer the soil, the easier and higher will the moisture ascend in it, and the longer after its ascent will it remain. If several glass tubes be placed in a vessel of water, the water will rise the highest in the smallest tube. Then, too, evaporation is not so rapid from a porous as from a hard body. The door-stone, after a shower, becomes dry a good deal sooner than the ploughed field. That the upper stratum of the earth is constantly, with more or less activity, drawing up the moisture from the strata beneath, will be manifest to any one who will take the trouble to put on his spectacles and walk in his own garden about sunset any warm summer's day. He will see the dry surface, especially in the paths and between the rows of his potatoes and beans, gradually assuming a moist appearance, until at length, before the twilight is gone, all the top of the ground will be wet. This does not come from the dew; for a dry, warm soil is the last place on which the dew falls; but it is drawn up by capillary attraction from the depths below. During the bright sunlight, this moisture was carried off by evaporation as fast as it came up; but when the sun had lost his power, it was left visible on the surface.

We have thus attempted to discuss, somewhat in detail, the subject of orchard culture in connection with some of the essential conditions of vegetable growth. It is worse than useless to set out trees, unless these trees be well selected, well planted, well pruned, well protected, and well fed. But let their roots have the freest range in a quick, warm, deep, moist, well-furnished soil, and they cannot fail to "bring forth fruit, some thirty-fold, some sixty, and some an hundred." We have no doubt that apple-raising is as much the mission and "manifest destiny" of New England, as cotton-growing is "the chief end" of Georgia and Mississippi. The nature of our soil, the peculiarity of our climate, our blazing sunshine in the summer, our commercial relations with all the world, the ice which crystallizes at our very doors, and which alone is necessary to keep our apples fresh and fair till their delivery at the ports of the remotest and hottest tropical nation, — these all invite us to devote ourselves and our farms to the production of fruit for exportation as well as for home consumption. Apples are no longer a mere luxury; they have, like potatoes, become a necessity. Money expended in scientific orchard culture is quite as sure to earn "one per cent a month," as it would be if invested in fancy stocks or fast horses. We know in this region not a few farms whose one acre of apple-trees yields more profit to the owner than all the other "ninety and nine." But besides the pecuniary advantages connected with fruit-raising, there are other considerations of a moral character not unworthy of notice.

No man can live among trees "exempt from public haunt," and make himself familiar with Nature in all her exhibitions of beauty, without becoming a purer and better man. In the old Zendavesta of Zoroaster we read that "to be a saint," according to the Magian religion, "a man must be the father of orderly children, *must plant useful trees*, must destroy noxious animals, must convey water to the dry lands of Persia, and work out his salvation by pursuing all the labors of agriculture."

EXCERPTS FROM SCHOOL REPORT.*

AMIDST all the foreign and domestic wars of Ancient Greece, there was one spot, the central island of the Cyclades, always consecrated to peace. Ionians, Persians, and Athenians, alike leaving behind shield and spear and the recollection of hard-fought battle-fields, met together at DELOS, and around the same altar joined in the worship of a common Deity. Not unlike those old warriors may we, whatever be our party names, pause for a moment amid the strifes and animosities of our political warfare, and, under the white flag of peace, make our united offering at the shrine of Letters. There is surely no one among us so warm with partisan zeal, or so engrossed with plans of personal preferment, as to be unwilling to attend to the present necessities of his children, or to consult for their future well-being and success. Even the few who may have failed to comply with that oldest and most honored command, given through Noah to a thinly-peopled world, are yet endued, it is hoped, with a patriotism so liberal and expansive as to enter with earnestness into any discussions which may relate to our system of common schools, — intimately connected as this system is, not only with the highest interests of our town, but with the true greatness of the State and the permanency of the government.

* Read at the annual town-meeting in Exeter, N. H., March 9, 1852, and ordered to be printed by the town.

PRIMARY INSTRUCTION.

A teacher of small children especially should be a sort of locomotive patent-office,—full of "all manner" of inventions. The young love novelty as much as they hate routine. To secure their interest, therefore, one must excite their astonishment and admiration, every hour of every day in the week, with some "new thing under the sun." The mistaken and ruinous notion is sometimes entertained, that, while the highest order of talent and acquisition is requisite in the instructor of advanced scholars, anybody will do for beginners. Wordsworth, throughout his huge octavo volume, has expressed no truer thought than that contained in the simple line so often quoted,

"The child is father of the man."

The teacher of the primary school sweetens or embitters the waters at the fountain. An infusion, which would poison the heart and the life of the child, might be poured into the man without especial harm. The dead horse which would pollute the spring might not seriously affect the flowing river. There is no grace, however winning, no virtue, however ennobling, no knowledge, however profound, no wisdom, however exalted, which may not find full scope for its highest exercise even in an infant school.

It has become a pleasant fashion in these latter days to bestow suitable testimonials of approval and appreciation upon those who, in responsible positions of trust or honor, have acquitted themselves like men. It is no unusual thing for sea-captains and clergymen, police-officers and statesmen, to receive from their friends gold medals or silver pitchers, as a reward for long-continued, faithful service. Now the elder (not *elderly*) Miss E. has not, it is true, commanded a ship, nor worn a white cravat on Sundays, nor carried the staff of a Marshal Tukey, nor has her eloquence fulmined from the Capitol, but she has been a laborious and successful teacher in this town for *twenty-five years*, during which time she has probably done more than any other single human being to give shape and direction to the young minds in this community. We beg leave to suggest, with all deference, to District No. 1, that some expression of respect and confidence, — some befitting testimonial of a grateful appreciation of unremitting labors, performed with more and more efficiency through a quarter of a century, might not be inappropriate or undignified.*

DISTRICT No. 1. — EAST GRAMMAR SCHOOL.

Female Instruction.

We have visited this school often, and uniformly with unalloyed gratification. Its seventy-eight scholars, in their quiet stillness, in their neat apparel, in their cheerful obedience to necessary rules, in their careful observance of the little courtesies of social intercourse, in their earnest interest in their studies, in the high-toned moral sentiment among them, furnish a good illustration of the subduing and quickening and purifying influence which an educated and accomplished woman must always and everywhere exert.

The recitations were brisk and thorough. There was no servile dependence on text-books, but a habit of self-reliance on the part both of teacher and pupils; no dull routine of stereotyped questions through which the class "like a wounded snake dragged its slow length along," but questions which, being invented at the moment, were fitted to excite in the learner intense thought and mental exertion. In arithmetic, for instance, written as well as oral, the

* In accordance with the suggestion of the Committee, the sum of $ 120 was at once subscribed and deposited in the Exeter Savings Bank, subject to the order of the teacher here mentioned.

great effort was not, as is too often the case, to cumber the memory with useless verbiage, but to quicken the reason and strengthen the understanding. But amidst the excitement of animated recitation, the most noticeable thing was the ease and stillness with which the machinery of the school-room worked in its gearing. Whenever we have been present, perfect order has prevailed without any apparent effort on the part of the teacher to enforce it. Boys who, in their untamed strength and reckless daring, would not flinch before any mere physical force, however crushing, have, like Bottom in "the most lamentable comedy of Pyramus and Thisby," been led, under her influence, to "roar you as gently as any sucking dove." In the very necessity of things this cannot be otherwise. The most potent forces in nature are always the most silent in their operation. A young man, however masculine in gender or rough-hewn in character, stands abashed in the

"light
Of a dark eye in woman";

he can no more shake off the power of female refinement and beauty, than he can escape from the law of gravitation.

HIGH SCHOOL.

The method of instruction is eminently thorough and scholar-like. The recitations are discussions of principles, rather than rehearsals of abstract, unintelligible rules. The student is taught to examine into the reason of things, and not to be content with the unsupported assertions of his text-book; to discriminate between the dogmatism of arbitrary authority and the deductions of rigid demonstration. As a result of this system of investigation, he soon comes to know what he does know, and to know what he does not know, — the two most important elements in all true scholarship.

The course of study pursued is liberal and comprehensive, embracing in the English department most of the branches usually taught in college. Indeed, a fault has been found with it by some, because it is so liberal, and requires so much time and persevering effort to go through with it. It does not seem to us, however, that we need be "frightened out of our propriety," ordinarily speaking, lest our children study too hard or know too much. It does not follow as a logical sequitur, that because "a little learning is a dangerous thing," therefore a good deal is, *a fortiori*, a deadly evil. The objection, too, is sometimes made to some of the branches prescribed, that they are not sufficiently practical, that they do not dovetail into the business of every-day life. We remember that, in Virgil's beautiful description of the games about the tomb of Anchises, the prize was not taken by the competitor whose arrow entered the mast, nor by the one who cut the string, nor yet by him who hit the dove in its upward flight; but the palm of victory was awarded to him whose far-ascending shaft kindled among the clouds, and marked its track with flames. It is not all of life to live. The process of digestion is not the only nor the highest function of organized existence. We have hearts as well as hands; intellectual aspirations as well as animal appetites. We might, however, say with entire truth, that every study which requires mental exertion is a practical one. It matters but little what the branch of study is, whether it belongs to the higher mathematics or to low Dutch, only let it demand patient, continuous, earnest thought, and it will be of service in this "working-day world." The solution of a hard problem in algebra strengthens and invigorates the mind, just as roast beef does the body. Besides all this, the school pursuits of our children should be fitted, not only to increase their money-making power, but also to widen the range of their vision and to multiply the sources of their happiness. The boy who has studied faithfully some treatise on astronomy, for instance, will ever after live in a new world; a new heavens will bend over his head; the stars, no longer mere "gimlet-holes to let the glory through," become the centres of revolving systems, and the universe, instead of being shut in within the confines of the old neighborhood, expands itself into the boundless realm of the Infinite One.

DISTRICT No. 2.

In this school, as in the High School, there has been the past year a very large increase in the number of visitors. This is not only in itself a pleasant indication of interest on the part of parents, but it is fitted to insure greater fidelity on the part of teacher and pupils. The apathy of the community on this subject is not merely strange, — it is altogether unnatural. The farmer, merchant, mechanic, lawyer, all alike pack off their children to a school-house whose interior they have never seen, and intrust their future destiny to an individual of whose character they know as little as they do of the dialect of the Choctaws. A lady will not permit everybody to scribble their names or their nonsense in her Album; yet, when she has become a mother, she allows without concern any person, whom the prudential committee may have hired *cheap*, to write on the white pages of her child's mind any lessons, whether of vice or virtue, which he may choose. The old monks of the Middle Ages had a way of erasing the ancient writings from parchment, that they might substitute the legend of a saint for a book of Livy. But there is no art of monk, no device of chemist, no tears of repentance even, which can blot from the child's mind the early impressions received in the school-room. They *strike through* like the red letters on our bank-bills. The importance of this topic might warrant a further discussion, but we shall be content with simply congratulating the citizens in District No. 2 that they have had a teacher the past year who, among other good qualities, had the faculty of exciting in parents an interest in their own children.

DISTRICT No. 3.

We would refer with especial commendation to the skill exhibited in drawing maps. There is no exercise more sure than this to interest children, — none better calculated to impress indelibly upon them the most important lessons in geography. Let a child draw a map of the United States, with the rivers, lakes, mountains, and principal towns belonging to it, and he will, when the work is done, have a more full and accurate knowledge of the geographical features of his own country than is possessed by the great majority of our teachers, not to say of our superintending committees.

The school-house, though surrounded with beautiful woods and rich fields, is not itself particularly ornamental to the landscape. It may be added, that it is no better than it looks.

DISTRICT No. 4.

A very commendable interest is felt by parents in the school, as has been exhibited from time to time by voluntary contributions in fuel; but, after all, a want of successful parental effort in a certain direction is still painfully evident in this District, — the whole number of scholars being but twenty. It should be mentioned, however, to its praise, that there has been since our last report an increase to its population of *three.*

It may be further stated, that the children, few as they are in number, are yet already altogether too numerous for the little box in which they are packed. Such a building is not large enough for any purpose of human instruction. It is too inconveniently small to tend one baby in, — too ugly in itself and in all its appointments to be looked at without danger of strabismus. A good-sized boy of high aims and expansive views would feel himself "cabined, cribbed, confined" in it, and in his attempts to study would find himself unconsciously babbling of brooks and green fields. We shall be pardoned for suggesting, that an edifice, not unlike a medium-looking goose-pen in airiness and amplitude of dimension, set up on a few cobble-stones on the edge of a rough and rocky road, surrounded with no play-grounds, and overshadowed by no tree, with no pleasant object without or within to address the eye or touch the heart, is not exactly the place to kindle the intellect and develop the moral nature of the young.

DISTRICT No. 5.

A few of the largest scholars appeared to good advantage at our last examination, but the mass of them were somewhat dull, especially in arithmetic. There is in fact very little in the school-house itself or around it calculated to "stir the divinity within them." We have expressed our mind in relation to this temple of Apollo and the Muses on former occasions. It certainly does not look any better now than it did five years ago. Indeed, we did not perceive any very striking difference. Perhaps the walls are a little browner, — the benches a little more *hackneyed*, — the *tout ensemble*, like the character of the First Consul, a little more "grand, gloomy, and peculiar." The stove-funnel, it should be observed, was, possibly in honor of our last visit, tied up and *securely* fastened with a bran-new tow string! The bricks, which at some remote period formed the hearth, have come to be "like angels' visits, few and far between," so that now, in the wild waste of the billowy floor, the solid land looms up like an island in an archipelago. Time, or somebody else, has in a good degree stripped the plastering from the ceiling, as

> "From a Tartar's skull they strip the flesh,
> Or peel a fig when the fruit is fresh."

It ought, perhaps, to be mentioned, too, that a small and necessary edifice belonging to the establishment, not consecrated to scientific purposes, after changing its position as often as an ambitious politician, has at length found rest on the windward side of the school-house, in immediate and fragrant contact with a window, which it darkens, where, in the summer season particularly, it is not destined, like Gray's unseen flower,

> "To *waste* its sweetness on the desert air!"

Aside from these slight variations, "all things since the fathers fell asleep continue as they were from the beginning."

DISTRICT No. 6.

The school in this District has been taught 35 weeks,— 23 in the summer by Miss L., and 12 in the winter by Mr. S. Miss L. had 30 different scholars; Mr. S. had 36. Miss L.'s intellectual qualifications were very good; those of Mr. S. were by no means deficient. Miss L. was gentle, and at the same time firm; Mr. S., so far from being tyrannous in his exactions of obedience, was as easy as an antiquated slipper. Miss L. made her pupils sing; Mr. S. did *not* make his dance. Miss L. was careful to keep the room neat and clean; Mr. S. was content to let it go dirty. With Miss L. the scholars studied hard most of the time; with Mr. S. they whispered hard all the time. In looking upon the exercises, as conducted by Miss L., at our examination, we were favorably impressed with the stillness which prevailed; in listening to the dissonant hubbub of Mr. S.'s young disciples we thought of what an old poet has said:

> "The earth and planets in their course
> Move along with silent force;
> The smallest chap that walks the footstool
> Makes more racket by a jugful."

Miss L.'s children made rapid progress up the hill of science. Mr. S.'s slid down the same hill. In a word, as Cicero hath it, Miss L. kept a good school; Mr. S. kept no school at all. It is possible that Mr. S., if he would revise and correct his notions of discipline, might yet become a successful instructor. We hope, however, that the experience of the past winter may satisfy this District, without further trial, that the masculine gender is not the only gender belonging to nouns, and that, when they get a good female teacher, it is for their interest to keep her.

DISCIPLINE.

If there is any place on the surface of the earth where *order* is the first and last and highest law, that place is the school-room. Without it there can be no such thing as progress. But in maintaining discipline, it is not necessary for the teacher to be rough and severe. He need not go armed and equipped with bludgeons or blunderbusses. He adds no weight to his authority by bloody threats "full of sound and fury, signifying nothing." But he must be prompt in decision, firm in purpose, and uniform in action. His laws should be few, but as immutable as the laws of nature; and the penalty of wilful transgression should be as certain as the decrees of fate. Or, as Tupper expresses it,

> "Be obeyed when thou commandest, but command not often;
> Let thy carriage be the gentleness of love, not the stern front of tyranny."

If, as will sometimes happen with the most skilful managers, corporal punishment becomes unavoidable as a last resort, the guilty culprit should even then be dealt with as old Izaak Walton dealt with the frog he used for bait, — "running the hook through his mouth and out at his gills, and in doing so using him as though he loved him." The operation, however, should never be a trifling one to the offender. It should be an event in his history to date from and to be remembered. He should, in after years, when clothed and in his right mind, look back upon it as the time when the devil was cast out of him, and a better and truer life commenced within him.

NON-ATTENDANCE.

The whole number of different scholars, over four years of age, who have attended the public schools in town at least two weeks during the year, is 780. The average number is 479. It will be seen from this, that 38½ per cent, or nearly two fifths, of the children of a suitable age to be in the school-room, have in effect been absent throughout the year. Who are these absentees, and where are they in their absence?

It must be obvious to every reflecting person, that 38½ percentage of absence is unnecessarily and ruinously large. We cannot stop to expatiate upon its pernicious effects in the derangement of classes, in the disturbance of recitation, in the actual loss of mental discipline to the irregular scholars themselves, and in the disgust which they acquire for school and all its exercises as a consequence of falling behind their more punctual classmates. The influence is evil, and only evil, and that continually. We have no doubt that it could be to a great extent remedied by parents, if they chose to feel a proper interest in the subject. If one half the effort were used in getting children into our schools which is used in getting voters to the polls, few would be left to stroll through the woods, or to loaf at the corners of our streets, or to smoke and swear in bar-rooms, or to drink and gamble in billiard-saloons and tippling-dens. It is a true saying of the Latin poet, "Facilis descensus Averni," — which, being interpreted, signifieth, the distance to perdition from a grog-shop is short and all the way down hill. The surest method of securing the young from vice is to keep them employed. The employment most appropriate to them is the pursuit of knowledge under the eye of a thorough and efficient instructor.

SOME OF THE QUALIFICATIONS CHARACTERISTIC OF A GOOD TEACHER.

We have examined during the year six individuals who proposed to instruct in this town, of whom we recommended five and rejected one. It must not be supposed, however, for a moment, that every person who can pass the strictest examination is fit to manage a school. It takes a peculiar man to be just the right sort of a teacher. He is an article compounded of various ingredients such as you cannot ordinarily buy at the apothecary's. As to his intellectual qualifications, his mind should be a fountain, and not a reservoir. His knowledge should gush up of itself, and not have to be drawn up by a windlass. He should be a man of ingenuity and tact, of various resources and expedients, and not a helpless creature of custom, plodding on day after day in the same old path like a horse in a bark-mill. He should be fresh in his feelings and sympathies, and not a petrified Medusa, — his heart should be young in all its pulsations, though his head may be as bald as Elisha's. Endued with a courage and resolution that know no defeat, he should, like Dickens's Raven, "never say die." He should be a man of the world as well as a man of books, — familiar with human nature not less than with Mitchell's Geography. He should be a scholar of some breadth as well as depth, knowing something more than the mere routine of daily study; and not a man whose half-dozen thoughts rattle in his vacant head like shrunken kernels in a bean-pod. His mental storehouse should be filled with the fruits of various and extensive reading, so that he need not be compelled to draw his illustrations for the recitation-room from the "Tales of *his* Grandfather" or from the treasures of a last year's almanac. In addition to his intellectual furnishing, he should be a man of integrity, of moral rectitude and purity of character, imbued with the spirit of truth and wisdom. If, beside all this, the light of a Christian faith should irradiate his scientific and literary acquirements, it would serve to give them a brighter lustre; even as "a lamp set in an alabaster vase brings out into bolder relief and clearer expression the beautiful figures which may be sculptured upon it." Let the common-school teacher possess qualifications like these, and he can do much, perhaps more than any single individual, for the renovation of human society. But he cannot do everything alone, and should not be condemned for other people's sins. He needs the active co-operation of the parent and the community. If, as it is sometimes said, he takes the child as the sculptor takes the marble from the quarry, there is yet one important difference: when the sculptor leaves his work for rest or relaxation, the half-formed statuary remains as he left it. But the pupil is never found as he was left. The self-developing power of the subtile element of life cannot be calculated by any rules of art. Excrescences may burst forth from him in some evil hour, which cannot be chipped off with hammer and chisel. And then, too, other hands besides the teachers have been busy upon him in giving form to his plastic nature. Silently and unobserved, mysterious influences, in the street and by the fireside, at noonday and beneath the quiet stars, have been at work. The character which promised to reveal, in the beauty and symmetry of its proportions, an Apollo Belvedere, has been touched by the spoiler, and has become a Caliban of misshaped ugliness.

While, therefore, we would exhort our teachers to elevate, term by term, the standard of their scholarship, we at the same time think the community should leaven their strictures and denunciations with the heavenly grace of charity.

ELECTION OF JUDGES.*

MR. CHAIRMAN: — Some gentleman has intimated the hope that there may be a free expression of opinion on the subject under consideration. On that hint, I propose to state, with all brevity, some of the reasons which will influence my vote when the question is taken. The report of the chairman of the Judiciary Committee, though somewhat complicated, must have appeared to all who heard it, or who have since read it, as exceedingly able and elaborate. Most of the changes suggested in the judiciary system will undoubtedly meet with the concurrence of the Convention and of our constituents. The most questionable clause, as it seems to me, is that which recommends that the appointment of the most important officers in the State be confined to the Governor.

Now, Sir, I am one of those radical democrats who believe that neither the integrity of the bench nor the security of the public interests requires the exception of even the judges of the Supreme Court from the officers to be elected by popular suffrage. The experiment has been tried, to some extent at least, in several States; and in no instance is it pretended that it has so far operated unfavorably. The eminent ability and unsullied purity of the bench in New York is strong, if not decisive evidence, that the people appreciate true worth and talent, and that every new responsibility imposed upon them tends to develop in them

* Speech in the Convention for the Revision of the Constitution of New Hampshire, December 18, 1850.

new energy to meet it. In this fact lies one of the most powerful arguments against refusing to the people the election of important officers of the government. Give them something to do worthy of their doing, something in which they have a deep personal interest, and they will bestow upon it such attention as its importance demands. It is only when the people are indifferent as to the result of an election, that they suffer themselves to become the tools of demagogues. The candidates for judges need not and cannot become, as some gentlemen fear, the centres of political contests; for, apart from all other considerations which would prevent it, it is not proposed by any one, so far as I know, to elect the judges of the Supreme Court annually, or even biennially. It is felt to be due to the legal talent and great responsibilities connected with the office of judge, to make the term of his service much longer than that of any other officer. Let him be elected not oftener than once in six years, and he is removed, of course, to a great degree, from the violence of party warfare. Partisans will rally around those candidates who appeal every year — and not once in six years — to the suffrages of the people.

The arguments which have been urged against allowing the people to elect the judges might be urged with the same force against allowing them to elect the Governor and Senate, and even the representatives to the State legislature. All such arguments are based, not upon convenience or economy, not upon the necessity of delegating power, but upon the assumption that the people are either ignorant or corrupt, or both, — an assumption difficult to prove, perhaps, to the satisfaction of the people themselves. But if the assumption were true, how do we remedy the difficulty by permitting them to do, through another, what we forbid them to do by themselves? Manifestly, we only "change the place and keep the pain." "What one does by another he does by himself," is an old maxim of common law. The truth is, if the people are fit to *delegate* power, they are fit to *exercise* power. This proposition is as indisputable as the old 47th Theorem in Euclid. Why are not the people as competent to elect those who shall decide what the law *is* in a controverted case, as to elect those who shall *make* the law which applies to such controverted case? Is it consistent in us to be indifferent as to our law makers, but overweeningly scrupulous in the matter of our law expounders? For myself, I should be as willing that the people should seat the judge on the bench, as to seat themselves in the jury-boxes. One thing is certain, when they cease to be intelligent and virtuous enough to do either, it is a matter of very little consequence who their judges are, or who elects them.

But the election of judges, as well as all other officers, by popular suffrage, is not only consistent with the safety of the people, it belongs to them as a *right* and a *duty*. That it is their right, nobody of course has any doubt. The Czar of Russia appoints his officers according to his sovereign pleasure; for he is regarded by his subjects as the source of all political power. But the proposition, that all power is inherent in the people, need not, of course, be demonstrated in New Hampshire. The right to choose their own rulers in the first place, and, in the second place, the exercise of this right in frequent elections, are the two prominent characteristics of a free people. The right itself distinguishes our government from a despotism; the frequent exercise of the right distinguishes it from an elective monarchy. But, Sir, the choice of all officers of the State is not only the right, it is the *duty* of the people, — a duty from which they have no right to shrink. I care not if we were sure that our State Executive would always be a man of inflexible integrity, of the most disinterested patriotism, of the most varied intelligence and profoundest wisdom, — a man free from all partisan virulence and party prejudices, — such a man as some of our Governors have been, — still my objections to clothing him with the appointing power would be equally strong. It is the system to which I am opposed, — a system which attempts to mingle and fuse together the disagreeing elements of a democracy and a monarchy. Aside from these considerations, the very situation of a Governor incapacitates him from doing right, if he were so disposed. His personal knowledge cannot extend to all who are suitable candidates for the office of judge or attorney-general. He must rely on the representations of others, — representations beset with motives of which he can know little or nothing, setting forth fictitious claims with all the exaggeration of partial friendship, or depreciating real merit with all the zeal of rival interest or the malignity of private hate. But if there are any candidates for office with whom the people are better acquainted than with all others, they are the very candidates whose election it is proposed to take from them. As jurymen or witnesses or suitors or spectators at our courts, they know the men whom they would elevate to the judicial office, and in whose hands they would be willing to trust their interests, whether property or reputation, or liberty or life. The people may not know anything of a candidate for Governor, except the fact that the omnipotence of a caucus demands their votes; but every eminent lawyer in the State, whether he be at the bar or on the bench, is known personally or by reputation to every intelligent man in the State, — to the citizen as well as to the Governor. Instead, therefore, of electing the Governor by the people, and then allowing him to appoint the judges, it strikes me as far more appropriate for the people to elect the judges with the power to appoint the Governor.

At all events, I know of nothing in the gubernatorial chair which should suddenly impart to the occupant any extraordinary endowments. I suppose that the citizen may know about as much the day before he is elected Governor as he does the day after; and I presume, further, that he does not of necessity lay aside his wisdom and integrity when he lays aside the robes of his office.

I am further opposed to clothing the Governor with the appointing power, because, in exercising that power, he is constantly liable to frustrate the will and outrage the feelings of the people. Many men, through the means and appliances which may be brought to bear upon the executive, are promoted to places of trust and power, who, if compelled to submit their claims to the intelligence of the people, would be permitted to occupy themselves in some more quiet and useful employment. Not a few individuals, who are now conspicuous in the public eye, would, if the people could reach them, have an opportunity to enjoy the *otium cum dignitate*, — "the dignity of private life." Many a man, too, condemned by the popular voice to political execution, has been saved through the intervention of executive clemency; and not only saved, but "made a ruler and a judge" over the very people by whom he had been tried and found guilty. I need not say, of course, that I do not refer to those officers in this State who now hold their appointments immediately from the Governor; for, so far as I know, there is but one voice in relation to our Supreme Judges and Attorney-General, and that is a voice of unqualified commendation. But such incongruities between the fundamental idea of a free government and its practical workings as have been described, are always liable to exist when the people, without even the pretext of convenience or economy, delegate to others the power which they should exercise themselves. The importunity and bribes of office-seekers, the indignation of disappointed ambition, the intimate connection between the bounty of the patron and the support of the client, are but too well fitted to produce corruption in high places. The candidate who may be the favorite of the executive may not be the favorite of the people. At any rate, he drinks not from the fountain of popular sovereignty, but from the pool at the Capitol, — *a pool stirred*, as I am told, *by no angel.*

But, Sir, I am still further opposed to conferring upon the Executive the authority to appoint the Judges of the Supreme Court and the Attorney-General, because the power of dispensing patronage tends to convert a republican magistrate — no matter whether he be a President of the United States or a Governor of New Hampshire — into a despot. Men look up to him for favor; they cringe before his power. They

> "Crook the pregnant hinges of the knee,
> Where thrift may follow fawning."

As a candidate for office, he has no lack of violent advocates; for he may have "the loaves and fishes" to distribute to his followers.

If there is any one thing which, more than all others, is sapping the foundations of our government, it is the patronage at the disposal of our national and State Executives. "To the victors belong the spoils" has come to be the watchword of the successful party, whatever its name. Men fight, not for principle, but for plunder. Nothing would contribute so much to soothe our party strifes and animosities as to strip every office of all power of rewards and punishments. The zeal of small-beer, bar-room politicians, who, like a certain personage in Shakespeare, can "con state without book, and utter it by great swarths," would be extinguished the moment you extinguish in them all hope of pay.

But without detaining the committee to discuss this point at greater length, I will only say, that, in my judgment, executive patronage and popular sovereignty are antagonistic elements in our government. Their union is an unholy alliance between despotism and democracy. The accumulation of power in the hands of the few implies an absorption of power from the many. The necessity of guarding against this centralizing influence cannot be too strongly urged. Political action should not be confined to the seat of government; it should extend to every hamlet and hillside in the State. When the limbs of the body politic begin to grow cold, and the blood to concentrate in the heart, we may know that the symptoms indicate danger, if they do not betoken dissolution.

It is on general principles like these, that I am opposed to the recommendation of the Judiciary Committee now under discussion, and in favor of giving to the people the election of judges, and all other important officers in the State.

PUBLIC BUILDINGS,

IN THEIR RELATION TO HEALTH, TASTE, AND CIVIL LIBERTY.*

AS the representative of the town, and in its behalf, I accept from you the keys of this edifice. Of the manner in which the committee, of whom you are chairman, have discharged the trust reposed in them, I need not say a word. The structure is here, and speaks for itself. It stands in our village, and we trust it will stand for centuries to come, not only a magnificent illustration of the liberality of the town, but also a monument to the taste of the architect, to the ability of the committee and master-builder, to the fidelity of the workmen, one and all. I think I merely give expression to the public sentiment, when I assure you that your services have met, as they deserved, the earnest approval of an intelligent and appreciating community; and this, I know, will be to you the highest possible reward.

I congratulate my fellow-citizens on the completion of a hall suited to the wants and befitting the character of the town. Exeter is one of the earliest settled towns in New Hampshire, and, in point of intelligence and literary fame, is second to no other in the State. And yet, while individual members of the community have been erecting over their own heads private edifices, which bespeak their wealth and do credit to their taste, the town has had no

* Speech delivered at the Dedication of the Town-House, Exeter, January 31, 1856.

public buildings which were not inconvenient, full of cramps within, and in their outward shape,

> "If shape it might be called, which shape had none,"

grotesque and forbidding.

An occasion of more than ordinary interest might call together in this village not less than eight hundred persons; but there has not been a room in town which could hold half of that number for an hour, without extreme personal discomfort, not to say positive injury to the health. The capacity of the "Lecture-Room," as it is called, undoubtedly the best room we have had for public purposes, is less than 25,000 cubic feet. To those of us who have sat and suffered there for years, it does not require much ciphering to show that the air in such a place, packed as it often is like a Calcutta Black-Hole with human victims, must be, long before the expiration of an hour, not unlike the "gruel thick and slab" which boiled and bubbled in the witches' caldron. One of the first and highest and most indispensable requisites in a hall is capacity for air and the means of keeping it pure. As I shall probably never have a better audience or a more favorable opportunity, I am sorely tempted to preach to you a few minutes on this subject.

The air around us is rendered unfit for respiration in three different ways. First, by the consumption of its vital element, or oxygen, as it is called. The most eminent physiologists assure us, that one man will consume the oxygen from twenty cubic feet of air in an hour. Of course eight hundred men will consume the oxygen from 16,000 cubic feet in an hour. In the second place, the air is rendered unfit for respiration by being surcharged with carbonic acid. It takes but three and a half per cent of this noxious gas to make the air a poison, — slow indeed, but still a deadly poison. Now one man will in one hour surcharge with carbonic acid fifty cubic feet of air. Eight hundred men will, therefore, poison in an hour 40,000 cubic feet. In the third place, the air is rendered unfit for respiration by becoming saturated with hurtful vapors. It has been found, by careful experiment, that one man will throw off from his lungs and skin not less than two ounces of pulmonary vapor and insensible perspiration in one hour. These two ounces will saturate one hundred and twenty-five cubic feet of air. Eight hundred men will, therefore, in one hour saturate 100,000 cubic feet of air. If, now, we bring our several results together, we shall see that eight hundred men in one hour will, in the three different ways which I have described, utterly vitiate 156,000 cubic feet of air. Now the lecture-room, as we have said, contains less than one sixth of this amount, or scarcely enough to last eight hundred men ten minutes or four hundred men twenty minutes. What, then, must be its condition, and what must be the condition of the unhappy creatures who have sweltered in it for a full hour and more? Of course, in such an atmosphere, slimy, sticky, ropy, thick as poor molasses, and fetid and sulphurous as the fumes which John saw rising from the pit in the Revelation, — I say, in such an atmosphere a man can no more be expected to generate an elevated thought or to make a brilliant speech, than Jonah could be expected to prepare a sermon or to write a psalm of praise in the whale's belly.

But in the construction of this hall the committee have paid some attention to the laws of health. Its capacity is 80,000 cubic feet, and, with some slight additional arrangements for ventilation, the air here may, however large the audience, be kept as pure as that which blows fresh from our northern hills.

But, besides the relation which this edifice sustains to health and physical comfort, there are other relations in which it is pleasant to look at it. The whole structure within and without wears the appearance of durability as well as architectural taste and beauty. It is natural for men to strive to perpetuate their memory. There is a yearning in every human heart for some kind of an immortality. The only immortality to which a town can aspire is that which may be wrought out for it by the genius and taste of its citizens. It matters not how green its fields, or how fertile its soil, or how prosperous its inhabitants: these all pass away with the changing seasons, or at most with the lapse of a generation. It is in the "thoughts that breathe and words that burn" on the pages of its eloquent writers; it is in the trees which line its streets in colonnades not less beautiful than those which once embellished the Parthenon and Basilicæ; it is in the public structures which tower above the humble dwellings around them, and which, in their massive strength, outlast the life of man; — it is in these, and these alone, that a town lives, — lives in the present, and will live, if it live at all, in the future. Athens, Corinth, Rome, survive in their works of art and in the monuments of their literature.

It is well to have something in a town to be proud of, — something which may not be subject to the fluctuations of a stock-exchange or the caprices of political parties. The poor man may sleep in a miserable hut, and that not his own. The rains and the winds may dispute with him the empire of his solitary room and bed of straw. But in the public edifices of a town he is a joint tenant with the millionnaire. He owns as much stock in its most costly structure as his wealthy neighbor. He may feel that he casts his vote on town-meeting day, or listens to discussions of questions in science or literature or politics on winter evenings, in *his own house.* There is no danger of having too many things in a town in which its citizens have a common interest and feel a common pride. For one, I rejoice to feel that here in Exeter we need no longer blush when we introduce a public speaker into our lecture-room, or stammer when a stranger, who, perchance, may have heard of the great names in our history, inquires for our Town-Hall. It was Keats who said,

"A thing of beauty is a joy forever."

A handsome edifice, like a beautiful landscape or a beautiful woman, is not only a pleasure to the eye, but, like them also, it cannot fail to exert a healthful moral influence. That our characters are modified by the objects, whether animate or inanimate, which surround us, is a law as fixed and immutable as the law of gravitation.

There is one other relation which this hall bears to the community, at which I will merely glance, and then relieve your patience. The town-halls of this country are the schools in which we learn the first and highest lesson in a republic: we learn how to govern ourselves as a political commonwealth. Every town is a republic; every town-hall is a hall of Congress; every town-meeting is a meeting of Congress; every citizen is a member of Congress. It is true, we may not get our eight dollars a day, but we get what is far better, — a knowledge of the nature and spirit and value of a free government. Give to the old king-ridden monarchies of Europe town organizations like our own, let the people assemble in their town-halls, and talk and vote and establish municipal regulations for themselves, and it would not be a generation before republican liberty would be triumphant from the White Sea to the Mediterranean, from the Bay of Biscay to the Ural Mountains. Whatever freedom there is, either in the Old World or the New, might be traced directly to popular gatherings in halls like this. It was the hall built by the Canton of Uri, in commemoration of the escape of Tell from the stormy Lake of Lucerne and the death of the tyrant Gessler, which for centuries was the beacon-light of liberty to the brave Switzers struggling with their

Austrian oppressors. It was in the tennis-court around the great hall of Versailles, whose doors had been shut against them by royal command, that the members of the National Assembly bound themselves by an oath never to separate until they had given a constitution to France. It was in old Faneuil Hall in Boston that Otis and Adams and Quincy denounced the oppressive acts of the British Parliament, and by their impassioned eloquence roused the people to fight the battles of freedom. It was in old Independence Hall in Philadelphia that the adoption of the Declaration of Independence was first announced, while the iron tongue of the bell in the steeple proclaimed in a loud voice, "Liberty throughout all the land unto all the inhabitants thereof."

May this hall, like that of Versailles, like the Tellesplatte on Lake Lucerne, like old Faneuil and Independence Halls, be, in all coming time, a rallying-place for freemen jealous of their rights and uncompromising in their devotion to universal liberty.

SELF-CULTURE.*

CHARACTER is a development. It is not the result of any one act, or of any one resolve, or of any one purpose of the will. But it grows into shapes of symmetry or ugliness just like an animal or a tree. Under the rings and scales of the worst-looking caterpillar there lie, all folded up and hidden from human view, the gorgeous wings of the summer butterfly. Wait a little, and the dull worm will become, in the blessed sunshine, the beautiful emblem of immortality. You will find even in the apple-seed, if you should examine it with a powerful microscope, the rudiments of the future tree. The massive trunk, the wide-spread branches, the downward-striking roots, with their thousand fibres and spongioles, all appear in clear and well-defined outline to the eye of science; and I know not, if your instrument be strong enough, but that you may see in the seed, not the tree only, but its fruit also, *tenera lanugine mala*, weighing down the limbs and blushing in the sunlight like the cheeks of Eve at her bridal hour, a "celestial rosy red." The fertile soil and gentle rains and genial atmosphere and gladdening sunshine do not change the nature of the seed or endue it with any new properties; they only warm it and feed it, supply to it the conditions of its development, but the whole process of assimilation is its own. Its growth into a tree is the result of its own mysterious vitality. It drinks up its nourishment from the

* Extract from a speech delivered before the Evening Classes of the Polytechnic Institute, St. Louis, February 11, 1859.

ground, or inhales it from the air, and so grows from within outwards. It only asks that the soil be enriched and cultivated, and the dead branches and capricious sprouts be trimmed away; all the rest it does itself, clothing itself in its gorgeous array of green leaves more beautiful than Tyrian purple of prince or silken robe of maiden, shedding fragrance from its opening blossoms as from a thousand swinging censers, and in autumn scattering its yellow fruit upon the frosty grass like apples of gold in pictures of silver.

The history of a tree may not be unlike the history of any young man who hears me. The best college in the country, the most accomplished instructors that ever graced the professor's chair, can only furnish the student with the materials for his development. If he appropriate them to himself, he will grow up like "a tree planted by the rivers of water." If he should be too indolent to chew his food and digest it, no human ingenuity can convert his shrunk muscles and feeble intellect into a stalwart manhood. He becomes, not a cedar of Lebanon, in which the birds sing, not a "high-haired oak," of which Homer sings, but a dry, leafless trunk, borrowing any temporary beauty with which it may be decked from some clinging vine. No, old Epicharmus is right: "The gods have placed sweat in the pathway to excellence." It takes labor to retrace one's steps from Avernus, and so it does to accomplish anything in this world. The *hic labor* and *hoc opus* of Virgil are inscribed upon every human undertaking. But labor is honorable; it is only the performance of it in ignorance and darkness which is a disgrace and a crime. The toil-hardened hand and the thought-furrowed brow are alike the heraldic emblems of Nature's nobility. The leather apron of Kawah, the blacksmith of Ispahan, was for centuries the banner of the Persian empire. The good Emperor Aurelius worked at the anvil, and, among other products of his skill, made the very sword by which he was slain. One of the finest pictures of the Iliad is the poet's representation of Vulcan at the forge fashioning the wonderful shield of Minerva.

Poverty is undoubtedly a misfortune; but the flowering almond-tree, it should be remembered, blossoms not on the leaf-covered, but the bare branches. Birds of paradise, we are told by naturalists, fly best against the wind; it drifts behind them the gorgeous train of feathers, which only entangle their flight with the gale. The only well-educated man, in the proper sense of the term, is the *self-educated* man. It matters not whether his youth is spent in academic groves or in the field of toil. The advantages of the one cannot, without untiring exertion on his part, produce in him a masculine vigor of thought, nor can the disadvantages of the other quench in him the thirst and the successful effort for a higher and intenser life. Every difficulty we conquer, whether it be a hard problem in mathematics or a crisis in business, gives acumen and power to our intellect. There is, therefore, an important truth in the superstition of the savage Otaheitan, who imagines that the strength and valor of the stalwart enemy he slays passes into himself.

> "So a wild Tartar, when he spies
> A man that 's handsome, valiant, wise,
> If he can kill him, thinks t' inherit
> His wit, his beauty, and his spirit."

. . . . .

Remember, that learning, in whatever degree possessed, was not intended to embellish the dreams of a dignified leisure, but to enrich human life with discoveries and possessions; that the common fatherhood of God, implying of necessity the brotherhood of men, demands that our talents, whether one or ten, be consecrated to those principles which underlie society and uplift the grovelling, struggling multitude; that only when humanity, disenthralled and elevated by the power of intellectual culture and a religious faith, shall stand up in its primal strength and beauty, will Rothermel's picture of the "Laborer's Vision of the Future" find its happy realization. When each member of the community, in whatever sphere of life he moves, shall, under the discipline of schools like this, *learn to think*,— to think for himself, to act in the radiancy of his own enlightened reason, to fear God, and therefore fear no one else,—then no longer shall spectres haunt the imaginations and fallacies pervert the judgments of men; and there shall rise upon the eye of the world the lineaments of a republic far transcending the loftiest conceptions of Plato,—a republic of which poets have dreamed and prophets spoken, the flowerage of centuries, the bloom and perfume of a Christian civilization.

THE END.

Cambridge: Printed by Welch, Bigelow, & Co.

www.ingramcontent.com/pod-product-compliance
Lightning Source LLC
LaVergne TN
LVHW020233110826
845151LV00003B/917

* 9 7 8 1 4 2 5 5 3 0 4 1 9 *